OCR

Psychology

AS

Alan Bainbridge | Priya Bradshaw | Sandra Latham | Fiona Lintern | Series Editor: Fiona Lintern

www.heinemann.co.uk

✓ Free online support
✓ Useful weblinks
✓ 24 hour online ordering

01865 888080

Official Publisher Partnership

Heinemann is an imprint of Pearson Education Limited, a company incorporated in England and Wales, having its registered office at Edinburgh Gate, Harlow, Essex, CM20 2JE. Registered company number: 872828

www.heinemann.co.uk

Heinemann is a registered trademark of Pearson Education Limited

Text © Alan Bainbridge, Priya Bradshaw, Sandra Latham and Fiona Lintern

First published 2008

12 11 10 09 08

10 9 8 7 6 5 4 3

British Library Cataloguing in Publication Data is available from the British Library on request.

ISBN 978 0 435806 99 6

Edited by Jane Anson
Designed by Hicks Design
Typeset by Phoenix Photosetting
Original illustrations © Pearson Education Limited 2008
Illustrated by Asa Andersson & Phoenix Photosetting
Cover design by Big Top Design Ltd
Picture research by Zooid
Printed in China (SWTC/03)

Websites

There are links to relevant websites in this book. In order to ensure that the links are up-to-date, that the links work, and that the sites are not inadvertently linked to sites that could be considered offensive, we have made the links available on the Heinemann website at www.heinemann.co.uk/hotlinks. When you access the site, the express code is 6996.

Contents

Acknowledgements

The authors and publisher would like to thank the following individuals and organisations for permission to reproduce material in the book.

Photographs

Page 13: Elizabeth Loftus. Page 14: © Dragan Trifunovic/iStockphoto. Page 21: Autism Research Centre. Page 24: Sophia Tsibikaki/iStockphoto; Tari Faris/iStockphoto; Andrey Shadrin/iStockphoto; iStockphoto. Page 27: Nancy Kaszerman/Zuma/Corbis UK Ltd. Pages 29, 30, 31: Great Ape Trust of Iowa. Page 41: Dr Judith Samuel. Pages 46, 180: JLP/Jose Luis Pelaez/Zefa/Corb/Corbis UK Ltd. Page 49: Jon Brenneis/Getty Images. Pages 51, 53, 55, 182: Albert Bandura. Page 57: Mary Evans Picture Library/Alamy. Page 59: Photo Collection Alexander All/Corbis UK Ltd. Page 60: Sami Sarkis Provence/Alamy; Medioimages/Corbis UK Ltd. Page 69: Wellcome Trust. Page 71: Owen Franken/Corbis UK Ltd. Page 76: Lester Lefkowitz/Corbis UK Ltd. Page 77: Time Life Pictures/Getty Images. Page 79: Rolf Haid/Dpa/Corbis UK Ltd. Page 80: SuperStock/Alamy. Page 85: 2004 Getty Images/Getty Images. Page 97: Eric Kroll/Alexandra Milgram. Pages 98, 99, 100, 179: Alexandra Milgram. Page 105: Alex Haslam; Bettmann/Corbis UK Ltd. Page 111: Hulton-Deutsch Collection/Corbis UK Ltd. Page 112: Joe De May. Page 113: Irving Piliavin. Pages 114, 185: Associated Press/TopFoto. Page 125: Corbis UK Ltd. Page 129: Henry Westheim Photography/Alamy. Page 133: Corbis UK Ltd. Page 134: 2003 Getty Images/Getty Images. Page 137: New Line Cinema/The Saul Zaentz/akg-images. Page 138: Ronald Grant Archive. Pages 140, 177: Getty Images. Page 141: British Psychological Society. Page 146: David J. Green – Lifestyle/Alamy. Page 184: Sami Sarkis Provence/Alamy. Page 186: Sophia Tsibikaki/iStockphoto; Tari Faris/iStockphoto; Andrey Shadrin/iStockphoto; iStockphoto.

Artwork and text

Pages 15–17: two tables and a quote from Loftus, E.F. and Palmer, J.C. (1974) 'Reconstruction of automobile destruction: an example of the interaction between language and memory', *Journal of Verbal Learning and Verbal Behavior* 13, 585–9. Reprinted with permission of Elsevier Limited.

Pages 22–24: three tables and a quote from Baron-Cohen, S. et al. (1997) 'Another advanced test of theory of mind: evidence from very high functioning adults with autism or Asperger syndrome', *Journal of Child Psychology and Psychiatry* 38, 813–22. Reprinted with permission of Wiley-Blackwell Publishing Limited.

Pages 31–33: three tables from Savage-Rumbaugh, S. et al. (1986) 'Spontaneous symbol acquisition and communicative use by pygmy chimpanzees (*Pan paniscus*)', *Journal of Experimental Psychology: General* 115, 211–235. Reprinted with permission of the APA.

Pages 72–73: four graphs and a quote from Maguire, E. et al. (2000) 'Naviation-related structural change in the hippocampi of taxi drivers', *Proceedings of the National Academy of Sciences USA* 97, 4398–4403. Reprinted with the kind permission of the author.

Pages 78–81: three tables and four quotes from Dement, W. and Kleitman, N. (1957) 'The relation of eye movements during sleep to dream activity', *Journal of Experimental Psychology* 53, 339–46.

Page 87 Quote from Sperry, R. (1968) 'Hemisphere disconnection and unity in consciousness', *American Psychologist* 23, 723–733.

Pages 99, 101, 103 Quotes from Milgram, S. (1963) 'Behavioural study of obedience', *Journal of Abnormal and Social Psychology* 67, 371–8.

Page 108: two graphs from Reicher, S. and Haslam, S.A. (2006) 'Rethinking the psychology of tyranny: the BBC prison study', *British Journal of Social Psychology* 45, 1–40. Reprinted with permission of The British Psychological Society.

Pages 116–117: two tables and a quote from Piliavin, I.M. et al. (1969) 'Good Samaritanism: an underground phenomenon', *Journal of Personality and Social Psychology* 13, 289–299. Reprinted with permission of the APA and the authors.

Pages 140–142 Three tables from Griffiths, M.D. (1994) 'The role of cognitive bias and skill in fruit machine gambling', *British Journal of Psychology*. Reproduced with the kind permission of The British Psychological Society.

Every effort has been made to contact copyright holders of material reproduced in this book. Any omission will be rectified in subsequent printings if notice is given to the publishers.

Introduction

Psychology is described as the study of human behaviour and experience and is a fascinating subject. Within this book you will discover how psychologists have attempted to answer the following questions:

- Do people make good witnesses?
- Can we communicate with animals?
- Where do phobias come from?
- Is observing aggression bad for you?
- Can your brain change in response to experience?
- What happens if the two hemispheres of the brain are separated from each other?
- What happens when ordinary people play the roles of prisoners and guards in a mock prison?
- Would we obey an order to kill another person?
- Would we help a stranger in trouble?
- What is multiple personality disorder?
- How do gamblers explain their behaviour?
- How reliable is the diagnosis of sanity and insanity?

These are only a few of the millions of questions that could be asked about why we behave as we do. Stop and think for a moment about the people you know. Have you ever wondered why they behave as they do? Were they born that way or have they become that way because of the way they were brought up? How different might they have been if they had been brought up in a different environment?

Psychologists propose theories that attempt to explain the behaviours they have observed. These explanations or theories can often produce hypotheses or testable statements. This means that psychologists can conduct research to test their ideas. This research can take the form of highly controlled laboratory experiments, naturalistic observations, questionnaires and interviews as well as in-depth case studies of individuals. All these methods have their strengths and weaknesses and you will become familiar with these as you progress through the book.

However, research in psychology is different from research in chemistry or physics. Psychologists study the behaviour of people as opposed to the behaviour of atoms or chemical compounds. People are all different. No two people have had precisely the same experiences, so there are many factors to choose from when attempting to identify possible causes for their behaviour, so it is unlikely that we will ever discover single causes for behaviours. It is far more likely that a complex interaction of factors (biology, family, peers, media, and so on) have produced the behaviour that the psychologist is investigating, so the conclusions that can be drawn are often tentative rather than definite. Psychologists will suggest that certain factors are involved in certain behaviours rather than stating this as fact.

Psychological research is also different from other research subjects as psychology is about studying people. People who agree to be part of psychological research bring not only their unique set of experiences to the research but also their own expectations of the research process. If someone comes to the laboratory to take part in research they will have their own ideas about the topic being investigated and may even want to support or disprove the researchers' ideas. Even where people are unaware of the aims of the research, they try to work out what is going on and behave appropriately. This means that they may affect the results and conclusions of the research – this doesn't happen in chemistry and physics! Of course, research is not always conducted in a laboratory; sometimes psychologists simply ask people questions. Even this seemingly straightforward approach can have its problems: if someone asked you about your behaviour as a child, your secret dreams and fantasies, or your rating of your own intelligence, would you be totally honest? Most of us want to present ourselves in the best possible light.

One solution may be to conduct research without people knowing that they are part of the research. This can be done in some situations, but often this kind of research is unacceptable on ethical grounds. Psychologists have to follow strict ethical guidelines laid down by the BPS (British Psychological Society) and APA (American Psychological Association), which ensure that research does not distress, deceive or otherwise mistreat participants.

So remember, as you read this book, that research in psychology is difficult to design and can be difficult to conduct. You need to be aware of the many other factors that might have affected the results, such as how many participants there were, their ages, their jobs, their education, where they lived, and so on. No single piece of research can represent people from all over the world.

One final point to keep in mind when you are reading the studies in this book is that psychology is meant to be about you. If you find the conclusions difficult to accept or cannot believe that you would behave as the people in the study did, then hold that thought! Why do you find this difficult to accept? How do you think you would have behaved? Think through your reasoning and share your opinions with your fellow students. Above all, psychology is about ideas, and ideas need to be discussed.

We hope that you enjoy this book.

Fiona Lintern

Series Editor

March 2008

About this book

In the first part of the book, Unit 1, a number of core studies on psychological behaviour are described and discussed. These are considered under five approaches: cognitive, developmental, physiological, social and individual differences. The second part of the book, Unit 2, considers the research methodology that is used to investigate psychological theories. The two parts are drawn together in the section on synoptic issues.

Exam Café

In our unique Exam Café you'll find lots of ideas to help prepare for your exams. You'll see an Exam Café at the end of each approach and at the end of the Investigations and Synoptic sections. You can Relax because there's handy revision advice from fellow students, Refresh your memory with summaries and checklists of the key ideas you need to revise and Get the result through practising exam-style questions, accompanied by hints and tips on getting the very best grades.

FREE! Exam Café CD-ROM

You'll find a free Exam Café CD-ROM in the back of the book. This contains a wealth of exam preparation material: interactive multiple-choice questions, revision flashcards, exam-style questions with model answers and examiner feedback and much more!

Core studies

The cognitive approach

Loftus, E. F. and Palmer, J. C. (1974) 'Reconstruction of automobile destruction: an example of the interaction between language and memory', *Journal of Verbal Learning and Verbal Behaviour*, 13, 585–9.

Baron-Cohen, S., Jolliffe, T., Mortimore, C. and Robertson, M. (1997) 'Another advanced test of theory of mind: evidence from very high functioning adults with autism or Asperger syndrome', *Journal of Child Psychology and Psychiatry*, 38, 813–22.

Savage-Rumbaugh, E. S., McDonald, K., Sevcik, R. A., Hopkins, W. D. and Rubert, E. (1986) 'Spontaneous symbol acquisition and communicative use by pygmy chimpanzees (*Pan paniscus*)', *Journal of Experimental Psychology: General*, 115, 211–35.

The developmental approach

Samuel, J. and Bryant, P. (1984) 'Asking only one question in the conservation experiment', *Journal of Child Psychology and Psychiatry*, 25, 315–18.

Bandura, A., Ross, D. and Ross, S. A. (1961) 'Transmission of aggression through imitation of aggressive models', *Journal of Abnormal and Social Psychology*, 63, 575–82.

Freud, S. (1909) 'Analysis of a phobia of a five-year-old boy', in *The Pelican Freud Library* (1977), Vol. 8, Case Histories, 1, 169–306.

The physiological approach

Maguire, E. A., Gadian, D. G., Johnsrude, I. S., Good, C. D., Ashburner, J., Frackowiak, R. S. and Frith, C. D. (2000) 'Navigation-related structural changes in the hippocampi of taxi drivers, *Proceedings of the National Academy of Science, USA*, 97, 4398–403.

Dement, W. and Kleitman, N. (1957) 'The relation of eye movements during sleep to dream activity: an objective method for the study of dreaming', *Journal of Experimental Psychology*, 53, 339–46.

Sperry, R. W. (1968) 'Hemisphere deconnection and unity in conscious awareness', *American Psychologist*, 23, 723–33.

The social approach

Milgram, S. (1963) 'Behavioural study of obedience', *Journal of Abnormal and Social Psychology*, 67, 371–8.

Reicher, S. and Haslam, S. A. (2006) 'Rethinking the psychology of tyranny: the BBC prison study', *British Journal of Social Psychology*, 45, 1–40.

Piliavin, I. M., Rodin, J. and Piliavin, J. A. (1969) 'Good Samaritanism: an underground phenomenon?', *Journal of Personality and Social Psychology*, 13, 289–99.

The psychology of individual differences

Rosenhan, D. L. (1973) 'On being sane in insane places', *Science*, 179, 250–8.

Thigpen, C. H. and Cleckley, H. (1954) 'A case of multiple personality', *Journal of Abnormal and Social Psychology*, 49, 135–51.

Griffiths, M. D. (1994) 'The role of cognitive bias and skill in fruit machine gambling', *British Journal of Psychology*, 85, 351–69.

Approaches and perspectives

Introduction

The OCR AS Psychology specification identifies five key approaches in Psychology: the cognitive approach, the developmental approach, the physiological approach, the social approach and the individual approach. A brief outline of each of these approaches is given below, and there is more information at the beginning of each section.

In addition to the five approaches, this specification identifies two key perspectives: the behaviourist and the psychodynamic perspective. You do not need to know these in detail at AS, although you need to be aware of some of the key points associated with each one.

Approaches

The five approaches

The cognitive approach

Cognitive psychology studies mental processes such as memory, perception, thinking, reasoning, problem-solving and language. We cannot see thinking or memory; we can only see the end results of these cognitive processes as they are displayed in behaviour. This means that psychologists have to use a variety of techniques to study cognitive processes. The three core studies look at:

◆ the effects of leading questions on eyewitness testimony
◆ a specific cognitive deficit associated with autism
◆ the ability of animals to use language.

The developmental approach

Developmental psychology takes a 'lifespan' approach to psychology and considers a range of changes that occur throughout our lives. This includes the study of the development of cognitive processes such as thinking, problem-solving and language and the development of social processes such as attachments to others and play. Developmental psychologists are interested in the many factors that contribute to making us the people we are and for this reason, have a great interest in the nature–nurture debate (see pages 8 and 180). The three core studies investigate:

◆ the effects of aggressive models on children's behaviour
◆ the effect of age, questioning style and task on cognitive skills
◆ the possible psychodynamic explanations for a childhood phobia.

The physiological approach

Physiological psychology (or bio-psychology) considers the extent to which behaviour and experience are determined by our biology. In particular, physiological psychologists have focused on studying the structure and functions of the brain and the nervous system. Technological developments such as MRI scanning have allowed them to study the brain in far more detail than was previously possible. The three core studies investigate:

◆ the relationship between eye movement and dreaming
◆ the functioning of the separated brain hemispheres
◆ the effects of long-term navigational experience on hippocampal volume.

The social approach

Social psychology looks at a range of behaviours that occur between people or groups of people. Many have direct relevance to many of the news stories you see every day, such as prejudice and discrimination, helping behaviour and aggression. Social psychologists are interested in the effects that environments (or situations) have on people's behaviour. The three core studies examine:

- what happens when people are ordered to give lethal electric shocks to another person
- what happens when people play the roles of prisoners or guards in a mock prison
- the factors affecting how people respond to emergency situations.

The individual differences approach

The individual differences approach is more difficult to describe than the approaches we have looked at so far. It looks at the differences between people, whereas the other approaches tend to look at factors that are common to all people. This approach covers the study of intelligence and personality as well as the definitions and explanations of normality and abnormality. The three core studies investigate:

- the reliability of psychiatric diagnoses
- a case study of multiple personality disorder
- gambling behaviour.

Perspectives

The behaviourist perspective

The behaviourist perspective assumes that all behaviour is learned. The person is described as a 'blank slate' at birth and their environment determines who they will be become. This puts behaviourism at the extreme 'nurture' end of the nature–nurture debate. The focus of behaviourism is the learning of behaviour, and behaviourists argue that only directly observable behaviour should be studied by psychology. The early behaviourists were Watson, Thorndike and Skinner, who all began their work in the early part of the twentieth century. They were also heavily influenced by the work of the Russian physiologist Pavlov. Behaviourism proposes a number of learning theories: classical conditioning (based on Pavlov's work with dogs) suggests that learning takes place through repeated association; operant (or instrumental) conditioning proposes that the consequences of behaviour (rewards and punishments known as

reinforcers) are the foundations of learning. Later theorists such as Albert Bandura proposed Social Learning Theory, which examined the importance of imitative learning and role models.

Behaviourism has been extremely influential in psychology. Although approaches such as cognitive psychology, which do examine 'invisible' behaviours, are now highly influential, the legacy of behaviourism is enormous. It was the influence of behaviourist ideas that encouraged psychology to use experimental methods and to develop as a scientific subject. Behaviourist applications are also widely used in education and treatments for disorders such as phobias. One of the core studies in the developmental section is an early piece of research by Bandura, investigating the effect of aggressive role models on children's behaviour.

The psychodynamic perspective

The psychodynamic perspective has its origins in the work of Sigmund Freud. Freud was a Viennese doctor working in the late nineteenth and early twentieth centuries and specialising in 'nervous' disorders. His work led him to propose the existence of the unconscious mind. Freud proposed that although we are unaware of the unconscious, it determines much of our behaviour. He suggested that we are motivated by unconscious emotional drives. He also claimed that different parts of our personality (id, ego and superego) are in constant conflict and that much of our behaviour can be explained in terms of the resolutions of these conflicts. Freud developed many therapeutic techniques for treating his patients, including dream analysis and free association (a technique where patients are encouraged to allow their thoughts to flow freely, saying whatever comes to mind). He claimed that once the unconscious conflicts and repressed memories and emotions were made conscious, they could be discussed and resolved. Freud's legacy is enormous. Apart from the many therapeutic techniques that have their roots in psychoanalysis, Freud was one of the first theorists to suggest that emotional or psychological disturbances could produce physical effects. One of the core studies in the developmental section of this book is one of Freud's original case studies concerning a 5-year-old boy's phobia of horses.

Methods

Psychologists use a variety of methods when conducting their research. The core studies include laboratory experiments, field experiments, observations, case studies, self-report and psychometric testing and correlations. You will need to know abut experiments, observations, self-report measures and correlations for the Psychological Investigations paper, and these methods are discussed in more detail on pages 153–60. Below is a brief introduction to the methods you will come across while reading the core studies.

Experimental methods

Experimental methods involve the manipulation and measurement of variables. In a standard laboratory experiment the researcher manipulates one variable (the independent variable) and measures the effect that this has on another variable (the dependent variable). A good example of a laboratory experiment is the core study by Loftus and Palmer, where the researchers manipulated the way that a question was asked and measured its effect on the response that the participants gave.

Sometimes experiments can be conducted in real-life situations. These are referred to as field experiments. An independent variable is still manipulated and a dependent variable is still measured, but not in a controlled laboratory environment. The core study by Piliavin et al. is a good example of a field experiment.

Other experiments are conducted with naturally occurring independent variables such as age or sex, which cannot be manipulated experimentally. These are referred to as natural experiments or quasi-experiments. The core study by Baron-Cohen et al. uses the naturally occurring variables of autism, Asperger's Syndrome and Tourette's Syndrome. The core study by Samuel and Bryant uses the naturally occurring variable of age and the core study by Maguire uses the variable of whether people are licensed London taxi drivers and the length of time that they have been licensed.

Try this ...

What do you think the strengths and weaknesses of each of these experimental approaches might be? Don't worry if you can't think of anything yet, we will be discussing the strengths and weaknesses of the methods used in each core study and there is more information on pages 153–60.

Observational methods

Sometimes psychologists simply observe behaviour in real-life situations or in the laboratory, without manipulating an independent variable. This can be extremely useful when it is not possible to manipulate variables or simply as a starting point for research. Observations usually involve the categorisation or rating of behaviour in precise ways.

Some studies are entirely observational, but more frequently researchers use observational techniques as a way of recording behaviour as part of an experiment. The core study by Bandura, Ross and Ross is an example of this kind of research. The researchers conducted a laboratory experiment but used observational techniques to code the children's behaviour. The core study by Rosenhan is another example of observation. In this study Rosenhan conducts a participant observation. This means that he (and some other researchers) posed as psychiatric patients in order to observe the interactions between hospital staff and patients.

Try this ...

What do you think the strengths and weaknesses of observational methods might be? See pages 155-6 for more information.

Questioning people (self-report measures)

Sometimes the best way to find out about people is to ask them questions. Several of the core studies use self-report techniques. Griffiths asks gamblers to self-report on the cognitive processes as they are playing fruit machines. Dement and Kleitman ask participants to self-report on the content of their dreams. Thigpen and Cleckley use a range of self-report measures in their case study of Eve, including psychometric tests, which are standardised tests measuring variables such as IQ and personality. Self-report measures have a range of strengths and weaknesses.

Try this …

Do you think people will always tell you the truth when you ask them questions? Think of as many reasons as you can to explain why people might not tell the truth.

Case studies

Case studies are in-depth studies usually of just one individual, although case-study research can also be used to study small groups of similar participants. For example, Thigpen and Cleckley studied an unusual case of a woman whom they diagnosed as suffering from multiple personality disorder. Sperry studied 11 participants who had all undergone the same brain surgery and Savage-Rumbaugh et al. studied two pygmy chimps to investigate their language abilities.

Try this …

Why do you think that psychologists might use case studies?

Correlations

Strictly speaking, correlation is a technique for data analysis rather than a research method. Correlation is used to establish whether there is a relationship between variables. Correlation involves the measurement of two variables and does not involve any manipulation. This is a very useful technique when variables cannot be manipulated for either practical or ethical reasons. Correlation is used by Maguire to investigate the relationship between the volume of grey matter in the hippocampal region of the brain and the length of time the participants had spent as licensed London taxi drivers.

Try this …

What variables in psychology can you think of that can't be manipulated?

Evaluation issues

As you read each of the core studies it is obviously important to make sure that you understand the study that has been conducted and can describe what the researchers did and what they found. It is also important that you begin to think critically about the material you are reading. This page will introduce some of they key evaluation issues that can be applied to psychological research. Keep these questions in mind as you are reading each study. At the end of each study there is an evaluation section, which will consider some of these issues in relation to the study and there is further information on these issues on pages 176–87.

Ecological validity

How like real life is the research? It could be argued that a piece of research conducted in an artificial environment such as a laboratory, where everyone knows that they are taking part in an experiment, is not going to produce the same results as a study conducted in a more realistic environment. Psychologists would say that such research is low in ecological validity. On the other hand, an observational study conducted in a real environment where the participants were unaware of the research could be considered to be high in ecological validity.

Application to everyday life

This is obviously similar to the issue of ecological validity, but is more concerned with the wider applications of the research rather than simply the environment in which the research was conducted. For example, a highly controlled laboratory experiment may have extremely useful practical applications.

Sample – representativeness and generalisability

Who were the participants in the research? Can we generalise the results beyond the original participants? For example, if a piece of research was conducted on male college students, can we use those results to tell us anything about female college students or about older people? Clearly no research can have a sample that represents the population of the whole world, and so care is needed when considering how far the results can be generalised.

Ethics

The ethical guidelines for psychological research are discussed on page 9, but in simple terms it is important to ask yourself whether the research should have been conducted. Did the research distress the participants or put them in embarrassing situations? Were people allowed to stop if they wanted to? Did they know exactly what they were going to be doing?

Nature–nurture

The nature–nurture debate is important in psychology. It considers the extent to which genetics and biology determine who we are and the extent to which our experiences make us who we are. Clearly both contribute, but as you read the core studies it is important to think about this debate. Does the study suggest a 'nature' explanation for the behaviour being studied, or does it suggest a 'nurture' explanation?

Individual vs situational explanations

Do we behave in the way we do because of individual characteristics (the kind of person we are) or is our behaviour determined by the situations that we find ourselves in? This is a fascinating question to ask yourself about your own behaviour, and as you read the core studies you should be considering this. Does the study suggest that the behaviour being studied was produced due to individual or situational factors?

Reliability

Reliability means consistency. In experimental terms it refers to the ease with which an experiment can be replicated. In observational terms it refers more to the consistency of measurement: if two or more observers were observing the same behaviours, would they record the same results? It also refers to the ability of a measure to give you the same result

each time it is used, for example each time you measure the same thing with a tape measure, you should get the same answer; it is difficult to devise psychological measuring instruments that have the same degree of reliability, but that is the aim! As you read the core studies, ask yourself how reliable the measurements are.

Validity

Validity refers to the accuracy of a measure. For example, if someone counted the number of questions that you got right in a test, would this be a valid measure of your intelligence?

Qualitative and quantitative measures

Research can produce different types of data. Some of the core studies collect data in the form of numbers; this is referred to as quantitative data. Others collect descriptions in words and this is referred to as qualitative data. Quantitative data are easy to analyse but may lose some of the 'richness' of people's own words. You should consider the strengths and weaknesses of each type of data as you read the core studies.

Control

This refers to the researcher's ability to control what is happening. Control can usually be exerted more easily in laboratory situations, as the researcher can set up an environment in the way that they want it. Researchers tend to have far less control in real-life settings. This means that in laboratory settings there are far fewer confounding variables (or extraneous variables). These are variables that haven't been controlled but may have an effect on the behaviour being measured. Psychologists often use control groups in their research; this gives the researcher a baseline to compare the results of the experimental groups with a group that has not experienced the same experimental manipulation.

Reductionism

If complex psychological phenomena are explained by reducing them to a much simpler level (usually a single factor), then this is referred to as a reductionist explanation. In some ways, all individual pieces of psychological research can be seen as reductionist, as most research selects one variable to investigate. However, when research is looked at as a whole a more complex picture emerges. Biological explanations are often considered to be more reductionist than social ones. As you read the core studies, consider the extent to which complex behaviours are being reduced to simpler levels.

Determinism

This is the argument that our behaviour is determined (or decided) by factors outside our control. These factors may be biological, such as genes or hormones, or situational, such as reinforcements received from others. The opposite argument is the free-will argument, which states that individuals are free to choose how to behave. Most psychological research suggests that our behaviour is determined by something – but as you read the core studies, try to identify exactly what the researchers are arguing determines the behaviour being studied.

Ethics

The British Psychological Society and the American Psychological Association issue ethical guidelines for those involved in conducting research. As you read each of the core studies you should consider the following questions:

◆ Was anyone harmed, either physically or psychologically, by this research?

If you think that they were, consider these questions:

◆ Do you think that the researcher should have conducted this piece of research?

◆ Were the costs of the research (e.g. the harm caused) worth it in terms of what was learned? In other words, was the research justified?

Try this ...

Before you read any further you might like to try and write a list of guidelines for psychologists – what do you think they should and should not be able to do?

The British and American guidelines are presented differently, but their messages are almost identical. The key issues that are discussed are as follows.

General issues

Researchers must always consider the potential consequences for the participants taking part in their research. Threats to their psychological well-being, health, values or dignity should be eliminated.

Consent

Wherever possible, the investigator should inform all participants of the objectives of the research before they take part. This ensures that participants are not just consenting to take part in any piece of research, but know exactly what they are letting themselves in for! Do you think that telling participants what the study is about might present problems for the researcher?

When research involves anyone under the age of 16 years, their parents or carers must give consent.

Investigators are often in a position of authority over their participants, who may be their students, employees or clients. Researchers should not be allowed to put any pressure on participants to take part in or to remain in an investigation. Finally, the payment of participants should not be used to persuade them to take more risks than they would have been prepared to take without payment.

Observational research has slightly different guidelines. In most cases participants should give their informed consent to being observed. However, it is considered acceptable to observe the behaviour of people in public places where they might expect to be observed by others; this might include places like shopping centres.

Deception

Researchers should not deceive their participants. The withholding of information or the misleading of participants is unacceptable if the participants are likely to object or to show unease once they have been debriefed. Very minor deceptions (such as not telling the participants exactly what the study is about) are generally seen as acceptable, but participants should always be given full details about the process that they will be following and what is likely to happen. Why do you think psychologists might deceive their participants?

Debriefing

Debriefing means telling the participants at the end of the study any information that they were not given at the beginning of the study. This might involve reassuring people that their performance on a test was within a normal range of scores, or simply answering questions about the research. If participants are debriefed properly then they will leave the research situation feeling the same (or better) than before they arrived. Participants should not be allowed to leave the research situation feeling worried or anxious about anything at all.

Debriefing does not excuse deception or any other unethical aspects of the research. It is not acceptable to significantly deceive someone and then claim that this is alright because you will debrief them at the end.

Withdrawal from the investigation

At the start of the investigation, the researchers should make clear to the participants that they have the right to withdraw from the research at any time they wish. They should also be made aware that this right is not affected by any payments or inducements that may have been offered for their participation.

Confidentiality

All information obtained about a participant during a piece of research is confidential unless agreed otherwise in advance. If a participant wishes to withdraw from the research then their data should be removed and destroyed. Video or other recordings can only be used with the express permission of the participants.

Protection of participants

Researchers have a responsibility to protect participants from physical and mental harm. Where research may involve behaviour or experiences that participants may regard as personal and private, the participants must be protected from stress and should be assured that answers to personal questions need not be given.

In cases of research involving children, investigators should also act with caution when discussing the results with parents, teachers etc.

This section has given you a brief introduction to the sort of information that you will meet throughout the book. Each of the core studies needs to be considered in relation to the method that has been used and the issues that the study raises. Try to think about the material you are reading, rather than simply trying to remember it: your thoughts and comments are important and you need to develop the ability to express them clearly. You should find that the studies covered in this book give you plenty to think about.

Cognitive psychology

Cognitive psychology attempts to explain our behaviour through an understanding of mental processes. We receive information through our senses (sight, hearing, taste, smell and touch) and cognitive psychology focuses on how we make sense of this information.

How are cognitive processes studied?

The processes investigated in cognitive psychology include perception, language, memory and thinking, along with the role of beliefs and attitudes and their formation. Cognitive processes are not easy to study because they cannot be directly observed, instead researchers must find ways to demonstrate what and how people think. Tests have been devised to measure cognitive functioning, but the validity of such tests is often criticised (whether they are really measuring the cognitive process they are intended to measure). Measuring attitudes is also difficult: the obvious way would be to ask questions, however people would not always tell the truth about their attitudes or beliefs. The most popular method for studying cognitive processes is the experiment, although its biggest disadvantage is the participant's awareness of being studied, which in itself can change the process being studied: features influencing a participant are known as demand characteristics.

Animals are also studied in an attempt to understand how cognitive processes work, and cross-cultural studies attempt to ascertain whether cognitive processes are the product of nature or nurture. Children are studied as a way of looking at how cognitive processes develop from birth.

The three core studies in this section will give you a flavour of cognitive psychology.

Loftus and Palmer (1974)

The study by Loftus and Palmer focuses on memory, eyewitness testimony in particular. It explores the idea that memory is not a photographic or precise version of events. Participants were shown film of car accidents and asked leading questions about what they saw. The researchers claim that the results demonstrate how information received after an event can distort an individual's recollection of what they witnessed.

Baron-Cohen et al. (1997)

The study by Baron-Cohen et al. investigates the core problem experienced by people with autism, a disorder involving social and communication difficulties. Theory of mind develops in most humans at around the age of 4 years, and is the ability to understand and predict what other people think and feel. This study attempts to measure the shortfall of advanced theory of mind skills in adults by using the 'Eyes Task'. The researchers claim that this study shows that the core deficit in autism is failure to develop a theory of mind rather than low intellectual ability. This has implications for understanding and helping people with autism.

Savage-Rumbaugh et al. (1986)

The study by Savage-Rumbaugh et al. describes the progress made by chimpanzees in language acquisition. Sign language was used since chimpanzees have similar hands to humans. The language use of Kanzi, a pygmy chimpanzee, was compared with that of a common chimpanzee. It was found that the pygmy chimpanzee was quick to learn new signs and his language use progressed further than the common chimpanzee. The researchers were confident that Kanzi learned to use language successfully.

Loftus and Palmer (1974)

Pause for thought

◆ Have you got a good memory?

◆ What sorts of things do you find easy to remember and what sorts of things do you find difficult to remember?

◆ Do you think you would make a good witness?

What is this study about?

Elizabeth Loftus and John Palmer have conducted research into eyewitness testimony. This is our memory for real-life events and this research has obvious practical applications for police interviews, courtroom practices and so on. Psychologists have identified many factors that influence the accuracy of our memory and this study considers just one of these factors.

This factor is *the way that we are asked about an event and how the information we receive after the event might affect our memory.*

Links to other studies

The study by Maguire et al. (pages 68–75) considers memory from a very different perspective.

What factors influence the accuracy of memory?

Try this ...

Find a video clip showing an event such as a robbery or an accident. Show this clip to two groups of people. Ask the first group to simply write down everything they can remember. Ask the other group some specific questions about the event.

1 Which group remembered the most information?

2 Which group remembered the most accurate information?

3 Did anyone remember anything that wasn't there or something that didn't happen?

4 Do you think that people might have been influenced by the questions that you asked?

You could repeat this the next day or a week later. How have people's memories changed?

Now think about the kind of factors that may have influenced their answers.

◆ Time of day
◆ Hunger
◆ Background noise
◆ Leading questions

What other factors can you think of?

This activity might demonstrate a difference between the two groups and may suggest that the way that people are questioned about an event can significantly affect their responses. Even if you did not find a difference between the groups you may have found that people's memories for events like these are not very accurate.

Finally, this exercise should have demonstrated the importance of *control* in psychological experiments – ensuring that as many factors as possible are kept constant.

How does information received 'after the event' affect memory?

Although the memory of an event is stored at the time of the event, research suggests that what has been stored can still change. The types of 'after the event' information that have been studied include the way witnesses are asked questions. Loftus and Zanni (1975) showed that people were more likely to recall seeing a broken headlight if the question was 'Did you see *the* broken headlight?' rather than 'Did you see *a* broken headlight?' However, it is possible that this simply reflects participants giving the answers they think they should give rather than supporting the notion that their memory has actually changed. This has obvious applications for eyewitness testimony.

Why are psychologists interested in eyewitness testimony?

Juries are very convinced by eyewitness accounts and will tend to return guilty verdicts when an eyewitness account has been presented by the prosecution. Even when the eyewitness has been discredited in some way, juries will still tend to be convinced by this information. Psychological research into memory strongly suggests that there are many factors that would make eyewitnesses unreliable and the Devlin Committee (1973) recommended that juries should be instructed that it is not safe to convict on the basis of eyewitness testimony alone.

The Devlin Committee was established in 1973 to investigate the use of eyewitness testimony in court. The committee studied a number of cases where the only evidence against the defendant was an eyewitness account and discovered that the defendant was found guilty in 74% of these cases, despite there being no corroborating evidence.

> **Try this ...**

Imagine that someone tells you that they saw two cars 'smash' into each other.

1   What sort of mental image might this information conjure up?

2   How fast do you think that the cars might have been going?

Now imagine that someone tells you that they saw two cars 'bump' each other and do the same thing again.

1   What sort of mental image does this information conjure up?

2   How fast do you think the cars might have been going?

You could try this exercise out on a few other people, perhaps other students who do not do psychology, or people in your family.

What problems might you encounter if you used other psychology students for a study?

Practical investigation idea

You could carry out an experiment based on Loftus and Palmer's work on eyewitness testimony. Perhaps you could investigate individual differences such as driving experience, age or gender to see if they influence the extent to which leading questions about speed have an effect.

Elizabeth Loftus

Figure 1.1 Elizabeth Loftus

Elizabeth Loftus is Professor of Psychology and Adjunct Professor of Law at the University of Washington in Seattle. She is considered to be an authority on eyewitness testimony and false memories and is often called as an expert witness in trials.

Weblink

See 'Websites' (page ii) for more information about Elizabeth Loftus and her work.

Loftus, E. F. and Palmer, J. C. (1974)

'Reconstruction of automobile destruction: an example of the interaction between language and memory', *Journal of Verbal Learning and Verbal Behavior* 13, 585–9.

What was the aim of the study?

The aim of the study was to see the effect of leading questions on memory of an event. Specifically the researchers wanted to find out if changing the verb used in a question about speed would have any effect on the speed estimates given by the participants.

Loftus and Palmer used two laboratory experiments to investigate the effect of leading questions on recall. In this study the verb used in the leading question is the independent variable and the estimate of speed given by the participant is the dependent variable.

> **Key terms**
>
> independent variable the variable that researchers manipulate in an experiment
>
> dependent variable in an experiment, the variable that is affected by the researchers' manipulation of the independent variable

Experiment 1

What was the methodology?

Forty-five student participants were shown seven clips of traffic accidents (these were segments taken from road safety films produced by the Evergreen Safety Council and the Seattle Police Department). The segments shown were between 5 and 30 seconds long. After viewing each clip the students were given a questionnaire that first asked them to 'give an account of the accident you have just seen' and then to answer some specific questions.

One of these questions, referred to as the critical question, asked about the speed of the vehicles. The students were divided into five groups of nine participants and each group was asked a different critical question.

Group 1   About how fast were the cars going when they *smashed* into each other?

Group 2   About how fast were the cars going when they *collided* with each other?

Group 3   About how fast were the cars going when they *bumped* each other?

Group 4   About how fast were the cars going when they *hit* each other?

Group 5   About how fast were the cars going when they *contacted* with each other?

What were the findings?

Average ratings of speeds for each condition were:

'smashed'	40.8 mph
'collided'	39.3 mph
'bumped'	38.1 mph
'hit'	34.0 mph
'contacted'	31.8 mph

Figure 1.2 Is this a smash or a bump?

U1
1

Loftus and Palmer (1974)

These results were analysed statistically and the differences in speed estimates between the conditions was found to be statistically significant.

Key terms

Statistical tests let you know how likely your results are to be due to chance. The lower the probability of a chance result, the more likely your results are to be due to the manipulation of the independent variable. If the probability of a chance result is less than 1 in 20 (written as $p<0.05$), we can say that there is a statistically significant difference between the conditions and accept our hypothesis

demand characteristics a feature of a procedure (other than the dependent variable) that influences a participant to try to guess what a study is about and look for clues as to how to behave

Loftus and Palmer were also able to analyse the accuracy of the speed estimates for four of the seven films. These four films were 'staged' crashes designed to show what happened when cars collide at different speeds. One collision took place at 20 mph, one at 30 mph and two at 40 mph.

Average estimates for these films were as follows.

Actual speed of cars (mph)	Average estimate of speed (mph)
20	37.7
30	36.2
40	39.7
40	36.1

You can see from this that people are not very good at estimating the speed that cars are travelling at.

Loftus and Palmer concluded from their experiment that the wording of the question did have an effect on the estimate of speed. The more severe-sounding verbs produced the higher estimates.

When the question had the word 'smashed' in it, people gave estimates that were, on average, 9 mph higher than when the question was asked using the word 'contacted'. They suggested that there are two possible explanations for this finding.

The first possible explanation is response bias factors. This means that the participant consciously biases their response in the direction of the verb used in the question. In other words, they give the answer that they think the researchers want. Factors like this that affect participant's responses are called demand characteristics.

There is a second possible explanation for the findings of this first experiment and this is that the question causes an actual distortion in the participant's memory representation of the accident.

The word 'smashed' leads the participant to represent the accident as being more severe than it actually was. From this explanation they propose that participants might also be more likely to 'remember' other details that did not actually occur but 'fit' with the 'memory' of the accident having occurred at high speed.

We cannot conclude that the wording of the question did influence the participants' speed estimates as they may have just been responding to demand characteristics.

Experiment 2 allows us to investigate the notion that a person's memory (representation) of an event may actually be changed by information that they receive after the event. Is it possible to cause a distortion in someone's memory so that they will 'remember' something that was not there or did not happen? This second experiment will also allow us to decide which of the two possible conclusions from Experiment 1 is the most appropriate.

What was the methodology?

This experiment was similar to the first experiment. One hundred and fifty student participants saw a 1-minute film that contained a 4-second scene of a multiple car accident and were then questioned about it.

As in Experiment 1, they were first asked to describe the accident in their own words and were then asked to answer a series of questions. The critical question was again asking about the speed of the vehicles.

In this experiment there were three groups. The independent variable is still the verb used in the question but the dependent variable is whether or not participants recall seeing broken glass. The students were divided into three groups of 50 subjects and each group was asked a different critical question.

Group 1 'How fast were the cars going when they hit each other?'

Group 2 'How fast were the cars going when they smashed into each other?'

Group 3 Subjects were not asked about the speed of the vehicles.

A week later subjects were asked further questions (they were not shown the film again) and the critical question was 'Did you see any broken glass?'

This critical question was one of ten questions on the questionnaire. There was no broken glass in the original film, but Loftus and Palmer predicted that the subjects who had been asked the 'smashed' question were more likely to say 'Yes'.

Why do you think that Loftus and Palmer predicted that participants who had been asked the 'smashed' question would be more likely to say 'Yes' to the question about broken glass?

Think about the second of their possible explanations for Experiment 1. They suggest that information received 'after the event' might become part of the memory we have of the actual event. So if you hear a question asking you about a 'smash' rather than a 'hit' this may make your representation of the event more severe. When you are asked a week later if you saw any broken glass, this might fit with the way you have now stored the memory and so you might say 'Yes'.

What were the findings?

Verb used in original question	No. of participants answering 'Yes' to broken glass	No. of participants answering 'No' to broken glass
Smashed	16	34
Hit	7	43
Control group (no speed question asked)	6	44

Sixteen participants answered 'Yes' to the question when they had heard the word 'smashed' a week earlier. Seven said 'Yes' when they had heard the word 'hit' and six of the participants who were not questioned about speed also said 'Yes' to the question about broken glass. There is a statistically significant difference between the 'smashed' group and the other two groups. There is no difference between the 'hit' and control groups.

This supports the argument that leading questions may cause an actual distortion in someone's memory of an event. In other words, the use of the word 'smashed' has a greater influence than simply increasing the estimate of speed given by the participants.

Loftus and Palmer suggest that the use of the verb 'smashed' distorts the memory of the event, making it more severe. This means that when participants are asked if they saw any broken glass they are more likely to say 'Yes' because broken glass fits with the modified image they have of the event.

This would offer some support for the second of the two explanations that Loftus and Palmer suggested for Experiment 1. Rather than simply a response bias they argue that they have demonstrated that the way the accident was represented in the memory after seeing the film was substantially changed by the use of the word 'smashed' in the speed estimate question. It is also interesting to consider the results from the 'hit' group and the control group. The fact that some people said 'Yes' to the 'broken glass' question suggests that our expectations play a part here. Broken glass fits with our general understanding of a car accident (our schema) and therefore people are likely to agree.

What did Loftus and Palmer conclude?

Loftus and Palmer suggested that there are two types of information which make up memory of a complex event: the information that we get from perceiving the event and the information that we get after the event. In this case the latter was the information suggested by the questions. Loftus and Palmer concluded that the questions actually altered people's memories.

Over time, the information from these two sources may be integrated in such a way that we are unable to tell from which source some specific detail is recalled. All we have is one memory.

(Loftus and Palmer, 1974, page 588)

Applying this explanation to this study would mean that when the participant first sees the film they form some representation of it in their memory. The experimenter then supplies further information in the form of the question they asked, for example that the cars smashed into each other. These two pieces of information become integrated and the participant is left with a memory of the accident that is more severe than in fact it was.

Key term

schema a framework of knowledge about some aspect of the world

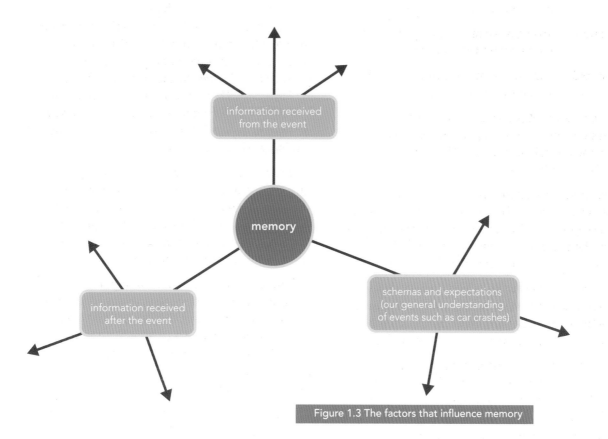

Figure 1.3 The factors that influence memory

Summary of main points

1 The verb 'smashed' in Experiment 1 led participants to estimate higher speeds than the other verbs.

2 The verb 'smashed' in Experiment 2 led participants to say 'Yes' to the question 'Did you see any broken glass?' more often than the verb 'hit'.

3 The conclusions are:

   a   Memory of events is not always reliable.

   b   Memory can be influenced by information that we receive after the event.

   c   Memory can be influenced by our schemas and expectations of events.

Evaluating the study by Loftus and Palmer

What are the strengths of the method used in this study?

The method used in this study was laboratory experiments. Loftus and Palmer manipulated the words used in the questions and measured the effect of this on recall. They did this in controlled conditions, keeping as many other variables as possible the same, thus allowing them to conclude that it was the words used in the questions that caused the differences in recall.

For example, they controlled the films that the participants saw. Everyone saw the same films, in the same room and were questioned about the films in the same way (with the exception of the manipulated independent variable, the verb used in the speed estimate question). They were all also asked questions immediately after the films were shown and the questions were in the form of a written questionnaire, meaning that no variance in the way questions were asked or any feedback from experimenter was possible.

This illustrates one of the major strengths of laboratory experiments: control. The more variables you have control over, the easier it becomes to draw conclusions about the effect of the independent variable on the dependent variable.

What are the weaknesses of the method used in the study?

Despite their many strengths, laboratory experiments have several weaknesses. The high level of control usually means that you have created an artificial situation that makes it difficult to apply your results to everyday life. This is referred to as low ecological validity and is discussed further below. Participants know that they are taking part in a laboratory experiment and this will affect their behaviour in a number of ways. They will be looking for clues as to how to behave (demand characteristics) and they will usually want to help the experimenters by giving them the results that they think they want. This could have had a major effect particularly on the results of Loftus and Palmer's first study.

How representative was the sample of participants?

Loftus and Palmer used student participants in both of the studies. It may be that students are not representative of the general population and therefore it will be difficult to generalise from the results of this study to people in general. Some differences between students and the general population may include:

◆ Students will usually be young and it is possible that people's memories are better when they are young.

◆ Students are used to taking in lots of information and then being asked questions about it. People who have not studied for many years may be less used to this.

◆ Students may be less experienced drivers than the general population and may therefore be less confident in their ability to estimate speed. This may have led them to be more influenced by the words in the questions.

◆ Students may be more susceptible to demand characteristics, especially if they are students of the researchers conducting the study.

What type of data was collected in this study?

Loftus and Palmer only collected quantitative data, that is, speed estimates and numbers of people saying that they had seen a broken headlight.

Quantitative data are very useful for making comparisons and allow statistical analysis to be conducted, but they are fairly superficial and do not tell us anything about why people gave the answers that they did.

A possible improvement might have been to ask people to rate how confident they were in the answers that they had given. This would allow us to analyse the results in more detail.

How useful was this research?

Given that it has just been argued that the study had an unrepresentative sample, you might feel that it was not very useful. However, despite the points made above, it is possible to identify a number of practical applications that arise from Loftus and Palmer's research.

The conclusion that leading questions can affect memory has important implications for interviewing witnesses, both by police immediately or soon after an event and also by lawyers in court some time later.

Interviewers should avoid leading questions and should be careful to word questions in ways that do not suggest an answer to the person that they are interviewing.

Check your understanding

What was the aim of the study by Loftus and Palmer?

Write a brief outline of the first and the second experiments in the study.

What can you conclude from the first experiment?

What can you conclude from the second experiment?

Suggest two strengths and two weaknesses of this study.

Exam Café

You should be able to describe the procedure and findings from the two experiments conducted by Loftus and Palmer. Remember that there are different numbers of participants in each experiment.

The first experiment had five conditions and the second experiment had three conditions. These are as follows:

Experiment 1
Five conditions, each using a different verb (*smashed, collided, bumped, hit, contacted*).

Experiment 2
Three conditions (*hit, smashed* and a control who was not asked this question).

You should be able to state the findings and conclusions from each experiment, and also give an overall conclusion.

U1
1

Loftus and Palmer (1974)

Baron-Cohen et al. (1997)

What is this study about?

Autism is a psychiatric disorder usually detected from the age of 4. Although often seen as a disorder of childhood, autism actually stays with an individual throughout their lifetime. Its main characteristics fall into three categories: impairments in social interaction, impairments in communication, and repetitive and stereotyped patterns of behaviour. In particular, autistic people: have poor eye contact, fail to develop friendships, don't recognise how other people might be feeling or how they might react to certain situations (empathy), fail to develop language, stick inflexibly to routines, and lack creativity and imaginative play.

Not all people with autism have these impairments to the same degree, and despite the social difficulties listed above, some have considerable abilities in one or two areas, for example drawing; these are known as islets of ability. Others are 'very high functioning', in other words they have a higher than normal IQ. This is rare however, as in most people with autism, intellectual development suffers as a result of their social difficulties.

So it can be seen that people with autism do not all experience the associated symptoms to the same degree, in fact there is a whole scale or continuum of autistic symptoms, ranging from the most severe to a mild version known as Asperger's Syndrome.

Theories of autism

Many theories have been put forward to explain why autism occurs. Some of the earliest focused on environmental factors, including poor parenting (Bettelheim, 1967) and interaction in families (Tinbergen and Tinbergen, 1983), but these have been rejected in favour of more biological explanations, including: a general intellectual impairment, a genetic defect, the result of an extreme male brain, and more recently the result of the MMR vaccination (the measles, mumps and rubella injection recommended for all children).

Baron-Cohen was one of the first researchers to propose a cognitive explanation of autism, where the core problem is seen as the inability to predict how others think or feel, a skill which the majority of humans develop automatically. This skill was termed 'mind reading', and since autistic children lacked this skill they are referred to as having 'mind-blindness'. Baron-Cohen suggested that 'reading' or predicting the mind of others (i.e. guessing what they are thinking or how they might react) was based on the ability to see things from their point of view. He called this a theory of mind, in other words a theory that an individual has about how minds in general work, including their own and that of every other human being.

In focusing on a cognitive explanation of autism, Baron-Cohen was rejecting all other explanations of autism. He particularly wanted to demonstrate in his study that autism was not due to intellectual impairment but was the result of the failure to develop a specific cognitive (mental) skill: a theory of mind.

How has theory of mind been tested?

Baron-Cohen had previously carried out research on autistic children; using the Sally-Anne test he had successfully shown that the majority of autistic children he studied did not display theory of mind skills. However, Baron-Cohen claimed that the tests designed for use with children did not assess the more advanced theory of mind skills found in normal adults, and it was the aim of this more recent study to use a new, adult test of theory of mind competence, which could tell us much more about these skills in adults with autism.

Links to other studies

The study by Samuel and Bryant (see pages 40–47) looks at the development of a different cognitive skill: conservation.

Key terms

Asperger's Syndrome a mild version of autism

theory of mind an individual's theory about how minds in general work, including their own and other people's

Sally-Anne test a simple test involving two dolls. One doll leaves the room, the other moves an object, the first doll returns and the child is asked where that doll will look for the object. It is assumed that basic theory of mind skills are required in order to pass this test

Try this ...

Write a list of situations where you 'mind-read' (use your theory of mind).

For each one, note down the consequences of not being able to mind-read, as in the case of autistic people.

Practical investigation ideas

An experiment could be conducted to test theory of mind skills in males and females. Take photographs or use magazine pictures of eyes as stimulus material. Subjects would have to decide which emotion is represented in each set of eyes.

Simon Baron-Cohen

Figure 1.4 Simon Baron-Cohen

Simon Baron-Cohen is Professor of Developmental Psychopathology at the University of Cambridge in the Departments of Experimental Psychology and Psychiatry. He has conducted extensive research into autism spectrum conditions at the psychological, diagnostic, and neuro-scientific levels.

Weblinks

To read the earlier study by Baron-Cohen, Leslie and Frith, and for the 20 most asked questions about autism, including definitions and characteristics of autism, look at the Rutgers University and Autism UK websites (see 'Websites' on page ii).

Baron-Cohen et al. (1997)

Baron-Cohen, S., Joliffe, T., Mortimore, C. and Robertson, M. (1997)

'Another advanced test of theory of mind: evidence from very high functioning adults with autism or Asperger Syndrome', *Journal of Child Psychology and Psychiatry*, 38, 813–22

What was the aim of the study?

This study attempted to provide support for a cognitive explanation of autism, specifically that autistic adults lack advanced theory of mind skills: the ability to predict the thoughts or behaviour of another person.

In order to show that an impaired theory of mind was a specific deficit associated with the autistic spectrum of disorders, this group was compared with a clinical control group of adults with Tourette's Syndrome, chosen because of the number of similarities these subjects had with the subjects with autism and Asperger's Syndrome:

1   They all had intelligence in the normal range.

2   They had all suffered from a developmental disorder since childhood.

3   These disorders all cause disruptions to normal schooling and peer relations.

4   These disorders are all believed to affect the same area of the brain.

5   They are all suggested to be genetic in origin.

6   These disorders all affect males more than females.

A third group of participants was made up of normal adults. Each group was tested on their advanced theory of mind skills using the 'Eyes Task' and their performance compared.

A secondary aim of the study was to investigate whether females would be better on this test of theory of mind than males. In the words of the researchers:

Folk psychology would lead us to expect that normal females may be superior to normal males in the domain of social sensitivity or empathy, but most previous theory of mind research has not used sufficiently subtle tests to evaluate if there is any basis to this.

Baron-Cohen et al., page 814

The independent variable in this study was the three different groups of subjects, while the dependent variable was performance on an advanced test of theory of mind (eyes task).

What was the methodology?

Since the participants were allocated to the three conditions depending on whether they were autistic/Asperger's Syndrome, normal, or had Tourette's Syndrome, the independent variable varied naturally, was *not* manipulated and so the method used was a quasi-experiment.

Subjects

Three groups of subjects were tested:

1   16 subjects (13 males and 3 females) with high functioning autism (4) or Asperger's Syndrome (12). All were of normal intelligence (mean IQ was 105.31), therefore unconfounded by mental handicap. They were recruited from a variety of clinical sources, as well as an advert in the National Autistic Society magazine, *Communication*.

2   50 normal age-matched adults, 25 males and 25 females, all drawn from the general population of Cambridge. None had any history of any psychiatric condition (as established by self-report). They were selected randomly from the subject panel held in the university department. They were all assumed to have intelligence in the normal range, i.e. an IQ above 85. A larger number of normal male and female subjects were tested to examine sex differences in theory of mind skills.

3   10 adult patients (8 males and 2 females) with Tourette's Syndrome, also age-matched with Group 1. They were all attending a referral centre in London (mean IQ was 103.5).

The location and the tasks

The Eyes Task, Happé's 'strange stories' and two control tasks were presented in random order to all subjects; this was to avoid order effects. The subjects were tested individually in a quiet room in their own home, in the researchers' clinic or in the laboratory at the university.

The test for theory of mind – the Eyes Task

The test comprises magazine photographs of the eye region of 25 different faces (male and female). All faces were standardised to one size and photos were all black and white, with the same region of the face selected for each photo: from midway along the nose to just above the eyebrow. See Figure 1.5 for a selection of the photographs used.

Each picture was shown for 3 seconds, with a forced choice between two mental state terms printed under each picture. The experimenter asks the subject 'Which word best describes what this person is feeling or thinking?' The maximum score on this test is 25.

Construction of the Eyes Task

Four judges (2 male and 2 female) discussed and decided on the target word to describe the mental state behind each pair of eyes. A 'foil' word was also selected which represented the exact opposite of the target word. These words were then tested on a panel of 8 judges (4 male and 4 female) who were all blind to (unaware of) the hypothesis of the study. There was full agreement on all the target words amongst the 8 judges. The mental state terms included both basic and complex mental states. See Table 1.1 for a sample of the mental state terms and the foils.

Pair of eyes	Target term	Foil term
1	Concerned	Unconcerned
2	Noticing you	Ignoring you
3	Attraction	Repulsion
4	Relaxed	Worried
5	Serious message	Playful message
6	Interested	Disinterested
25	Decisive	Indecisive

Table 1.1 Target mental state terms, and their foil terms

Baron-Cohen et al. (1997)

Key terms

order effects effects such as improvement in performance, boredom or tiredness, that occur as a result of the order in which conditions or tasks are experienced

quasi-experiment an experiment where the independent variable varies naturally without the need for manipulation by the experimenter

Validity of the Eyes Task

The Eyes Task was designed to be a 'pure' theory of mind test, at an advanced level. In order to make sure that the Eyes Task was really measuring theory of mind, i.e. that the test was valid, subjects in the two clinical groups were also tested on Happé's 'strange stories', also a test for an advanced theory of mind. The idea behind this was that since both were tests of the same thing (theory of mind) then if subjects had difficulties with one of these tasks they should also have difficulties with the other.

This way of checking the validity of a measure is called concurrent validity, and is based on the assumption that two measures of the same thing should produce similar results.

Control tasks

In order to check whether poor performance on the Eyes Task in Group 1 (autistic/Asperger's) was due to other factors, two control tasks were administered.

Gender recognition task

This involved looking at the same sets of eyes as in the experimental task, but this time identifying the gender of the person in each photograph. This task involved a social judgement, i.e. whether someone looks like a man or a woman, rather than involving mind-reading. This task was done to check whether poor performance on the eyes task was due to general deficits in face perception or social perception rather than a lack of theory of mind skills. The maximum score on this task was also 25.

U1
1

23

Basic emotion recognition task

This involved judging photographs of whole faces displaying the basic emotions (based on those described by Ekman: anger, disgust, fear, joy, sadness, and surprise). This was to check whether poor performance on the Eyes Task could be attributed to a problem with recognising basic emotion expression rather than a lack of theory of mind skills. Six faces were used and examples can be seen in Figure 1.5.

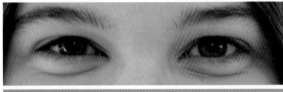

Figure 1.5 Can you judge how these people are feeling?

Try this ...

In pairs, one person makes facial expressions while the other person identifies the emotion intended. Reverse roles.

What were the findings?

Do people with autism lack a theory of mind?

The results from the Eyes Task show that the subjects with Tourette's Syndrome did not differ from normal subjects on this task, but both control groups performed significantly better than the group with autism or Asperger's Syndrome.

On the Happé's 'strange stories' no subjects with Tourette's Syndrome made any errors, but the subjects with autism or Asperger's Syndrome made errors and were significantly impaired on this task, compared to the control groups.

On the gender and emotion-control tasks, there were no differences between the groups.

Group	Eyes Task	Gender recognition task
Autism/ Asperger's Syndrome (16)	16.3	24.1
Normal (50)	20.3	23.3
Tourette's Syndrome (10)	20.4	23.7

Table 1.2 Mean performance on the Eyes Task and the gender recognition task

Do females have a more advanced theory of mind?

In the normal group, as predicted, female subjects performed significantly better than male subjects on the Eyes Task.

Sex	Eyes Task	Gender control
Males (25)	18.8	24.0
Females (25)	21.8	23.8

Table 1.3 Mean performance by males and females in the normal group

What did Baron-Cohen et al. conclude?

Baron-Cohen et al. confirmed that adults with autism or Asperger's Syndrome, despite being of normal or above average IQ, performed poorly on the Eyes Task, an advanced test of theory of mind. They concluded from this that the core deficit involved in autism is the lack of an advanced theory of mind.

The researchers justify the theory of mind explanation for the poor performance of the autism/Asperger's Syndrome group in the following ways:

◆ Poor performance of this group could not have been due to low intelligence because these subjects were in the normal or above normal range of IQ. In fact, some of the subjects with autism or Asperger's Syndrome had university degrees, yet scored poorly on the Eyes Task, strongly suggesting that this aspect of social cognition is independent of general intelligence.

◆ Neither could it have been due to developmental neuropsychiatric disability, since the subjects with Tourette's Syndrome were unimpaired on this task.

The researchers claim that the Eyes Task was a valid measure of theory of mind because:

◆ the target words are mental state terms

◆ the target words are not just emotional states but include terms describing cognitive mental states, suggesting that this task is not just an emotion perception task

◆ the pattern of results from the Eyes Task mirrored the pattern of performance on Happé's 'strange stories', another test of advanced theory of mind

◆ the poor performance on the Eyes Task was not mirrored on the two control tasks, suggesting that the poor performance by subjects with autism or Asperger's Syndrome was not due to the stimuli being eyes, or to basic emotion recognition.

A second finding was that females performed significantly better on the Eyes Task than males; from this the researchers concluded that within the normal population, females have more advanced theory of mind skills than males. Baron-Cohen et al. suggest that this may reflect sex differences in the rate of development of theory of mind in early childhood, and also mirrors female superiority in language development and male superiority in spatial skills, which might explain why men tend to be good at map reading.

Try this ...

Draw a graph of the three groups of participants' mean performance on the Eyes Task and the gender-recognition task. What conclusions can you draw from the findings?

Key terms

Happé's 'strange stories' a test of advanced theory of mind skills that involves answering questions on a selection of stories and the characters in them

IQ intelligence quotient, a numerical representation of intelligence. IQ is derived from dividing mental age (result from an intelligence test) by the chronological age

Tourette's Syndrome a neurological disorder characterised by recurring movements and sounds (called tics)

Weblinks

You can read about Asperger's Syndrome on the Asperger Foundation and BBC websites, see 'Websites' on page ii.

To read about Happé's 'strange stories', look at the Autism Research Centre website, see 'Websites' on page ii.

Summary of main points

1 Previous tests of theory of mind skills were only suitable for children up to the age of about 6.

2 Baron-Cohen et al. wanted to test the theory of mind capabilities of adults.

3 The 'Eyes Task' is a test of advanced theory of mind skills.

4 Subjects with autism or Asperger's Syndrome were significantly impaired on this task compared to a group of age-matched normal adults and a clinical control group with Tourette's Syndrome.

5 This provides evidence for impaired theory of mind skills in very high functioning individuals on the autistic continuum.

Baron-Cohen et al. (1997)

Evaluating the study by Baron-Cohen et al.

What were the strengths and weaknesses of the method used?

There are many strengths of the method used in this study. First, the method was experimental, which allows 'cause and effect' to be established. It was possible to control variables that could have an effect on the subject's performance, for example to test the subjects individually and to administer control tasks. The fact that the experiment was conducted in a laboratory made it easier to apply these controls.

The method used was also a quasi-experiment, which has the advantage of studying naturally occurring conditions. The experimenter did not have to manipulate anything as the subjects were naturally in the three categories of normal, having autism or Asperger's Syndrome, or Tourette's Syndrome. In some experiments where the experimenter has to create conditions, more ethical issues can arise.

A further strength relates to establishing the validity of the Eyes Task through the use of a second measure of advanced theory of mind skills, Happe's 'strange stories'. This established concurrent validity, making sure the test was indeed measuring theory of mind.

The fact that this group did get some of the questions on the Eyes Task correct (mean score was 16 out of 25) would suggest that they did have theory of mind skills, perhaps an analysis of which mental states they got wrong might give more indication of the level of these skills.

The main weakness of a laboratory experiment can be a lack of ecological validity. The laboratory can be a strange environment for the participant; subjects with autism could easily feel disorientated by their surroundings. This could have affected the way they performed, especially since an autistic characteristic is the need for routine and familiarity.

In addition, the Eyes Task was unusual rather than 'lifelike'. The researchers point out that even though it is a 'very advanced test' of theory of mind, it is still simpler than the real demands of live social situations and was therefore low in ecological validity. Specifically, the photographs were static in a way that the real social world never is. It might therefore have been more realistic to use films rather than photographs.

The task required the subjects to study photographs of just the eye section of the face. In everyday life we can generally use cues from the whole face, for example the mouth can give clues about emotion and mental state. To study part of the face in this way could be considered reductionist. In addition, a characteristic of autism is the avoidance of eye contact, which would of course put this group at a disadvantage.

Although the study does not immediately appear to have many ethical issues, the situation could have induced stress in the subjects as any test conditions can, this would break the ethical guideline of protection.

How representative was the sample of participants?

The way in which individuals are affected by autism varies and it would therefore be difficult to generalise from the performance of the 4 autistic adults and 12 with Asperger's Syndrome in the study.

A further criticism is the small number of adults in both of the clinical groups: 16 in the autistic/Asperger's Syndrome group and only 10 in the Tourette's Syndrome group, raising the question of whether these groups were representative. It may have been difficult, however, to find participants with these disorders willing to take part in the study, especially high functioning autistic adults, who are quite rare.

What type of data was collected in this study?

The data collected in this study were quantitative, consisting of the numbers of the scores of each subject on each of the tests administered. Since the researchers believed that the Eyes Task measured whether the subjects had a theory of mind, they saw no need for qualitative data to be collected. However, qualitative data often gives more in-depth explanations and more open-ended questions could have provided reasons for the answers given by the subjects.

How useful was this research?

Research is only useful if it provides valid measurement, and the criticisms of the Eyes Task outlined above do question how useful this study is. However, it seems that most people on the autistic continuum do lack a theory of mind and this knowledge can inform various techniques for people educating and interacting with autistic people.

Many techniques have been developed to encourage theory of mind skills, for example teaching autistic children to recognise facial

expressions using picture cards. Some autistic people have developed their theory of mind skills, for example Temple Grandin, an American woman who developed strategies to understand and predict the thoughts and behaviour of others.

Figure 1.6 Temple Grandin

It would seem that autism can be a lonely disorder to have, considering that the main difficulty is interacting with other people and understanding that they have thoughts and feelings too.

Any research that helps us to understand autism more fully must therefore be considered useful, and further investigation into why autistic children fail to develop a theory of mind would develop our understanding even further.

> ### Key term
>
> cause and effect refers to the ability to establish that one variable is having an effect on another. By controlling all variables other than the independent variable, you can be sure it has caused any effect found. In Baron-Cohen et al.'s study it was clear that the characteristics of autism caused poorer performance on the Eyes Task, as all other variables were controlled

Try this …

Suggest some questions that could have been asked in the study to provide qualitative data.

Weblinks

You can read about teaching children to recognise facial expressions on the *Times* website, and about Temple Grandin on her website, see 'Websites' on page ii.

Check your understanding

What is meant by 'theory of mind'?

What conclusions can be drawn from this study?

What control measures were used in this experiment?

Suggest two strengths and two weaknesses of this study.

Suggest an alternative way in which theory of mind could be investigated with more ecological validity.

Exam Café

You should be able to describe the aim and method used in this study. The design was quasi-experimental and you should be able to explain this. The dependent and independent variables are important for you to know, along with how they were operationalised. The sample was made up of autistic people, 'normal' people and people with Tourette's Syndrome; you need to know how and why these participants were selected for this study along with the limitations of the sample. You should also be able to describe the conclusions that can be drawn from this study and the strengths and weaknesses of the method and procedure used.

Baron-Cohen et al. (1997)

Savage-Rumbaugh et al. (1986)

Pause for thought

◆ What is the difference between language and communication?

◆ How is the communication used by animals different to the language used by humans?

◆ If animals could use language in the same way as humans, what implications would this have?

What is this study about?

There has long been debate about whether other species can use language in the way humans can. Many studies have focused on attempts to teach language to apes, since they are the most genetically similar animals to humans, but until fairly recently, these were rejected as being irrelevant to an understanding of the evolution of human language, and too lacking in scientific rigour to be taken seriously.

Herbert Terrace, a psychologist at Columbia University, New York, published a paper stating that the apes in these studies were merely mimicking their instructors and had no sense of grammatical structure. He compared the performance of apes to the behaviour of rats and pigeons in laboratory experiments, which appeared to understand requests often with the promise of some reward for appropriate behaviour. At the same time, Thomas Sebok, a linguist at Indiana University, commented that the researchers were either victims of self-delusion or guilty of fraud.

As a result of these claims, funding for ape-language studies was not easily available and many creditable journals refused to publish what little research there was. That is until a little pygmy chimpanzee called Kanzi was born in 1980. The study of Kanzi at the Language Research Centre in Atlanta provided a fresh challenge to the cynical views of Terrace and Sebok. This study utilised more scientific procedures for assessing language use and there was a consensus that the new data on chimpanzees went further than previous ape

studies in making us question the nature of human uniqueness. Data were systematically collected on Kanzi and his younger sister Mulika.

Of the four great ape species, only the pygmy chimpanzee (*Pan paniscus*) has not, prior to this study, been the subject of language acquisition studies. This is mainly because of the difficulty in obtaining these animals. They are rare, both in captivity and in the wild, and it is presently illegal to export them from their severely threatened native habitat in Zaire, Africa.

The pygmy chimpanzees differ in many ways from other great apes in their social communication; eye contact, gestures and vocalisations are all considerably more frequent and more elaborate than in other apes. Also male–female ties appear to be exceptionally close, and males, at least in captive groups, participate in infant care. Food sharing is also a frequent behaviour even between adults. In contrast, in common chimpanzees the male–female ties are weak, the males do not participate in infant care and the majority of food sharing occurs only between mother–infant pairs.

Previous research on pygmy chimpanzees also suggests that they are more intelligent than other apes. For example, when a pygmy chimpanzee and a common chimpanzee were raised together for several years and numerous physical and behavioural differences between the two animals were noticed, it was concluded that the pygmy chimpanzee was an extraordinary animal.

So, because the pygmy chimpanzees are more developed in gestural, visual and vocal communication the researchers felt that they would be better prepared than other apes to acquire language.

Comparisons were made with two common chimpanzees (*Pan troglodytes*), who were reared by people in a language-using environment from 1975 to 1983. They were assigned to the Language Project at 1½ and 2½ years of age respectively, and were removed from their mothers before coming to the Language Research Centre. At the time of the report they were 9 and 10 years of age.

There is no common agreement on what constitutes language. However, numerous features have been identified as common to all human languages, some of which can be seen in Table 1.4.

The authors of this study claim that Kanzi approached some of the key criteria of language, including grammatical rules, both in his use of 'words' on a lexigram, and in his ability to comprehend complex spoken sentences, a first in ape-language studies.

Feature of language	Definition
Displacement	The ability to speak about the present, past and future. It is widely believed that humans are the sole species capable of this
Arbitrariness	There is no natural connection between a word or sound and the thing it denotes, we cannot tell the meaning of a word simply by looking at it or hearing it
Productivity	The ability to invent new signals in order to describe new ideas
Cultural transmission	The language used around us, by our family, determines the language we speak

Table 1.4 Four main features that differentiate human language from animal communication

Key term

lexigram a visual symbol system, a board covered with geometric symbols that brighten when touched

Links to other studies

A link can be made with the study by Bandura, Ross and Ross (see pages 48–55), since they also used observational methods to record the imitation of aggressive acts in children.

Practical investigation ideas

You could visit a zoo and observe primate behaviours including grooming, feeding, mating, gestures, vocalisations, parent–infant behaviour. You could compare two species of primates. Whatever you decide to observe, a behaviour checklist will enable you and other observers to know what you are looking for, and you can easily collate quantitative data for comparative purposes from the checklist.

Figure 1.7 Sue Savage-Rumbaugh

Sue Savage-Rumbaugh is a scientist at the Great Ape Trust of Iowa – a research centre dedicated to studying the behaviour and intelligence of great apes. The first and only scientist doing language research with bonobos, she joined the Great Ape Trust following a 23-year association with Georgia State University's Language Research Centre.

Weblink

You can watch a talk by Savage-Rumbaugh and film footage of Kanzi on YouTube, see 'Websites' on page ii.

U1

1

Savage-Rumbaugh et al. (1986)

Savage-Rumbaugh, S., McDonald, K., Sevcik, R. A., Hopkins, W. D. and Rubert, E. (1986)

'Spontaneous symbol acquisition and communicative use by pygmy chimpanzees (*Pan paniscus*)', *Journal of Experimental Psychology: General*, 115, 211–35

What was the aim of the study?

To study the language acquisition of two pygmy chimpanzees (*Pan paniscus*), Kanzi and Mulika compared with two 'common' chimpanzees (*Pan troglodytes*) Austin and Sherman.

To describe the first instance in which a non-human species has acquired symbols without specific training towards that goal.

What was the methodology?

This report describes the data gathered from an in-depth longitudinal study of the rearing of two pygmy chimpanzees. The data were gathered across a 10-year span and the study reports on a 17-month period.

It is important to note that the researchers claim that the present project was not an experiment and was not undertaken with the intent of producing the findings described. However, comparisons were made between the pygmy chimpanzees and two common chimpanzees, who were taught language with the same visual-graphic symbol system. In this way the study ended up having a quasi-experimental design, where the naturally occurring independent variable was the species and the dependent variable their respective language acquisition.

Subjects

In 1986, when the report was written, the pygmy chimpanzees, Kanzi and Mulika, were being reared in a language-using environment, with access to their mother. Kanzi, the main subject of this study, was aged 4 when the report was written. His sister Mulika was 3, and the two common chimpanzees, who had also been reared in a language-using environment, were 9 and 10 years of age.

The communication system

The main medium of communication used with all the animals was a visual symbol system, a lexigram consisting of geometric symbols that brighten when touched, which is treated as the equivalent of uttering a word. Kanzi's keyboard was connected to a speech synthesiser so that words were spoken when he touched the symbols on the board. A lexigram was used because it is thought that apes cannot produce human-like vocalisations.

When outdoors, Kanzi and Mulika used a 'pointing board', a thin laminated panel containing photographs of all the lexigrams. These were not suitable for Austin and Sherman, as their broad hand movements made it difficult to distinguish which symbol they were selecting.

Spoken English accompanied the experimenters' lexigram communications, and gestures were also used with all subjects. Most gestures were informal, spontaneous and natural accompaniments to speech. The experimenters also used approximately 100 American Sign Language gestures.

Figure 1.8 A lexigram

Rearing environments

Kanzi and Mulika's rearing environment after separation from their mother was similar to that of Sherman and Austin; they were all with people who used the visual symbol system around them throughout the day. However there were some major differences between their environments and exposure to lexigrams:

◆ Sherman and Austin were in a training setting, whereas Kanzi and Mulika were in an observational setting

U1
1

Savage-Rumbaugh et al. (1986)

- Sherman and Austin's keyboard did not have a speech synthesiser because tests revealed that they did not understand spoken English words

- Sherman and Austin did not use a keyboard outside the laboratory.

Apart from these differences, other aspects of the rearing environment were similar, including: attachment to caretakers, opportunity to interact with and observe people, exposure to human speech, exposure to gestures, photographs, novel objects, types of formal tests, discipline, opportunity to watch television etc.

No formal training was ever attempted with Kanzi and Mulika; people modelled symbol use during their communications with each other and with the chimpanzees. During all daily activities including playing, eating, resting and travelling in the woods, people commented on and emphasised their activities both vocally and visually by pointing to the appropriate lexigrams on the keyboard. For example, when a teacher was tickling Kanzi they would comment vocally and using the keyboard: 'teacher tickle Kanzi'.

Sometimes Kanzi and Mulika would observe the keyboard being used and at other times they would ignore it. In this way they were observing rather than being trained.

Figure 1.9 Kanzi communicating with the lexigram

Data recording

From Kanzi's first use of the lexigram at the age of 2½ years, a complete record was kept of all his utterances for 17 months. The same was kept for Mulika from 11 to 21 months. Each utterance was classified as it occurred, first as correct or incorrect and next as spontaneous, imitated or structured, as shown in Table 1.5.

Classification	Definition
Correct	Appropriate utterances
Incorrect	Inappropriate utterances
Spontaneous	Any utterance initiated without prior prompting, querying or attempts to elicit a specific utterance
Imitated	Any utterance which includes any part of a companion's prior keyboard utterance
Structured	Any utterance initiated by questions, requests, or object-showing behaviour on the part of the companion, e.g. 'What is this?'

Table 1.5 Classification of utterances

Vocabulary acquisition criteria

Two criteria had to be met before a word could be included in Kanzi and Mulika's vocabulary:

- symbol production should appear to be appropriate

- the word should occur spontaneously on 9 out of 10 occasions, followed by demonstration of concordance on 9 of 10 additional occurrences. (Concordance referred to use of the word backed up by a behavioural confirmation, e.g. if Kanzi requested a trip to the tree house he would be told 'Yes, we can go to the tree house'. He would then have to lead them to the correct location for 'tree house' to be confirmed in his vocabulary.)

Controls

Along with the strict vocabulary acquisition criteria, various controls were undertaken to ensure that data had been accurately recorded at the time they were witnessed (real time). An analysis was done of 4.5 hours of videotape in

Savage-Rumbaugh et al. (1986)

which real-time coding was checked against the videotape. The scoring was done independently by two different observers.

There was 100% agreement over which lexigrams Kanzi used and whether or not they were used correctly in context. However nine utterances were noted on the videotape that were not seen by the real-time observer.

Formal tests of ability to produce and receive communications

Kanzi and Mulika were also tested in everyday situations. For example if Kanzi had scattered a number of objects on the floor, he would be asked to help pick them up in a certain order. If he failed any of these tasks he was shown what to do. These tasks were not associated with rewards and only used lexigrams that Kanzi knew. Similar tests were carried out with Mulika.

At the end of the 17-month period covered in this report Mulika and Kanzi were tested on all the items in their vocabulary. These tests were carried out as a control measure to confirm that Kanzi and Mulika's symbol usage was not being cued by the setting or the companions involved.

These were blind tests and the order of presentation and location of the stimuli were carefully controlled so that the experimenter had no prior knowledge that could bias the responses. Similar tests were carried out on Austin and Sherman.

What were the findings?

Use of gestures

Between 6 and 16 months of age both Kanzi and Mulika spontaneously began to use gestures to communicate preferred directions of travel and actions they wished to have performed. Similar gestures were observed in Sherman and Austin when they were older (between 2 and 4 years).

Kanzi and Mulika's gestures were often more explicit than Sherman's and Austin's, for example if Kanzi wanted a hard nut opened, he would offer it to a person. If the person did not understand that this was a request to crack the nut, Kanzi would slap the nut with his hand, followed by taking a small rock and placing it on top of the rock and illustrate what he wished to have done.

Vocabulary

Symbols	Age acquired (months)
Orange, peanut, banana, apple, bedroom, chase, Austin	30
Sweet potato, raisin, ball, cherry, peaches, coke, bite	31
Melon, jelly, tomato, orange drink	32
Trailer, milk	33
Key, tickle	34
Coffee, juice, bread	35

Table 1.6 Kanzi's symbol acquisition

Symbols	Age acquired (months)
Milk	17
Key, t-room, surprise	20
Juice, water	22
Groom	37
Egg	40
Hamburger, water, M&M, surprise	41
Clover, Matata (her mother), TV, orange juice	42
Mulika, carrot	43
Grab, tree house, blanket, blackberry	44
Mushroom trail	45
Refrigerator, hot dog	46

Table 1.7 Mulika's symbol acquisition

Formal tests of ability to produce and receive communications

Kanzi and Mulika did well on formal tests from the beginning. They seemed to understand that the experimenters were not communicating about something that was going to happen as they touched a symbol, but rather were posing a specific question.

Sherman and Austin, when first asked to label an item in a test, appeared to anticipate that they would receive the item as a consequence of touching the symbol. When they did not, they became confused and consequently, labelling had to be introduced slowly.

The researchers also summarised four main differences between the pygmy chimpanzees and the common chimpanzees:

◆ Kanzi and Mulika comprehended the lexigrams with far more ease, and used them far more spontaneously without the need for training, than Austin and Sherman did.

◆ Kanzi and Mulika were far more able to comprehend spoken English words.

◆ Kanzi and Mulika used lexigrams far more specifically (e.g. to differentiate between coke and juice) than Sherman and Austin, who used broader categories, e.g. food.

◆ Kanzi was able to refer to requests involving others. Austin and Sherman never formed requests in which someone other than themselves was the beneficiary.

What did Savage-Rumbaugh et al. conclude?

The results suggest that pygmy chimpanzees exhibit symbolic and auditory perceptual skills that are distinctly different from those of common chimpanzees. The researchers comment that it is surprising that two closely related species differed so greatly in their capacity to acquire a functional symbolic communication system, specifically in their ability to comprehend spoken speech.

They go on to suggest that this finding minimises the significance of the behavioural differences

between humans and apes, and also point out that the findings highlight the power of culture learning, and that pygmy chimpanzees have the capacity to understand speech.

Summary of main points

1 Observational data were collected on Kanzi and Mulika's use of language.

2 Language use was also assessed through formal testing.

3 The researchers concluded that pygmy chimpanzees are close to humans and have shown the capacity to learn spoken language.

4 The researchers commented on the small sample size but claimed the subjects were representative of their species.

5 The researchers suggested that further research needs to be conducted to assess more carefully the effects of the variables of rearing and species.

Try this …

Using the data in Table 1.8, draw a graph to illustrate the performance of Kanzi, Mulika, Sherman and Austin on the formal tests.

Key terms

blind test the use of an experimenter who does not know the details of a study and so cannot influence the outcome

culture learning the role of culture and socialisation in learning language

Savage-Rumbaugh et al. (1986)

Subject	Type of test							
	Match symbol to English		Match symbol to photo		Match photo to symbol		Match symbol to speech synthesiser	
	Correct	Incorrect	Correct	Incorrect	Correct	Incorrect	Correct	Incorrect
Kanzi	98	2	97	3	93	7	79	21
Mulika	98	2	88	12	98	2	n/a	n/a
Sherman	n/a	n/a	7	93	100	0	n/a	n/a
Austin	n/a	n/a	10	90	100	0	n/a	n/a

Data are % of total number of total trials administered. n/a = no tests were administered

Table 1.8 The performance of Kanzi, Mulika, Sherman and Austin on the formal tests administered

Evaluating the study by Savage-Rumbaugh et al.

What were the strengths of the method used?

This study was an improvement on previous studies on language acquisition in primates, mainly in respect of the many controls that were implemented by the researchers.

Data gathered under rigorous controls such as the formal tests, are more likely to be valid and reliable as they are less open to bias and subjectivity. It is also respected far more than the anecdotal evidence gathered in some previous studies.

The fact that this was a longitudinal study also brings strengths. Longitudinal studies allow in-depth data to be collected and also allow development over time to be studied. It would not have been possible to see the development of Kanzi and the other chimpanzees in a study done over a short period.

Kanzi and the researchers would roam from place to place in the land around the centre. This suggests that the environment had high ecological validity.

What are the weaknesses of the method used?

The issue of ethics is an obvious one in a study involving animals. Animals are vulnerable and unable to express their desires as humans can, and this begs the question of whether studies on animals should take place at all. It is clear that the researchers looked after Kanzi and the other chimpanzees, as the animals' desire to be with their human companions is reported throughout the study, but is it ethical to 'humanise' the chimpanzees as was done in this and other similar studies?

The chimpanzees engaged in human pastimes including watching television, drinking coke and wearing a backpack; even their hunting and feeding habits were shaped by the study in that food was readily available to them, and included items such as sweets, which are not their normal diet and might harm them.

It would have been difficult for the chimpanzees to return to a natural habitat where they had no interaction with humans. There are also reports of the chimpanzees getting frustrated with the constant testing, shown by 'scratching themselves all over', and it could be argued that frustrating animals in this way could harm them. However, the researchers point out that as infants Kanzi and Mulika did have access to their mother, which is an improvement on some earlier studies.

A further weakness was the failure to control the chimpanzees' rearing environments. There were differences in the rearing environments between Kanzi and Mulika on one hand, and Sherman and Austin on the other. These differences could have led to the differences in performance between the two species. A more controlled study would give the two species identical rearing environments and procedures.

How representative was the sample of participants?

The researchers recognised that the number of subjects involved in the study was small. They felt that the differences that emerged between the two species were significant and worthy of consideration, especially since the chimpanzees used were all representative of their species. Whether this is true is uncertain and similar studies on a larger sample of both species would need to be carried out before these results could be generalised.

Were Kanzi and Mulika using language?

Kanzi and Mulika displayed several of the features of language including grammatical structure, combinations, and the use of words to convey requests and to refer to objects and people not in front of them.

However, many features of language were not displayed, and some critics would argue that they did not use language in the complete sense and not in the complex way that humans do.

What type of data was collected in this study?

The main type of data collected in this study was quantitative, consisting of the number of words in the chimpanzees' vocabularies and the number of correct responses in the formal tests administered. This type of data allows comparisons between the chimpanzees to be made easily. However the validity of the data relies on the validity of the tests, which do not allow for comments on and observations of behaviours that may have occurred during the tests, in this way the data could be considered as reductionist.

How useful was this research?

This is a difficult question to answer, especially given that the main aim of psychology is to understand human behaviour and experience. Psychologists often study animals in their quest to understand humans, and basic similarities mean that animals provide a less complicated version of humans, epitomising the role of instinct and biology.

The chimpanzees displayed many of the characteristics of a human child learning language, for instance the role of the simple associations made between words and objects before comprehension develops. This helps us to analyse how human children learn language. In turn it is possible to identify and help children who display difficulties early in the language acquisition process.

Another obvious use that emerges from studies on language acquisition in species such as chimpanzees is that they help us to discover the potential for animals to use language in the way humans do, and to progress and evolve to the status of humans. This has dramatic implications for the way we may live alongside animals in the future.

Weblinks

You can listen to the Radio 4 interview 'A life with Kanzi' on the BBC website, see 'Websites' on page ii.

Check your understanding

Describe the methods used to collect data in this study.

Identify two of the control measures used in this study.

Describe the criteria used to determine whether a new word had been learnt by the chimpanzees.

Describe the main results of this study.

Exam Café

It is important to note that this study was not intended to be an experiment but the paper does describe the comparison made between the pygmy chimpanzees and the common chimpanzees, which suggests a quasi-experimental design.

Other methods used include observation and the overall longitudinal design, which you should be able to describe in detail.

The issues relating to the generalisability of the sample and the ethics of animal research in psychology are also important details for you to understand, and you should also be able to describe the conclusions that can be drawn from this study, along with the strengths and weaknesses of the method and procedure used.

U1

1

Savage-Rumbaugh et al. (1986)

ExamCafé
Relax, refresh, result!

Hot tips

What I wish I'd known at the start of the year…

Sam

Make sure you read the exam question carefully and think about what you're going to say before you start writing. I've wasted lots of time in exams writing down everything I could remember about a study and then realising that I needed to be writing about something else.

Refresh your memory

A common question in the examination asks you to consider possible changes to the core study and the effects that these changes might have. To help you think about this, complete the table below: for each of the three studies, think about how changes would affect the results.

Study	Alternative sample	Different method	Different ways of measuring	More ethical	Improvements
Loftus and Palmer			See student answer		
Baron-Cohen et al.					
Savage-Rumbaugh					

Get the result!

Sample answers

Exam-style question

We are going to look at a student response written under exam conditions to the following question:

Outline an alternative way of measuring the cognitive process in your chosen study and discuss any methodological implications this alternative may have. (8 marks)

Student answer

The cognitive process measured in the Loftus and Palmer study was the reliability of memory, specifically the effect of leading questions on eyewitness testimony. This was measured by asking questions about the speed cars were travelling at in film clips of car crashes. Another way that the reliability of eyewitness testimony could be measured would be to show real-life scenarios acted out and to ask questions relating not just to speed but to other features including colours, clothing and personal characteristics of the actors involved.

This would have several effects including a greater ecological validity due to the use of real people rather than just film clips. In addition, the results would relate to memory for a wider range of information which is more relevant to real-life eyewitness testimony, for example in criminal cases where witnesses often have to remember a wide range of details about incidents they have witnessed.

Examiner says:

This is a good answer and is clearly focused on an alternative way of measuring eyewitness testimony. The alternative has been clearly described and the effects have been well discussed.

How can this question be related to the other two studies in this approach?

Baron-Cohen et al.

The cognitive process investigated in the Baron-Cohen study is theory of mind, and the way this was measured was using the Eyes Task. Alternative measurements could include scenarios like the 'Sally-Anne test', where the participants are shown two dolls and asked to predict how they will behave, based on what they believe. This method has shortcomings in terms of ecological validity, the extent to which the results relate to behaviour of humans outside the laboratory, and it does not measure advanced theory of mind skills.

You could think of other ways to measure theory of mind, perhaps involving watching film clips or using photographs of full faces, or you could suggest an observation of participants in their everyday lives.

For any suggestion of alternative measurement you need to consider the methodological implication as requested in the question.

Savage-Rumbaugh et al.

The Savage-Rumbaugh study was looking at language use in chimpanzees and you need to consider alternative ways that this language use could have been measured and what implications this would have.

Since the chimpanzees were using sign language, you could try using deaf people to communicate with the chimpanzees. This would rule out the influence of other cues that may be picked up during the communication process.

Alternatively the chimpanzees could be filmed and a content analysis could be carried out on the footage. You could use more formal tests that you feel would measure language use by the chimpanzees.

Whatever your suggestion you must consider the methodological implications that would arise as a result of the changes: validity and reliability are important issues to consider.

Developmental psychology

Developmental psychology is the study of the psychological changes that occur throughout a person's lifespan. Much of the work carried out focuses on children and adolescents, as many rapid and significant changes occur during this period. There has recently been a growing interest in changes that occur later in life, and this is no doubt due to our increasing longevity.

The changes that are of interest to psychologists cover a wide range of topics that include cognitive processes such as thinking, conceptual understanding and problem-solving, and social processes such as developing relationships and the acquisition of moral understanding.

Developmental psychologists will often focus on fundamental questions about the nature of children and adults, particularly whether children are qualitatively different from adults or are just 'little adults in the making'. Within this debate children could be different from adults due do to their lack of life experiences or because they have different qualities, such as how they think.

Adults' views of childhood have changed significantly throughout history, and have provided psychologists with a framework to approach the study of development. One view is that children's development is dependent on their experiences. The other view is to consider development as a staged process where each stage requires different strategies and skills.

Samuel and Bryant (1984)

This study replicates two earlier pieces of research: the first by Piaget on how children may have qualitatively different thought processes from adults and how these thought processes can be seen to have different cognitive developmental stages; the second by Rose and Blank, which questions Piaget's methodology and how this may have impacted on his findings.

Samuel and Bryant do not contest Piaget's views, and support the view that children think differently from adults, but they do question the rigidity of the stages during childhood development and Piaget's methodological approach. They see children as being different from adults and cognitive development as being organised into discrete stages that are common to all children.

Bandura, Ross and Ross (1961)

This study focuses on a social process, and particularly on how children learn about behaving aggressively, and therefore this could be linked to the development of moral understanding. The researchers take the view that children learn from their experiences, and they designed an experiment that provides a range of ways of seeing aggressive behaviour. They argue that children develop views of the world by observing 'models' and considering the type of social reward certain behaviours might receive. Bandura, Ross and Ross attempt to identify common features that could account for children behaving aggressively.

Freud (1909)

Freud's psychoanalytical theory suggests that unconscious processes as well as events of which we are conscious affect our behaviour. He regarded events in early childhood as having an impact on later behaviours and therefore considered the role of experience to be of considerable importance in understanding development. Significantly, he placed the experiences into different stages and viewed these as having different thought processes.

Samuel and Bryant (1983)

Pause for thought

◆ Is there a 'type of thinking' you find difficult, for example maths, science or ICT?

◆ Why don't we teach long division to three-year-olds?

What is this study about?

Identifying and studying diversity is not an easy task and this study attempts to deal with how individuals of different ages may think and learn. Behaviourists would argue that children and adults learn in similar ways and that we learn more by having more experiences. This study will consider evidence that children think and learn in qualitatively different ways from adults.

Piaget: what he found out

Jean Piaget was one of the most dominant psychologists of the twentieth century. His main area of study was the cognitive development of children. Piaget developed his interest in how children think early in his career while he was working in Alfred Binet's laboratories in France devising IQ tests. He became interested not only in what children could or could not do, but why they made the mistakes they did. Piaget's undoubted genius lay in his ability to devise imaginative tasks for children that would allow him to have an insight into their thought processes. The overall conclusion was that children's thinking was not the same as adults' and that thinking, or cognition, developed through a series of stages (see Table 2.1).

1 The sensorimotor stage: between birth and about 18 months children learn via their senses.

   My food is warm and mushy. It makes me happy.

2 The pre-operational stage: between 18 months and about 7 years when symbols (such as words) and general rules become important.

   When I say Yum Yum, I get a bowl of the warm mushy stuff.

   For the child the sound 'Yum Yum' represents the feeling of being hungry and wanting this satisfied by banana custard.

3 The concrete operational stage: between 7 and 12 years when thought experiments become a possibility but are still limited by the present world and how it is.

   I like this banana custard well enough, but what if I made it thicker and turned it into a cake-type thing?

4 The formal operational stage: between 12 years and above when thoughts are governed by logical reasoning and cause and effect can be considered.

   OK I need one pint of milk, three mashed bananas, two spoons of custard powder, one cup of flour and an egg. Ah, the perfect banana custard cake.

Stage	Age
Sensorimotor	0–18 months
Pre-operational	18 months–7 years
Concrete operational	7–12 years
Formal operational	12 years+

Table 2.1 Piaget's stages of cognitive development

This study concentrates on the features of thought in pre-operational children. Piaget noted that at this stage children cannot:

◆ *conserve*, that is, understand that if the shape of something is physically changed it will still have the same mass, volume or number

◆ *reverse mental operations*, that is, they can only accept what they observe in the present and, for example, would not be able to understand that a pool of water was once an ice cube.

Weblink

To read more details about Piaget, see 'Websites' on page ii.

Try this …

Collect a variety of bottles that have the same volume but are different shapes. Ask friends who are not familiar with psychology to put them into what they think is an order of increasing volume.

Now fill them up from a measuring jug. Stand back and watch them be amazed! Is it just pre-operational children who cannot conserve volume?

Challenges to Piaget's theory of cognitive development

Piaget's findings had a huge impact on teaching and learning in the 1960s and 1970s and were even the foundation of a major government policy that suggested that primary-school teachers should become 'facilitators' of learning.

Before Piaget, most teaching was didactic, with the teacher telling the pupil what to do. Piaget's findings provided evidence that children are motivated to learn better when they explore their own thinking within each stage. He saw children as active little scientists.

This view is problematic for many. For example, Donaldson (1978) felt that it presents a limited understanding of learning and that the stages simply reflect the progression of a scientific thought process that ends with logical reasoning. Donaldson thought that the context in which learning took place was being ignored and particularly that learning is normally a social event.

Try this …

Devise a simple quiz for the same group of friends. Ask a number of questions and every so often re-ask one of the questions asked previously and note what your friends say.

Do they keep to the same answers or try new ones? Does this give you any insight into the effect of asking a question twice?

Judith Samuel

Judith Samuel is a Consultant Clinical Psychologist with Oxfordshire Learning Disability NHS Trust. Her main area of research is concerned with people with intellectual disabilities.

Figure 2.1 Judith Samuel

Links to other studies

Baron-Cohen et al. (pages 20–27) also grapple with the considerable problem of designing investigations related to children's thought.

Bandura, Ross and Ross (pages 48–55) show how the actions of those around us impact on our thoughts and behaviour.

Samuel, J. and Bryant, P. (1983)

'Asking only one question in the conservation experiment',
Journal of Child Psychology 22(2), 315–18.

What was the aim of the study?

This study is centred on how we can gain an understanding of the thought processes of young children. Piaget's well-established four-stage theory was beginning to come under question because it was developed:

◆ considering only scientific logical thought

◆ using methodologies that were seen as inappropriate for young children.

A previous study of learning by Rose and Blank (1974) was based on Donaldson's views about the importance of context on pre-operational children's ability to conserve. They had suggested that the reason for the children's mistakes in Piaget's tasks was due not to poor understanding but to the manner in which Piaget posed the questions. The suggestion was that the error was due to a social misunderstanding and not a cognitive one.

It is worth reviewing both Piaget's conservation tasks and those designed by Rose and Blank to help us understand the significance of the Samuel and Bryant study.

During the original investigation on conservation (of number) Piaget had shown 5- to 8-year-old children two rows of counters. He then asked them if the two rows contained the same number of counters and they normally said 'Yes'. This is the *pre-transformation question*.

Piaget then changed (transformed) one of the rows by making the spaces between counters wider but kept the total number of counters the same.

The children were then asked, again, if there were the same number of counters in each row. This is the *post-transformation question*. This time significant numbers of children got the answer wrong. They thought the more widely spaced row had a larger number of counters. Piaget assumed that this was because the children could not reverse their mental operations, saw that the counters were taking up more space and so intuitively reasoned that this must mean there were more.

The Rose and Blank study had developed Donaldson's ideas by considering whether asking two questions might be confusing for children. Normally, if a child is asked the same question twice it is not unreasonable for them to assume that this is because the first answer is incorrect. Therefore they changed their response to the second question and got the answer wrong.

The children were behaving socially correctly in this context and they responded to the demand characteristics of the procedure. The second question had an impact on the children's ability to carry out the conservation task.

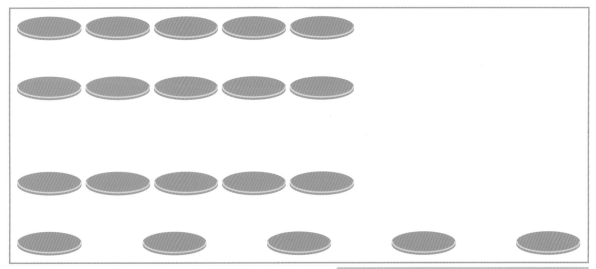

Figure 2.2 Two sets of counters as used by Piaget

Rose and Blank dropped the first, pre-transformation question and found that significant numbers of children now gave the correct response. This indicated that the children did have a better cognitive understanding of the task than Piaget would have expected a pre-operational child to have.

Samuel and Bryant 'simply' took Rose and Blank's investigation one step further by repeating this procedure with three conservation tasks, using a wider age range of children.

Key terms

demand characteristic a feature of a procedure (other than the independent variable) that influences a participant to try to guess what a study is about and look for clues as to how to behave

independent measures design a method that involves comparing the results from separate groups or populations

What was the methodology?

The participants were 252 boys and girls from a variety of Devon schools and pre-schools. They were placed into four age-controlled groups (A, B, C, D) of 63 each. These four groups were each divided into three subgroups to match the experimental conditions shown in Table 2.2.

Each experimental subgroup therefore contained 21 children and a total of 84 children were subject to each experimental condition.

Each child carried out three different conservation tasks using different materials:

◆ counters for number

◆ plasticine for mass

◆ liquid in a glass for volume.

They had four trials for each material, making a total of 12 trials for each child. Each child was only tested in one experimental condition. The results for the four age groups were therefore compared in an independent measures design.

There are three independent variables in this study: age, experimental condition and the material used in the conservation task.

Experimental condition	Procedure	Group A (mean age 5 years 3 months)	Group B (mean age 6 years 3 months)	Group C (mean age 7 years 3 months)	Group D (mean age 8 years 3 months)
Standard	Using the pre- and post-transformation questions as Piaget did	21	21	21	21
One-judgement	The question was only asked after transformation	21	21	21	21
Fixed-array (control)	The children only saw the objects after they had been transformed and were then asked the question	21	21	21	21

Table 2.2 Table showing protocol used in Samuel and Bryant's study

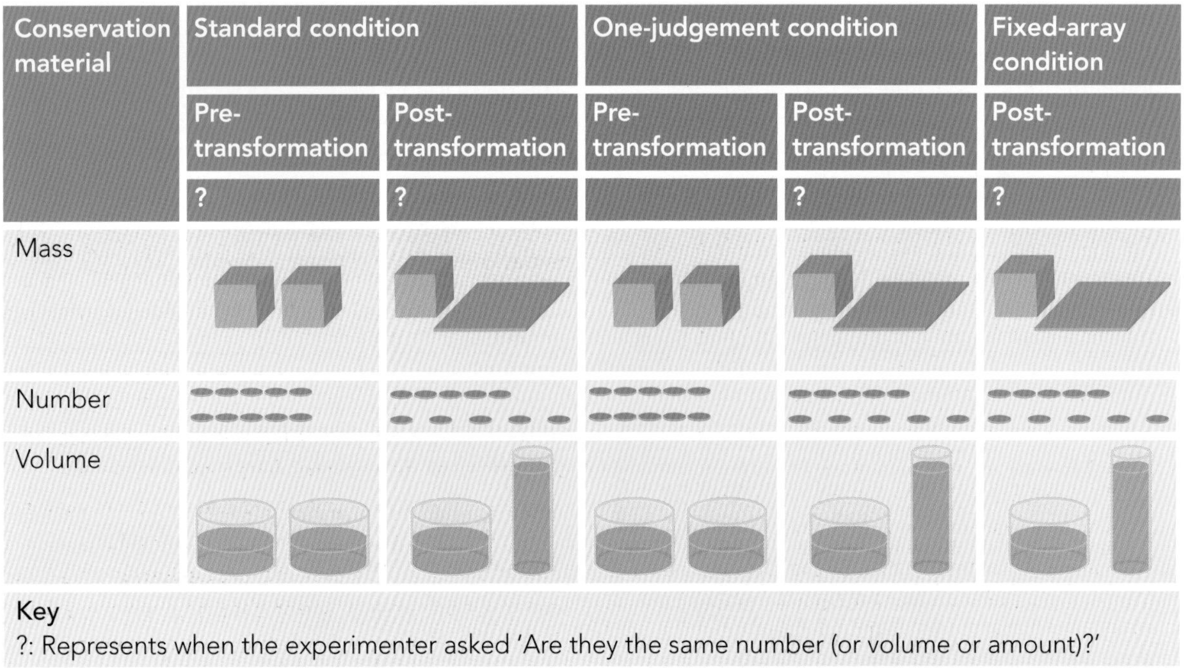

Conservation material	Standard condition		One-judgement condition		Fixed-array condition
	Pre-transformation	Post-transformation	Pre-transformation	Post-transformation	Post-transformation
	?	?		?	?
Mass					
Number					
Volume					

Key
?: Represents when the experimenter asked 'Are they the same number (or volume or amount)?'

Figure 2.3 How the transformations look

What were the findings?

The findings were recorded as the number of errors made during the conservation tasks. An error was recorded when the child incorrectly stated how the number, volume or mass had changed.

Table 2.3 shows the mean number of errors. As there were twelve trials the maximum error would be 12 and the minimum error 0.

The data in Table 2.3 show the findings for two of the independent variables: age and experimental condition.

Age: The mean number of errors decreases as the children get older, showing that their ability to conserve gets significantly better with increasing age.

Experimental condition: The mean number of errors is lower for the one-judgement condition. This is when only one post-transformational question is asked. The highest number of errors was recorded for the children who were only asked one question in the control condition. This is when the children did not see the transformation take place but were asked if the quantities were the same.

The data in Table 2.4 show the findings for the third independent variable, the material tested in the conservation task. It can be seen that children are more successful and so make fewer errors when conserving number compared with volume and mass.

Age	Experimental condition		
	Standard	One-judgement	Fixed-array (Control)
5 years 3 months	8.5	7.3	8.6
6 years 3 months	5.7	4.3	6.4
7 years 3 months	3.2	2.6	4.9
8 years 3 months	1.7	1.3	3.3

Table 2.3 Mean number of errors in each condition

What did Samuel and Bryant conclude?

The findings provide a 'winners all round' scenario, as although Piaget's ideas are not de-bunked, the criticisms levelled at him by Donaldson and others appear to be supported.

Children clearly can conserve better than Piaget thought they could, and this is shown to be related to the context in which the tasks are presented. When children are asked two questions in the standard Piagetian approach they make more errors than in the one-judgement condition. This is not because of an inability to conserve material, but rather it is due to the demand characteristic of the procedure. The fewer errors for the one-question procedure indicate that they do have the cognitive understanding to conserve.

The result for the fixed-array condition is interesting, as this further confirms that children do have an understanding of conservation. The number of errors for the fixed array is the highest of all and this suggests that children need to use the knowledge gained from their original, pre-transformation, observations to answer correctly. What this shows in relation to the standard and one-judgement conditions is that despite the fact that the children observe a physical change in appearance, they have sufficient knowledge to understand that the amount of material has not changed. In other words, pre-operational children can conserve number, mass and volume better than Piaget assumed.

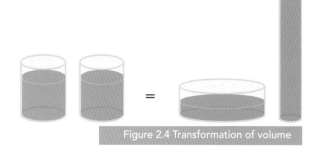

Figure 2.4 Transformation of volume

The original insight provided by Piaget still holds, as the ability to conserve in all conditions does get better as the children get older. The important finding is that if we are to use research to provide an understanding of how children think, then it is vital that the procedure is carefully considered, as even minor changes can have a significant effect on the results. Children may think differently from adults, but the difference may not be as great as Piaget thought.

Summary of main points

1   Children perform better in the conservation task if they are asked one question after the material has been changed.

2   The ability to carry out a conservation task correctly increases with age.

3   Number is conserved better than mass or volume.

Material tested	Experimental condition		
	Standard	One-judgement	Fixed-array (Control)
Mass	1.5	1.2	1.7
Number	1.5	1.0	1.5
Volume	1.8	1.6	2.5

Table 2.4 The mean errors across all ages for the material used in the conservation task

Evaluating the study by Samuel and Bryant

What are the strengths of the method used in this study?

The design of this study was more complex than that of Rose and Blank as it included three independent variables – age, experimental condition and the material being conserved. It therefore advances our understanding of how children may carry out a conservation task.

This study has an experimental design and therefore seeks to have tight control on the independent variables in an attempt to make clear links between cause and effect. The independent variables were controlled by:

◆ having a different procedure for each experimental condition

◆ each conservation task being repeated four times to eliminate the possibility that responses were due to error or chance; the tasks were also presented in random order to reduce the possibility of order effects

◆ putting the children into groups with defined age limits; this could be regarded as a quasi-experiment as the ages were not manipulated, they were simply the ages of the children.

Was the study ethical?

The study can be assumed to be ethically sound, as although the procedure may be unusual, the possibility of distress is fairly limited.

What are the weaknesses of the method used in the study?

Despite Donaldson's original criticism, that if we are to understand how children think we must take the context into account and design investigations that children can relate to, this study is laboratory based and far removed from a child's usual experiences, and is therefore still lacking in ecological validity. It could be said that as the design is so similar to Piaget's original study, all this study does is 'fine tune' Piaget's theories and add more evidence to the idea

Figure 2.5 Children are capable of a greater understanding than Piaget thought

that children's thinking develops into a type of scientific logical reasoning.

A feature related to the presence of an adult could be that the children felt compelled to engage with the task and may have completed the experiment despite the fact that it was dull and uninteresting. Many investigators seek consent from care givers but do not always seek the assent of the children. It is not clear whether Samuel and Bryant did this.

Pordopas (1987) suggested an alternative explanation that relates to the methodology. He considers that the increased error recorded when two questions are asked is the result of the child's short-term memory being interfered with. If only the adults had given the children some space, silence and time to think!

How representative was the sample of participants?

There were 252 children in the sample, which can be considered large enough to provide a representative sample. Samuel and Bryant tested children aged 5–8 years, which allowed them to draw conclusions about the age at which children begin to be able to conserve. All the children came from one area of England (Devon), which might mean that they are not representative of children from other areas of the country. For example, if teaching methods in Devon were different from other counties, this might affect children's cognitive abilities. This is not a major criticism of the study, and it is likely that the findings are representative of children in most western cultures.

Why might the findings not represent cognitive development in non-western cultures?

What type of data was collected in this study?

The data are quantitative and allow statistics to be used to indicate the probability that the behaviours observed were due to chance. A particularly robust statistical test was used that enables the data to be used confidently.

How useful was this research?

Children's cognitive development is shown to be affected by environmental influences, in this case how the questions are asked. This provides the possibility that our abilities are not fixed at birth but can be changed by social interactions throughout our lives, especially when we are young.

The social context of how children learn is very important and needs to be considered in education, as children will not respond well to just being told to do things. These 'social cues' are very important and effective learning may not take place without them.

This study highlights the need to pay considerable attention to research methodology as seemingly insignificant events can have wide-ranging effects on the findings.

Check your understanding

Why did Rose and Blank want to change Piaget's procedure?

What are the characteristics of a pre-operational child?

What could the child be thinking when the post-transformation question is asked?

What was the effect of age on the number of errors?

Consider the three experiments: Piaget, Rose and Blank, and Samuel and Bryant. How do the experimental conditions differ?

Exam Café

Why did Samuel and Bryant have three experimental conditions?

To answer this, you need to consider carefully what each condition was trying to show. Clearly, the standard condition was just a replication of Piaget's method. But why was only one question asked in the one-judgement condition? This should be easy for you to answer (hint: demand characteristics). The more difficult condition to explain is the fixed array. How might this give insight into reversing mental operations?

Bandura, Ross and Ross (1961)

Pause for thought

◆ Do you think children are born naughty?

◆ Why are some people more aggressive than others?

◆ How often have you copied something somebody said, or how they behaved?

What is this study about?

This study has the 'transmission of aggression' as its focus. This is not meant to refer to some strange technology that enables aggressive behaviours to move around the population. Bandura, Ross and Ross were interested in individuals and their social interactions and in particular how these interactions might account for aggressive behaviours. To investigate this, they would have to grapple with two main questions, the first dealing with the *origin* of aggression and the second with the possible mechanism for transmission.

◆ Are human beings naturally aggressive?

◆ If aggression is not innate, then how do we learn to be aggressive?

Bandura and colleagues had already shown that children will imitate the actions of adults when the adults are present. This further investigation was intended to test whether children would imitate adults even if they were not present and the children were in a different setting. The focus on aggression also allowed differences in aggressive behaviour between the genders to be investigated.

Links to other studies

See Freud (pages 56–62) for a different view on the origin of aggressive behaviour.

See Reicher and Haslam (pages 104–111) on the social origins of behaviours.

Social Learning Theory (SLT)

Bandura, Ross and Ross's idea that children may learn behaviours by observing others was underpinned by what was known as Social Learning Theory (SLT), which had been developed about 20 years earlier as an alternative to behaviourist views on learning.

Many people were becoming unhappy with the simple notion that human behaviours could be explained and understood in terms of responses to environmental stimuli. Human behaviour was far too complex for this stimulus–response view of the world, which did not take into consideration internal processes, such as thinking.

Cognition, or thinking, was central to SLT, which regards humans as social beings who are continuously observing others and making judgements about the value of the behaviours they see.

These judgements can be linked to behaviourist theory, as it is suggested that individuals observe the interactions between others and identify those behaviours that provide social rewards or punishments. This is regarded as observational learning. If a behaviour is observed by an individual to obtain a reward then it is more likely that this will be imitated later.

SLT refers to this process as 'modelling'. We often read about 'role models', that is, people who have sufficient status or notoriety to exert great influence on those who observe them.

ExamCafé
Relax, refresh, result!

Relax and prepare

What I wish I'd known at the start of the year…

Mike

Re-read the study you want to revise. Do this a few times if you can, or even record yourself reading and listen to this a few times. When you do this, concentrate on what is happening to the participants. Now write a short story from their point of view. This will help you get a feel for what it may have been like to be part of this study.

Daphne

What's really important is to concentrate on revising the bits you don't know. Revising is about trying to make sure you know as much as possible, and this means being honest and finding the gaps in your knowledge. For each study, consider what you knew about the topic before you started the course. For example, how did you think children developed aggressive behaviours? Now record what new information the study has given you. You could make a 'What I knew before' and 'What I have learnt' list.

Refresh your memory

You will often be asked to comment on the way a psychologist carried out a study. To do this, you need to know what they did and why they did it. This is more than just describing the methodology, as it requires you to consider why a study was designed that way it was. This will help you to get more marks in the exam, as knowing why is harder than just describing. Try copying and completing the table on the next page .

Study	What type of data were collected?	What was the sample?	How was the study carried out?	What are the strengths?	What are the weaknesses?	How could the study be improved?
Freud	Qualitative data to obtain a detailed account		Case study of one child			
Bandura, Ross and Ross		72 children between 3 and 5 years old			The conditions set up were not related to real-life expectations, e.g. the children questioned the model's behaviour	
Samuel and Bryant			Investigated three types of conservation under three different conditions to extend previous findings			Use observations from normal play or teaching contexts

Sample answers

Exam-style question

We are going to look at a student response written under exam conditions to the following question:

Outline an alternative sample that could be used in your chosen study. Discuss any methodological implications this alternative sample may have. (8 marks)

Student answer

In the study by Bandura, Ross and Ross there were 72 participants. This may sound like quite a large sample but they were not all subject to the same experimental condition. The investigation actually had 8 experimental groups and this meant that there were only 6 children in each group. The children were selected from a university nursery and aged between 3 and almost 6. The sample chosen by Bandura and colleagues therefore has a number of problems.

Each group is too small to make reliable generalisations: children from a university nursery may not be representative of the wider population and children between 3 and 6 behave very differently.

An alternative to the sample used by Bandura, Ross and Ross would be to use more children in each experimental condition. If these conditions had 20 or more children then it is more likely that the behaviour observed could be interpreted and then generalised to other children. It might still be difficult to generalise their findings as the children represented a particular social group and so it would be useful to have a sample that had children from a variety of social and cultural backgrounds. The children's ages were only a few years apart but when they are this young they do behave very differently. The sample could therefore also be improved by having children of the same ages in each experimental group. It is possible that 3 year olds will react differently from children who are nearly 6.

Examiner says:

This is very helpful as it suggests that you clearly know the details of this study.

Examiner says:

It might have been better to include the points from the list below in this paragraph as this would help your argument flow better.

Examiner says:

This is useful as you are showing what features of the sampling you wish to address, but see the comment above.

Examiner says:

Good point. You could add some examples to make the point clearer.

Examiner says:

A fair point. You could add some suggestions as to how the response to the experimental condition may differ.

How can this question be related to the other two studies?

You need to be prepared to be able to answer the question about alternative methods for each of the three studies, therefore it is useful for you to consider what the alternatives may be, as in the examples below.

Freud

This is a case study on one young boy. An alternative would be either to observe a girl or to gather data from more children. If Freud had observed a girl it would have enabled him to compare her behaviour with that of Hans. Observing more children makes it more likely that findings can be generalised.

Samuel and Bryant

This study was essentially an extension of previous investigations and one of the changes was to use a wider age range of children. A useful alternative would be to repeat this experimental design but with children from a variety of cultures and social groups. This would enable the findings to be generalised more widely within the population.

Physiological psychology

Physiological psychology attempts to explain human behaviour through an understanding of biological and neurological processes. This approach assumes that behaviour can be explained in terms of the physiological workings of the body and the brain. Physiological psychologists study the structure and function of different parts of the brain and the nervous system. This has led to an overlap between psychology and neuroscience.

What techniques do physiological psychologists use to study the brain?

One of the earliest techniques for measuring brain activity is the electroencephalogram (EEG). This involves electrodes attached to the scalp, which detect brain activity. The study by Dement and Kleitman used EEG measurements of brain activity during sleep.

More recent techniques include PET scans, which can provide coloured images of brain activity. These allow researchers to identify which areas of the brain are active in response to different kinds of stimuli. MRI scans can provide details of the size of different brain structures and can reveal the location and precise details of brain damage. MRI scans are used in the study by Maguire et al. to calculate the size of the hippocampus.

Physiological psychologists also use case studies. Occasionally people suffer extreme and unusual forms of brain damage, and studying them can tell us a great deal about the functioning of normal brains. The core study by Sperry used this approach, as he was able to study a small number of people who had undergone radical brain surgery as a treatment for epilepsy.

Maguire et al. (2000)

The study by Maguire et al. uses the MRI scanning technique. Maguire hypothesised that experiences can cause changes in the brain. For this research it was suggested that people who use navigational skills constantly in their work might show corresponding changes in the part of the brain that deals with this skill: the hippocampus. Maguire and her colleagues compared the hippocampal size of licensed London taxi drivers with a control group, and found that the taxi drivers had a significantly larger hippocampal volume.

Dement and Kleitman (1957)

The study by Dement and Kleitman is a very early study of sleep and dreaming. The participants were volunteers who agreed to sleep in a laboratory with electrodes attached to their scalps to measure their brain activity. The researchers were able to make one of the first scientific demonstrations of the relationship between the stages of sleep and the occurrence of dreaming.

Sperry (1968)

The study by Sperry investigated a small number of people who had had their corpus callosum severed. The corpus callosum is the bundle of fibres connecting the left and right hemispheres of the brain. These people had this extreme surgery to control their epilepsy; severing the corpus callosum does not cure epilepsy, but it prevents the seizures from spreading across from one hemisphere of the brain to the other, and can significantly reduce their severity. In a series of ingeniously devised experiments, Sperry was able to demonstrate the functions of the different hemispheres.

Maguire et al. (2000)

◆ Not long ago, the only way to examine the brain was during an autopsy. Brain-scanning techniques have had a dramatic impact on brain research, allowing researchers to examine living brains and to see what happens when a certain task is performed.

◆ How do you think this has changed psychology?

◆ Do you think that your experiences cause physical changes in your brain?

◆ In what way do you think this might happen?

Background

The hippocampus is a part of the brain located in the medial temporal lobe and making up part of the limbic system. Humans and other mammals have two hippocampi, one in each side of the brain. Their major function appears to be an involvement in memory and spatial navigation. The name comes from the Greek word for 'seahorse' and refers to the shape of the hippocampus.

Key terms

limbic system a set of brain structures including the hippocampus and the amygdala that support a variety of functions including emotion and long-term memory

hippocampus the part of the brain that is concerned with memory and spatial navigation

The exact role of the hippocampus is still disputed, but psychologists and neuroscientists agree that it plays an important role in the formation of new memories about experienced events, sometimes referred to as episodic and autobiographical memory. Some researchers have argued that the hippocampus ceases to play a role in the retention of memory once it has been consolidated. This is supported to some extent by the fact that damage to the hippocampus usually results in an inability to form new memories, although access to memories formed prior to the damage may also be affected. However, memories established many years before the damage are sometimes spared, supporting the idea that consolidation over time may 'transfer' the memory out of the hippocampus to other parts of the brain. This has proved to be a difficult area to research and the precise role of the hippocampus is still being investigated. Damage to the hippocampus does not affect all aspects of memory: the learning of new skills such as playing a musical instrument

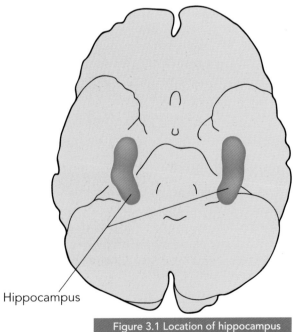

Hippocampus

Figure 3.1 Location of hippocampus

appears to be untouched and this suggests that such abilities depend on a different type of memory (procedural memory), which does not involve the hippocampus.

The following case study gives some clues about the role played by the hippocampus.

> HM is a much-studied patient who had severe epilepsy. As a drastic solution he had surgery, which removed the front two-thirds of his hippocampus on both sides of the brain, an area of surrounding tissue about 8 x 6 centimetres and the amygdale. After the surgery, HM had no memories of the previous 2 years. His memories until the age of 25 were largely intact but there was nothing after that. He was unable to acquire new memories and could hold on to information for only a few minutes. Researchers who have known HM for many years have to be introduced to him every time they see him.

Weblink

To find out more, see 'Websites' on page ii.

The role of the hippocampus in navigation

Neuroscientists know that the hippocampus is involved in spatial memory. It seems to be particularly important in navigation. Small mammals and birds that rely heavily on navigational skills have larger hippocampi relative to their brain and body size than animals that rely less on navigational skills.

It has also been shown that the hippocampus can increase in size when needed: animals and birds have a greater hippocampal volume during seasons when navigational skills are more important, such as when they are involved in food-storing behaviours.

Studies on rats have shown that neurons in the hippocampus have spatial firing cells called place cells, which fire when the animal finds itself in a particular location; some appear to be sensitive to direction and to head movements. Place cells have also been found in humans involved in finding their way around a virtual-reality town (they had had electrodes implanted in their brain as part of surgical treatments for epilepsy).

The discovery of place cells suggests that the hippocampus might act as a cognitive map – a neural representation of the layout of the environment. This may not be strictly true, as other research suggests that the hippocampus may be associated with more fundamental navigational processes, such as basic spatial memory (environmental stimuli such as the location of food, water, prey or predators), or simple mental maps. However, it is clear that an intact hippocampus is required for even the most simple spatial memory tasks.

So, without a hippocampus, we would not know how to get to where we wanted to be, or be able to remember where we had been.

However, it is also true that some people have better navigational skills than others, and there may be some truth in the claim that men are better map-readers – research has shown that males are better at such skills because they have a greater hippocampal volume.

Eleanor Maguire

Figure 3.2 Eleanor Maguire

Eleanor Maguire is a Principal Investigator working at the Wellcome Trust Centre for Neuro-imaging at University College London. The centre was founded in 1994 and is regarded as a centre of excellence for neuro-imaging. Eleanor Maguire has conducted several studies related to the one being discussed here and describes her research interests as aiming to establish how we internally represent large-scale space and our personal experiences. She has also investigated the effects of a variety of disorders (such as dementia) and their effects on memory representations.

Maguire, E. et al. (2000)

'Navigation-related structural changes in the hippocampi of taxi drivers',
Proceedings of the National Academy of Science, USA, 97, 4398–403

What was the aim of the study?

This study attempts to determine whether changes could be detected in the brains of humans who have extreme experiences of spatial navigation. The researchers predicted that if there were any differences in the brains of those who rely heavily on spatial navigational skills in their working life, then these differences would be found in the hippocampus. The assumption being made here is that the hippocampus has 'plasticity', that is that the volume of grey matter here can change in response to learning and experience.

Who were the participants?

The researchers decided that a suitable sample for this study would be London black-cab drivers, who have to pass a series of tough tests before being licensed to drive one of the famous black cabs. The training is referred to as 'the Knowledge' and takes at least two years to complete.

The participants were 16 male licensed cab drivers who had passed 'the Knowledge'. All were right handed and were between 32 and 62 years of age with a mean age of 44. They had all been licensed for at least 18 months, although the range was from 18 months to 42 years with

What is 'the Knowledge'?

Potential black-cab drivers have to be aged 21 or over and must apply to the Public Carriage Office before beginning their training. The licence for the whole of London requires drivers to have a detailed knowledge of the 25,000 streets within a six-mile radius of Charing Cross, as well as a more general knowledge of the major routes throughout the rest of London. Candidates are given 'the blue book', which contains 320 different routes through London. Whilst training, candidates often follow licensed cab drivers on mopeds with map holders attached to their handlebars, trying to learn all the routes. They have a written test on the first 80 routes and then an interview-style examination on the other 240.

When they have got through the 320 central London routes they start learning the suburban ones, and after that they take a cab-driving test in London. Finally they take another written and map test. It can take several years to become fully licensed.

Cab drivers are an ideal sample for a study looking at structural brain changes from spatial navigation. The researchers scanned cab drivers and non-cab drivers (the control group), and were able to compare the scan results of the two groups to see if there are any differences. Having a sample of people with a range of years of navigating experience also allows the researchers to examine the effect of spatial experience on brain structure over time.

Figure 3.3 A small part of the area that London cab drivers have to know

a mean of 14.3 years. The average time spent training before passing 'the Knowledge' was 2 years (range 10 months to 3.5 years). Some had trained continuously and some had trained on a part-time basis. They were all described as having healthy medical, neurological and psychiatric profiles.

The researchers also needed a control group to compare with the cab drivers. As the data were collected through brain-scanning technology, the researchers simply selected 50 scans from the structural MRI scan database at the same centre where the cab drivers were scanned. All these scans were from healthy, right-handed males aged between 32 and 62, to match the general profile of the cab drivers. The mean age and the spread of ages were similar in both groups. None of the control scans were from cab drivers.

What was the method?

The method is best described as a quasi-experiment. The researchers did not manipulate the independent variable in this study and they simply used two existing groups of participants – cab drivers and non-cab drivers. The data were collected through two different techniques of analysing MRI scans. These were voxel-based morphology and pixel counting. These data were also correlated with the length of time the cab drivers had been licensed.

What is an MRI scan?

MRI stands for magnetic resonance imaging. An MRI scan works by aligning atomic particles in the body tissues by magnetism and then bombarding them with radio waves. This causes the particles to give off radio signals that differ according to what type of tissue is present. A computer software program then converts this information into a 3D picture. A brain scan taken like this looks like a greyish X-ray, which shows clearly where the different types of tissue are. The analysis of the scan in this study was able to calculate the volume of grey matter in the hippocampus.

What are voxel-based morphology and pixel counting?

Voxel-based morphology (VBM) and pixel counting are ways of analysing scan information to give a measure of brain volume. A pixel represents the image in two dimensions and a voxel in three dimensions. VBM has been used to identify changes in a variety of neurological disorders, including schizophrenia and temporal lobe epilepsy. It has also been used to identify structural abnormalities such as those found in patients suffering from multiple sclerosis and Alzheimer's disease. It has also been used in studies that have attempted to identify the impact of learning on brain structure. Studies have shown that learning to read music, learning a second language and even learning a complex motor skill such as juggling corresponds to changes in the grey and white matter. This study looks at the changes corresponding to navigational skills and experience.

U1

3

Maguire et al. (2000)

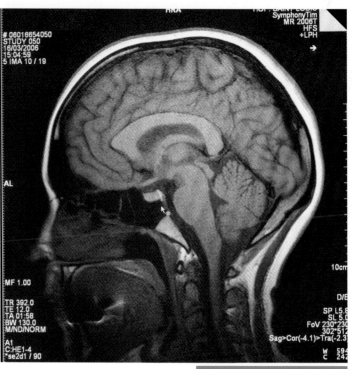

Figure 3.4 An MRI scan

What were the results?

The analysis of the scans using the VBM technique showed that the brains of the cab drivers showed significantly increased grey matter volume in the right and the left hippocampi. This difference was found in the posterior hippocampus only. The control group had relatively greater grey matter volume in the anterior hippocampus relative to the cab drivers. No other differences were found between the brains of the two groups.

The pixel-counting technique showed that there was no significant difference in the overall volume of the hippocampi between the cab drivers and the control group, but did confirm the regional differences described above. The posterior hippocampus was greater in the cab drivers and the anterior hippocampus was greater in the control group.

Interestingly, while the volume of the right posterior hippocampus showed a positive correlation with the length of time as a cab driver, the results are reversed when we look at the anterior hippocampus. Figure 3.6 shows that there was a negative correlation between the volume of the anterior hippocampus and the length of time spent as a cab driver.

The researchers also looked to see if there was a correlation between the volume of the posterior hippocampus and the length of time that each of the cab drivers had spent as a cab driver. This was significant in the right posterior hippocampus.

Note: one individual was removed from the data used in the correlation. This was a cab driver who had 42 years' experience and although his results were in line with the others, his experience was so much greater than theirs that it was decided not to include his data in this analysis.

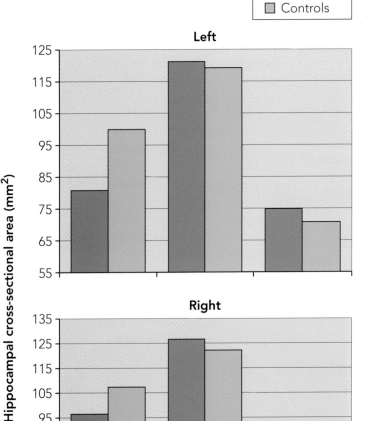

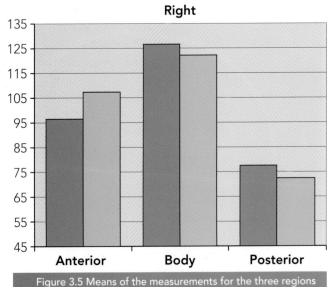

Figure 3.5 Means of the measurements for the three regions of the hippocampus

Time as taxi driver (months)

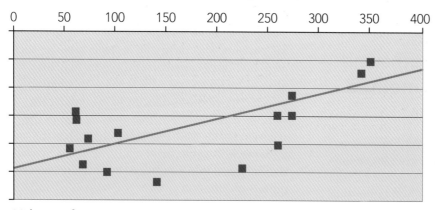

Volume of grey matter in posterior hippocampus

Time as taxi driver (months)

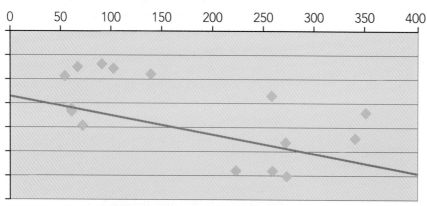

Volume of grey matter in anterior hippocampus

Figure 3.6 Graphs to show the relationship between time as a taxi driver and hippocampal volume

Conclusions

These results do suggest evidence of differences between the hippocampi of licensed cab drivers compared with those of control group. They further suggest that the more experience a cab driver has, the larger the volume of his posterior hippocampus.

This suggests that 'professional dependence on navigational skills in licensed London taxi drivers is associated with a relative redistribution of grey matter in the hippocampus'.

(Maguire et al., page 4402)

What exactly does this mean? This difference could have been there before these individuals took 'the Knowledge' and perhaps this predisposed them to jobs where navigational skills were important. However, the results of the correlational analysis suggest that some change

may have taken place since they qualified. These results showed that the longer they had been a cab driver the greater the volume of their right posterior hippocampus. This would strongly suggest that the hippocampus increases in size with use over time.

Summary of main points

1   Cab drivers had a significantly greater volume of grey matter in the posterior hippocampus, whereas the control group had a greater volume in the anterior hippocampus.

2   There was a correlation between the amount of cab-driving experience and the volume of grey matter in the posterior hippocampus.

Evaluating the study by Maguire et al.

What are the strengths and weaknesses of the method used?

This study is best described as a quasi experiment, as the researchers used an already existing independent variable (whether people had passed 'the Knowledge' or not) rather than manipulating a variable themselves.

In some cases it is more difficult to draw conclusions from this kind of research as the difference between the groups may have been due to some other factor.

If the researchers had simply analysed the scan data, it would be difficult for them to conclude that the differences were due to the differing experiences of the two groups.

However in this study the addition of the correlational analysis that strongly suggests a relationship between the length of time the participants had been licensed cab drivers and the posterior hippocampal volume allows the researchers to suggest that the hippocampus increases with size as a result of navigational experience.

What are the strengths and weaknesses of the data collected?

The data collected are quantitative and were collected using precise measuring equipment. This means that the data are unlikely to have been subject to any biases in collection and it is not possible that the participants could have responded to demand characteristics in any way. MRI scans are a precise measuring tool giving a detailed view of the brain. Their advantages and disadvantages are described below.

Advantages include that the scans are safe, painless and non-invasive. No X-rays or radioactive material are used in an MRI scan. There is very little in the way of preparation for an MRI scan. Patients can eat and drink as normal before the procedure and simply have to remove all metal objects such as jewellery.

However this means that they are not suitable for patients who have any metallic devices such as plates or pacemakers. Problems may also arise in trying to use MRI scans with children or patients who are difficult to communicate with, as it is important that they lie still in the scanner. Lastly, MRI scans are unsuitable for patients who suffer from claustrophobia, as they are enclosed in a small space for a significant period of time.

Was the sample representative?

Clearly cab drivers are not a representative sample of the general population. However, the researchers are not attempting to apply these results to the population as a whole. They have examined a specific group of people who have specific skills, and have concluded that their brains show some significant differences when compared to the control group. In applying these results in a broader context they are simply able to say that these results suggest the brain's ability to change in response to experience.

Looking at the issue of sample in a slightly different way, the choice of cab drivers for this study is an excellent one. They are a discrete group of people who have a specific set of knowledge and experience. Not only do they all have good navigational skills, but they all have good navigational skills relating to one specific area of the country, making their experiences very similar.

The researchers did not include any women or any left-handed men in their sample and this exclusion gives them high levels of control over potential confounding variables as discussed above.

However it might be suggested that these findings may not be precisely replicated in groups of female cab drivers or in left-handed cab drivers. This is not a criticism of the study that has been conducted, but as research continues in this area these may prove to be fruitful areas of investigation.

Was the study useful?

The use of scanning technology to investigate the brain is proving to be invaluable to psychology. In a slightly broader context than this study, the results suggests that the brain shows some 'plasticity', that is, it is able to change in response to the environmental demands placed upon it. At the end of their article, Maguire et al. suggest that the finding that 'normal activities can induce changes in the relative volume of grey matter in the brain' means that there are positive implications for those who have suffered brain injury or disease, as there is a possibility that the grey matter of the brain can in some way 'mend itself'.

Nature–nurture

This research supports the nurture side of the nature–nurture debate.

The initial analysis of the scan data could indicate either innate differences in the hippocampal volume of those who become cab drivers and those who don't, or it could indicate changes as a result of experience.

In this study it is the correlational data that indicates the role of learning and experience (nurture). As hippocampal size increases with length of time spent as a licensed cab driver, this gives strong support to the nurture argument.

However, this does not mean that there is no role for nature here. It may still be that there are innate differences (in the size or the plasticity) of the hippocampus that give some people an advantage where navigational skills are required.

Check your understanding

Outline the results of this study.

What do the results of this study tell us about the nature–nurture debate?

Describe the participants who were used for this study.

Comment on the usefulness of the research by Maguire et al.

Try this ...

What other occupations require specialist knowledge of this kind?

Perhaps future research will discover other examples of changes in grey matter as a result of experience.

Exam Café

You should be able to explain the aim and the method of this study in some detail. Make sure you understand that Maguire et al. did not conduct an experiment in the true sense of the word, as they had no control over whether someone was a licensed taxi driver or not, or how long they had been working for.

However, they compare two groups (cab drivers and non-cab drivers) and you should be able to describe the results of this comparison.

They also correlate the measure of hippocampal volume with the length of time someone has been a cab driver and you should be able to describe these results. You should also be able to describe the conclusions that can be drawn from this study.

Dement and Kleitman (1957)

Pause for thought

◆ Have you ever woken up in the middle of the night, aware that you have been dreaming? How easy would it be to describe the content of your dream to someone?

◆ How accurately do you think that you could estimate how long you had been dreaming for?

What is sleep?

Sleep consists of a number of stages. These stages can be shown by distinctive patterns produced during electroencephalography.

> **Key term**
>
> electroencephalography a non-invasive method for measuring the electrical activity of the brain by recording from electrodes placed on the scalp. The resulting traces (printed out by the machine) are known as an electroencephalograph (EEG). They represent the activity of a large number of neurons and are sometimes called 'brainwaves' due to the wave-like patterns seen on the traces (don't use this term, as the brain does not broadcast electrical waves).

Stage 1 sleep is characterised by lowered heart rate, muscle tension and body temperature and is similar to states of deep relaxation and hypnosis. An EEG recording of brain activity would show alpha waves that have a frequency of 8–12 cycles per second (Hertz). People can be woken easily from this stage of sleep.

Stage 2 sleep is characterised by slower and larger EEG waves and by the presence of sleep spindles. These are bursts of high-frequency waves (12–16 Hertz) lasting for about 1 second. This is a deeper sleep than Stage 1, but people can still be woken relatively easily.

Figure 3.7 An electroencephalograph machine

Awake, relaxed

Stage 1 sleep

Stage 2 sleep

Stage 3 sleep

Stage 4 sleep

REM sleep

Figure 3.8 Traces produced during electroencephalography

In *Stage 3* sleep delta waves are seen. These are large, slow waves of around 1–3 Hertz. People in Stage 3 sleep do not easily respond to external stimuli and are quite difficult to wake up.

Stage 4 sleep is characterised by delta waves of about 1 Hertz and is the deepest of the four stages of sleep. Metabolic activity is low and people are difficult to wake, although noises that are personally significant, such as their baby crying, will waken them quite easily.

It takes about 30 minutes to reach Stage 4 sleep. We spend another 30 minutes in this stage, and then the cycle of sleep reverses through Stages 3 and 2. Instead of entering Stage 1 sleep again, we enter a phase of 'active sleep'. This is where an EEG shows a desynchronised pattern, which indicates an aroused subject. Metabolic activity increases, as does heart rate, although the body is more or less paralysed and this is the hardest stage to wake someone from. It is the deepest stage of sleep and is called 'rapid eye movement (REM) sleep' as rapid eye movements can be observed under the closed eyelids. It is sometimes called 'paradoxical sleep' because the subject is deeply asleep but the brain shows an EEG pattern similar to that of being awake. People typically spend 10 or 15 minutes in REM sleep and then descend through the stages to Stage 4 sleep. This cycle takes around 70–90 minutes and is repeated five or six times during a night's sleep.

Why do we sleep?

Restoration theory suggests that non-REM (NREM) sleep *restores bodily processes* that have deteriorated during the day and that REM sleep *stimulates protein synthesis* which replenishes brain processes.

Evolutionary theory proposes that sleep serves a *survival function* by keeping animals safe from predators. Hibernation would be seen as an extension of this process.

Why do we dream?

Some more recent theories have concluded that we sleep because we have a psychological need to dream. Theories of dreaming include the following.

◆ Reorganisation of mental structures. It has been suggested that REM sleep is involved in the organisation of schemas (the cognitive structures that make up our knowledge and understanding) and this is supported by the finding that complex cognitive tasks lead to an increase in the time spent in REM sleep and also by the fact that babies spend so much time in REM sleep.

◆ The activation synthesis model proposes that dreams are an 'active interpretation' of the signals produced by the cortex during REM sleep. Crick and Mitchinson (1983) suggest that this is a way of sorting out all the information that has been taken in during the day and hence dreaming is about the brain deciding what to keep and what to forget.

◆ Freud (1900) saw dreams as the 'royal road to the unconscious' and psychoanalytic therapists still use dream interpretation as a way of interpreting the patient's hidden desires and thoughts.

The study by Dement and Kleitman is an early laboratory study that established a link between REM sleep and dreaming.

William Dement

William Dement has been Professor of Psychiatry at Stanford since 1963, and has worked on sleep since 1952. He spent many years as chairman of the National Commission on Sleep Disorders Research.

Figure 3.9 William Dement

Try this ...

Keep a pen and paper next to your bed. Whenever you are woken by an alarm clock or the phone ringing (as opposed to waking naturally), try to recall whether you were dreaming or not. If you were, write down as much of your dream as you can remember. Could you remember your dream in detail?

Dement, W. and Kleitman, N. (1957)

'The relation of eye movements during sleep to dream activity',
Journal of Experimental Psychology 53, 339–46.

What was the aim of the study?

Dement and Kleitman subtitle their article 'an objective method for the study of dreaming'.

Although we started by outlining some key information about sleep, the focus of this study is dreaming. Dement and Kleitman claim that a relatively subjective topic can be made objective if it is shown that it is associated with (or correlated with) a physical phenomenon that can be measured objectively. An earlier study by Aserinsky and Kleitman (1955) observed periods of rapid eye movement during sleep and found that subjects were more likely to remember their dreams if woken during these periods than at other times. Such periods of rapid eye movement were shown to appear at regular intervals during sleep and were related to cyclic changes in the depth of sleep as measured by an EEG.

The study is an attempt to determine the relationship between eye movement and dreaming. It was one of the earliest experimental investigations into the relationship between eye movements and dreaming. Dement and Kleitman used three approaches to do this, each one addressing a different research question. They describe their three approaches as follows.

Approach 1 'Dream recall during REM or quiescent periods was elicited and this was done without direct contact between experimenter and subject, thus eliminating the possibility of unintentional cuing by the experimenter.' (Dement and Kleitman, page 339)

In other words, Dement and Kleitman wanted to see whether their subjects were more likely to remember dreams if woken during periods of REM than if woken during periods of NREM. They designed a technique that would allow the subjects to be woken without an experimenter present, as the presence of an experimenter might have influenced the subjects' ability to recall and describe their dreams.

Approach 2 'The subjective estimate of the duration of dreams was compared with the length of eye movement periods before awakening, reasoning that there should be a positive correlation if dreaming and eye movements were concurrent.' (Dement and Kleitman, page 339)

In other words, Dement and Kleitman wanted to see whether subjects were able to estimate how long they had been dreaming for and whether their estimates correlated with the length of time they had been in REM sleep.

Approach 3 'The pattern of eye movement was related to the dream content to test whether eye movements represented a specific expression of the visual experience of dreaming or merely a random motor discharge of a more active central nervous system.' (Dement and Kleitman, page 339)

In other words, Dement and Kleitman wanted to see whether the content of the dream showed a relation to the pattern of eye movement.

Based on these approaches, the researchers formulated three research questions:

1   Will people be more likely to report dreams if they are woken during periods of REM than during periods of NREM?

2   Can people accurately estimate the duration of their dreaming?

3   Is the direction of eye movement during REM related to dream content?

Try this ...

Dement and Kleitman stated research questions rather than hypotheses. See if you can rewrite the questions above as hypotheses. Should they be experimental hypotheses or correlational hypotheses? Try to identify the variables in each hypothesis.

Who were the participants?

The participants were seven adult males and two adult females. Five of the participants were studied intensively and minimal amounts of data were gathered from the other four, with the intention of confirming the results from the first five.

How was the study conducted?

The study was a laboratory experiment. The participant reported to the sleep laboratory just before their normal bedtime. They had been asked to avoid caffeine and alcohol on the day of the experiment but otherwise to eat and drink normally.

Electrodes were attached near the eyes to measure the eye movement and to the scalp to measure the brain's electrical activity (to determine depth of sleep). The participant then went to bed in a quiet, dark room in the laboratory. The electrodes were attached to an EEG machine, which ran continuously throughout the night.

At various times during the night the participant was woken up to test their dream recall. They were woken by a doorbell and spoke into a tape recorder near the bed. They had to state first whether they had been dreaming, and if they had, to report the content of the dream.

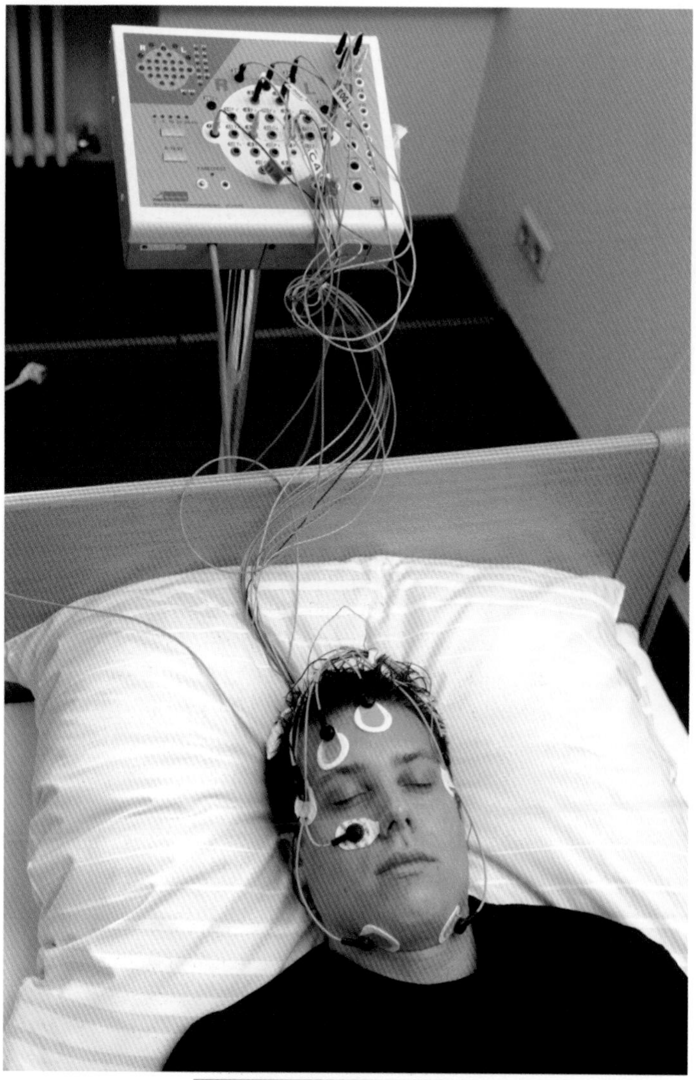

What were the results?

Question 1 Will people be more likely to report dreams if they are woken during periods of REM than during periods of NREM?

The researchers observed that all subjects showed periods of REM during sleep. It was not possible to give a mean length of REM periods for these subjects, since most were disturbed by the doorbell ringing. However, REM periods where people were not woken by the doorbell varied between 3 and 50 minutes, with a mean of about 20 minutes. Dement and Kleitman also noted that the length of REM periods tended to increase, the longer the subject was asleep. Eye movements were not constant during these periods, but occurred in 'bursts of one or two, up to fifty or a hundred movements' (Dement and Kleitman, page 340).

The REM periods occurred at fairly regular intervals during the night. The frequency of occurrence seemed to be relatively constant and characteristic to the individual. The average for the whole group was one REM period every 92 minutes and the range was from 70 to 104 minutes. Awakenings had little effect on the frequency and regularity with which REM periods occurred.

Altogether, 351 awakenings took place. For one subject this was done to a pattern, three REM awakenings followed by three NREM awakenings and so on. For others the pattern of awakenings was determined by random number tables. One subject was told that he would be woken only when the recording indicated that he was dreaming but was in fact woken randomly. One subject was simply woken randomly 'at the whim of the experimenter'.

Figure 3.10 Would you sleep normally like this?

Key term

random number tables computer-generated lists of random numbers

Woken during REM sleep		Woken during NREM sleep	
Recalled dreams	No recall	Recalled dreams	No recall
152	39	11	149

Table 3.1 Dream recall during REM and NREM sleep

All subjects were more likely to recall dreams when woken from REM rather than NREM and the patterns of awakenings did not seem to influence them, although some were better able to recall their dreams than others. The subject who was woken to a definite pattern was no more accurate than the others (although there was a pattern he might have learned). The subject who was misled to believe that all awakenings were when he was dreaming was no less accurate than the others.

The results show that participants were much more likely to recall dreams in REM sleep than in NREM sleep. This gives us an answer to question 1. Although some dreams were recalled on awakenings from NREM sleep, the researchers suggest that these were memories of dreams from earlier periods of REM sleep.

Question 2 Can people accurately estimate the duration of dreaming?

To begin with, subjects were woken after varied periods of time spent in REM sleep and simply asked to estimate how long they had been dreaming. The experimenters finally decided that this was too complex and too difficult for the participants.

A second series of tests was done where subjects were woken randomly, either 5 or 15 minutes into REM sleep, and were asked to decide whether they had been dreaming for 5 or 15 minutes.

The results show that participants were mostly accurate in their estimation of dream length. This gives us the answer to question 2. Interestingly, one participant was responsible for a large proportion of the incorrect estimates.

Question 3 Is the direction of eye movement during REM related to dream content?

Initially the researchers asked the subjects to try to account for every eye movement by stating chronologically in which directions they had looked during their dreams. The researchers had to abandon this idea as subjects could not recall their dreams in such detail.

Figure 3.11 A person sleeping normally

51 tests		60 tests	
Woken after 5 minutes of REM		Woken after 15 minutes of REM	
Correct	Incorrect	Correct	Incorrect
45	6	47	13

Table 3.2 Estimate of length of time spent dreaming

In the final approach, subjects were awoken when one of four main patterns of eye movement (determined by the placing of the electrodes) had persisted for at least 1 minute and were asked to describe what they had been dreaming about. A total of 35 awakenings were collected from the nine participants. These four patterns and the types of dreams reported are shown in Table 3.3. As can be seen, periods of mainly vertical and horizontal eye movements were rare.

These results support the idea that eye movement is related to dream content, and this is further supported by measuring the eye movements of awake subjects looking at close and distant objects. This gives us an answer to question 3.

Summary of main points

1 People are more likely to report dreams if they are woken during periods of REM than during periods of NREM.

2 People can estimate the duration of dreaming to an extent.

3 The direction of eye movement during REM seems to be related to dream content.

Type of eye movement	No. of times observed	Examples of dream content
Mainly vertical eye movements	3	• Standing at the bottom of a cliff and looking up at climbers • Climbing ladders and looking up and down • Throwing basketballs at a net
Mainly horizontal eye movements	1	• Watching two people throw tomatoes at each other
Both vertical and horizontal eye movements	21	• Looking at close objects • Talking to groups of people • Looking for something • Fighting with someone
Very little or no eye movement	10	• Watching things in the distance • Staring at an object • Driving a car and staring at the road ahead

Table 3.3 Dream content reported for four patterns of eye movements

Evaluating the study by Dement and Kleitman

What are the strengths and weaknesses of the method used in the study?

This study was conducted in a laboratory. Laboratory studies have high levels of control over variables but may lack ecological validity (see below). The researchers were able to control the environment in which the participants slept, the manner in which they were woken and their caffeine and alcohol intake. High levels of control such as these make conclusions easier to draw and reduce the chance of confounding variables. The study used the EEG to measure brain activity and this allows precise and objective measurements to be taken.

Try this …

Explain why Dement and Kleitman used a doorbell to waken the participants.

Was the sample representative?

The sample was very small indeed. Only nine participants were studied in total and only five of these were studied intensively. This is a very small number of participants to generalise from. You could argue that physiological processes are likely to be the same in all people, and it is true that much physiological research uses small numbers of participants. It is also possible that sleep patterns and, in particular, relationships between eye movements and dreaming, vary from person to person. For example, in this study the researchers note that most of the incorrect guesses about the duration of dreaming came from one person; they also note that there were differences in participants' abilities to recall the details of their dreams.

It could be suggested that the conclusions drawn from Dement and Kleitman's research would be strengthened if the same relationships were established in a larger sample of people. On the other hand, the data from the four further participants appeared to confirm the data from the first five, which suggests that similar results would be found in larger groups of participants.

It should also be remembered that this study was one of the first to attempt to study dreaming in this way and that Dement and Kleitman went on to conduct many more studies after this early one.

What type of data were collected?

The data collected in this study were mostly quantitative. In relation to the first two research questions, the data are simply numbers of participants who could or could not recall dreams or could or could not accurately estimate the length of their dreams.

Quantitative data are relatively easy to collect and can be analysed statistically. However, they reduce complex qualitative phenomena to numbers and this often results in a lack of detail in the data.

The data collected in relation to the third question were more qualitative, as here participants were asked to describe the contents of their dreams. This gives richer and more interesting data, but such data are difficult to use for comparisons and are hard to analyse statistically.

Was the study ecologically valid?

The research studied participants who went to sleep in a laboratory with electrodes attached to their heads. It is unlikely that this bears much relation to sleep in a normal environment. It is possible that being in such an artificial condition meant that the participants' sleep was disturbed and, if this was the case, the researchers would not have been studying normal sleep patterns.

The participants were also woken several times during the night and asked about their dreams. Again, this is unlikely to happen normally and may have had an effect on the way the participants slept. However, research conducted outside the controlled conditions of the laboratory would have been unable to measure brain activity and eye movements in such an objective manner.

Was the study useful?

Try this ...

Does this study establish that dreaming takes place in REM sleep? What other interpretation could there be?

The conclusions reached by Dement and Kleitman have been replicated by many other researchers. When the research was first conducted, little was known about the relationship between eye movements and dreaming, so Dement and Kleitman's research really did add new information to our knowledge about sleep.

It is difficult, nearly 50 years later, to understand what a major breakthrough this study represented. The use of an EEG to record brain activity in a sleeping subject was also relatively new, and it was not until research like that in this study was carried out that it became clear that dreams could be studied in an objective way. Dement and Kleitman's research generated many other studies into sleep and dreaming.

Try this ...

Outline one change that you could make to this study and discuss the effects that this change may have on the results.

Was the study reductionist?

Arguably, Dement and Kleitman have reduced a complex phenomenon (dreaming) to a simple physiological measure. This could be seen as oversimplifying the subject matter. However, it allowed research into this area to be conducted in a scientific manner and the relationship between eye movements and dreaming to be established.

Check your understanding

What were the three research questions investigated by Dement and Kleitman?

Briefly outline the procedure of this study.

What are the key findings from this study?

Hint: you should give findings in relation to the three questions.

Exam Café

You need to separate out the three research questions. Make sure that you can explain what Dement and Kleitman found in relation to each one. Remember too that finding that people recall more dreams in REM sleep than in NREM sleep does not show that dreaming only occurs in REM sleep.

You should also remember that this was a very early laboratory study and technological advances now allow researchers to observe brain activity in much more detail, as shown in the study by Maguire et al.

Sperry (1968)

Pause for thought

◆ What do you already know about the structure of the brain?

◆ Have you heard people talking about 'left-brain' and 'right-brain'?

◆ What do you think this means?

◆ How does information travel from one hemisphere to the other?

How does information reach the brain?

The brain is made up of two halves called hemispheres. The left hemisphere receives information from the right visual field and the right side of the body. The right hemisphere receives information from the left visual field and the left side of the body. The corpus callosum is a bundle of nerve fibres that connect the two hemispheres, allowing information to be transferred between them.

What functions do the two hemispheres have?

The two hemispheres have very different functions. The left hemisphere is sometimes described as the 'words' hemisphere, as it controls the ability to speak, understand language and reason things out. The right hemisphere is the 'pictures' hemisphere and specialises in tasks such as drawing, spatial awareness (judging where you are in space) and intuitive tasks.

Background to the study

The language abilities of the left hemisphere were first identified in the nineteenth century through the work of Broca and Wernicke. In 1861 Broca published a case study of a patient who could only say the word 'tan', although his ability to understand language seemed normal. 'Tan' (as he is referred to in the case study) died shortly after admission to hospital and an autopsy showed an area of damage in the lower part of the left frontal lobe. Broca's work led to this region becoming known as Broca's area.

In 1874 Wernicke reported on a number of patients suffering from a different type of language disorder. These patients could speak, although what they said had little, if anything, to do with the conversation going on at the time. These patients appeared to have little understanding of words, could not respond to

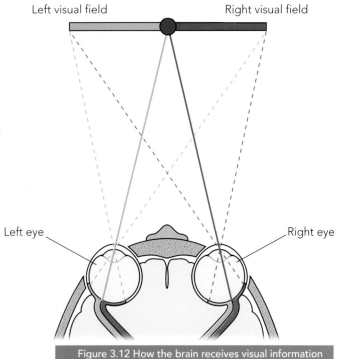

Figure 3.12 How the brain receives visual information

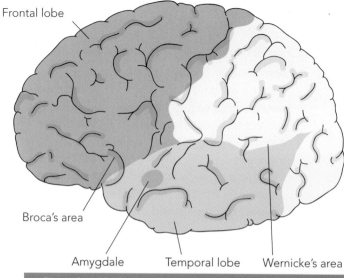

Frontal lobe

Broca's area

Amygdale   Temporal lobe   Wernicke's area

Figure 3.14 The brain seen from the left, showing Broca's area and Wernicke's area

but in extreme cases epilepsy can cause collapse, tremor and loss of consciousness. Because the brain is such a good conductor of electrical impulses, the attack spreads rapidly and an attack that begins in one hemisphere will spread rapidly to the other hemisphere via the corpus callosum.

In the 1940s an extreme solution to severe epilepsy was developed. The corpus callosum was cut, thus preventing the spread of an epileptic attack from one hemisphere to the other, but also making it impossible for the hemispheres to transfer information between them. Considering the scale of the brain damage caused by this operation, 'split-brain' patients (as they became known) showed remarkably few side effects and most gained significant relief from their epilepsy.

Green (1994) comments that 'Researchers in the 1940s were baffled as to what the corpus callosum might be doing in the normal brain, if cutting it had such minor effects. Some were reduced to proposing that it was simply there to hold the two hemispheres together!' (page 60).

Sperry realised that the 'split-brain' patients provided researchers with an opportunity to study the functions of the two hemispheres in ways that would never be possible experimentally. His major contribution to this area was in the design of apparatus that allowed information to be sent to just one hemisphere. The core study reports on the findings of Sperry's groundbreaking research in this area.

Roger Sperry

simple questions, repeat simple phrases or follow instructions. Autopsies revealed damage to the top of the left temporal lobe, a region of the brain now referred to as Wernicke's area.

Although the work of Broca and Wernicke has since been refined, these basic findings are still valid, and were the first scientific indication of hemisphere organisation. These findings demonstrate that the two hemispheres are not equivalent in terms of the cognitive tasks that they perform. When these studies were published there were no techniques available to study the brain (such as the various scanning procedures we have today) and results were almost always based on autopsies. However, in the 1950s, testing procedures developed by Sperry allowed researchers to explore the different abilities of the hemispheres on a number of verbal and non-verbal tasks.

Key terms

corpus callosum the bundle of nerve fibres that connects the two hemispheres of the brain

neurospecificity the way in which neurons are hard-wired to attach to one another in certain predetermined ways during the development of the brain

Sperry worked with epileptic patients. Epilepsy is a violent and uncontrolled electrical discharge in the brain that disrupts normal brain functions. In some people such attacks are barely noticeable,

Figure 3.15 Roger Sperry

Sperry was born in 1913 and grew up on a farm in Hartford, Connecticut. He studied for a degree in English, a Masters degree in psychology and was awarded a PhD for his research in zoology. He worked at the Yerkes Laboratory for Primate Biology before being appointed to a Professorship in Psychobiology at the California Institute of Technology (Caltech) in 1954. Sperry was awarded the Nobel Prize in 1981.

What was the aim of the research?

Sperry was attempting to study the functions of separated and independent hemispheres.

Who did Sperry test?

Sperry investigated 11 participants who had already undergone radical surgery to sever their corpus callosum. Two of these are described in some detail. The first was a man who had been having seizures for more than 10 years, with an average of two major attacks each week. He had also begun to suffer from recurring seizures that fail to stop and have a very high risk of death. Since having the surgery this patient had had no seizures, had significantly reduced his medication and reported an overall improvement in his well-being.

The second patient, a woman in her thirties, is also described as seizure free since her operation more than 4 years previously; medical staff also reported a normal EEG pattern in this patient. Based on the successful outcome for these patients, surgery was conducted on 9 further patients.

It is important to remember that Sperry did not conduct this operation himself, nor was this operation conducted for the purpose of his research. As he simply took advantage of being to use the very small number of people who had had this operation, we can describe his sample as an opportunity one, and the method a natural experiment, as the independent variable was not manipulated for the purposes of the research. These patients underwent serious surgery for medical reasons and Sperry realised that they offered an opportunity to investigate the functional outcomes of this surgery. In his words 'the behavioural, neurological and psychological effects of this surgical disruption of all direct cross-talk between the hemispheres' (page 723).

What was the procedure?

Sperry used specially designed apparatus that allows information to be presented to just one hemisphere. The individual's vision is divided into the left and right visual fields and their hands are screened from their own view. The subject has one eye covered, as the tiniest eye movement could allow information to be transferred to the other visual field. They centre their gaze on a designated fixation point on a screen in front of them. Stimuli (words or images) can be flashed on this screen for 1/10 second or less. This is too fast for the person's eye to move and allow information into the other half of the visual field. Remember that information from the left visual field goes to the right hemisphere and vice versa (see Figure 3.12). If you imagine that you are looking straight ahead, the view on the right side of your nose is the right visual field and the view on the left is the left visual field. Participants in this study have one eye covered to add further control to the study, as the tiniest eye movement could allow information to be transferred to the other visual field. By flashing the stimuli to the right or the left of the fixation point, the experimenter controls which visual field receives the information.

For tactile tasks, objects can be placed in one of the subject's hands (which are screened from view) and thus the sensory information is received only by the corresponding hemisphere. The subject then has to find the object again (usually from a grab bag) with either the same or the opposite hand.

It may help to think about this as two individuals: the surgery has left the individual with no means of communication between the hemispheres of their brain. In everyday life however, the effects of this are difficult to see, as sensory information is received by both visual fields or a combination of sight and touch (not to mention the other senses). Information cannot cross the corpus callosum but it is received by both hemispheres. If we imagine this as two individuals, this procedure is almost like presenting visual information to person A, then asking person B what person A had seen.

What were the findings?

Sperry describes the results of his studies as showing that these patients act as if they have two minds in one body. He says that:

Instead of the normally unified single stream of consciousness, these patients behave as if they have two independent streams of conscious awareness, one in each hemisphere, each of which is cut off from and out of contact with the mental experiences of the other. In other words, each hemisphere seems to have its own separate and private sensations, its own perceptions; its own concepts; and its own impulses to act; with related volitional, cognitive and learning experiences. Following the surgery each hemisphere also has thereafter its own separate chain of memories that are rendered inaccessible to the recall processes of the other.

(Sperry, 1968, page 724)

Sperry's article contains a huge number of findings. Some of the most important ones are summarised below:

◆ If the visual fields are divided and one piece of information is sent to the left visual field (and hence to the right hemisphere) it is only recognised again if 'seen' by the same visual field. The right visual field (and left hemisphere) simply has never 'seen' it before.

◆ Visual material shown to the right visual field (left hemisphere) can be described in speech and writing. If the same material is shown to the left visual field (right hemisphere) the participant insists that he did not see anything. However, if instead of asking him to tell you what he saw, he is asked to use his left hand to point to the object among a collection of other objects he is able to select accurately the item he has 'just insisted he did not see'.

◆ Even more interestingly, if a different figure is flashed to each hemisphere (for example, a dollar sign to the left visual field and a question mark to the right visual field) and the participant is asked to draw what he has seen with his left hand, the participant will draw the figure seen in the left visual field. But if you ask him what he has drawn he will tell you that he drew the object that appeared in the right half of the field. As Sperry notes 'the one hemisphere does not know what the other hemisphere has been doing' (page 726).

Figure 3.16 The apparatus used by Sperry

- Objects put in the right hand (left hemisphere) can be described and named. Participants simply make wild guesses about objects put in their left hands (right hemisphere) and may even be unaware that anything at all is present. However, they can still select it correctly from a collection of other objects. Unlike a 'normal' person however, they can only do this with the same hand that the object was originally placed in. If two objects are placed one in each hand, each hand can then search for its own object but will in the process reject the object that the other hand is looking for. It is simply as if two separate people are working at the task.

These findings show that the hemispheres are operating independently. Again, if you think of this in terms of two separate people (or two brains) working at this task, it may be easier to understand these results.

Sperry and his team were also fascinated to discover what goes on in the 'speechless' right hemisphere, and their results suggest that it is capable of complex tasks, although it is not able to express itself verbally. The research showed that the right hemisphere was able to:

- select similar items to a target item (e.g. a watch rather than a clock)

- perform simple arithmetic operations

- understand both written and spoken words, although the right hemisphere is not able to express this understanding verbally (e.g. if the word 'eraser' is flashed to the left visual field (right hemisphere) the subject can select an eraser from a collection of objects using the left hand, but can't name it)

- identify objects: if asked to select a piece of cutlery, the left hand can select a fork, but the individual may well report that they have chosen a knife or a spoon. Both hemispheres heard the instruction, but only the right hemisphere knows which item has been selected. The left (talking) hemisphere does not know the correct answer

- understand fairly complex instructions (find something used to remove dirt – soap, find something inserted in slot machines – coin)

- show appropriate emotional reactions: if nude photos were flashed to the right hemisphere the subject typically denies seeing anything but may blush or giggle, suggesting that the picture was registered at some emotional level.

This last finding suggests that emotional responses may be transferred across

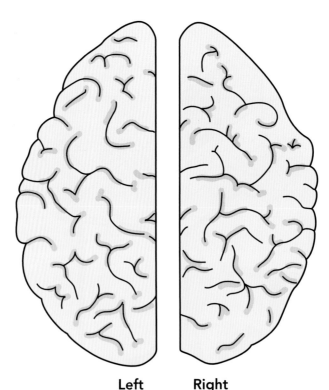

- Logical components
- Sequences
- Language

- Whole picture
- Patterns
- Images
- Music
- Creativity

Left **Right**

Figure 3.13 Some of the functions of the two hemispheres of the brain

hemispheres. One possible explanation may be the presence of other pathways between the hemispheres.

The corpus callosum is the only pathway between the cortical areas of the hemispheres – that is, the areas dealing with a variety of higher cognitive processes. But as Carter explains, there is another pathway called the anterior commissure, which connects the deep subcortical regions of the brain known as the limbic system. 'Here in this cerebral underworld, raw emotion is generated; alarm bells are set off in response to threat; false smiles are registered; and lust first twitches at the sight of an attractive other' (Carter, 2000, page 67). This means that although the cognitive expressions of emotional responses cannot be transferred across hemispheres, basic emotional responses from a more primitive part of the brain can be.

How do these patients manage in everyday life?

Many of the problems described above only arise when information is flashed for fractions of a second using complex apparatus that does not allow for eye movements that would automatically mean the material was in both visual fields.

Many effects only occur when people are prevented from seeing their hands (which would allow information to go to both hemispheres) and many other effects are easily compensated for by speaking aloud, which transfers much information to the other hemisphere in a more indirect way. However they do have problems with short-term memory and orientation, and find reading and other tasks requiring mental concentration tiring.

Exaggerated head movements have been observed in some 'split-brain' patients while reading, which is presumably a strategy developed to ensure that information is received by both visual fields and hence both hemispheres.

Weblinks

There are a number of websites that you may find interesting and which provide a good basic introduction to this area (see 'Websites' on page ii). You will be able to read background information on Sperry's research and why he won the Nobel Prize, and take part in activities, such a game in which you have to work out which part of the brain is doing what.

Summary of main points

1. The hemispheres have different functions. Language skills are based in the left hemisphere.

2. Information received by only one hemisphere is not accessible to the other hemisphere.

3. Information received by the left hemisphere can be responded to verbally.

4. Information received by the right hemisphere cannot be responded to verbally, although this 'minor' hemisphere can respond in a variety of non-verbal ways.

Evaluating the study by Sperry

Sperry's work was a major contribution to psychology. He was awarded the Nobel Prize for Medicine in 1981. He argues that these studies revealed the true nature of the two hemispheres for the first time.

His work has been supported and extended by others, and the conclusion that the two hemispheres are separate spheres of consciousness with their own private sensations, perceptions, thoughts, feelings and memories is now well accepted.

The apparatus designed by Sperry was also a significant breakthrough, allowing for the scientific study of these patients for the first time.

However, more recent research has suggested that the degree of separation between the hemispheres in normal people is perhaps not as great as once thought.

For example it has now been demonstrated that the right hemisphere has some understanding of language and that the left hemisphere may have responsibility for the production of imagery.

This more recent view sees the functioning of the two hemispheres as less separate and more integrated. Studies of normal patients show that the two sides of the brain do not operate in isolation but form a highly integrated system. Most everyday tasks involve a mixture of right and left brain skills.

What are the strengths and weaknesses of the method used by Sperry?

Sperry conducted a natural or quasi-experimental design. One weakness of this type of design is that it does not give the researcher full control over the independent variable (whether someone had their corpus callosum severed).

However, quasi-experimental designs allow researchers to investigate variables that are not able to be investigated in strict laboratory experiments.

Sperry's research can be seen as similar to a collection of detailed case studies conducted with highly controlled and objective laboratory equipment and procedures. The major strength of Sperry's work is definitely the techniques that he developed, which allowed the functions of the two hemispheres to be studied in ways that had previously been impossible.

Was the sample representative?

Sperry had 11 participants who had already undergone surgery to sever their corpus callosum. This would normally be considered quite a small number, but it would have been impossible to find large numbers of people who had had this operation (Green estimates that only around 60 people in total have had it).

Two questions need to be considered:

◆ Are these 11 people representative of everyone who has had this operation?

◆ Can the results of this study tell us anything about the functioning of the 'normal' brain?

The results suggest that all 11 participants experienced similar effects, so it would be safe to conclude that anyone who had this operation would experience these effects.

However, as Sperry did not control the independent variable in this study, he was not able to test these participants prior to the operation. It is possible that their brain functioning may have been atypical (different from the norm) before the operation and this would make it more difficult to draw conclusions about the functions of the hemispheres in non-separated brains.

It has been argued that the long-standing abnormalities in these patients' brains might have caused significant reorganisation of their brains. It is also possible that there are significant individual differences that have not been considered in this study.

What type of data was collected in this study?

There are examples of both quantitative and qualitative data in this study. The majority of the data are quantitative, as Sperry simply records whether something could be identified or not.

These are the important data in this study, as it is from these that Sperry is able to draw his conclusions about the different functioning of the two hemispheres.

However, the results are illustrated with some revealing qualitative examples of the experiences of the 'split-brain' patients, which add significantly to our attempt to understand their experiences. For example, the description of patients giggling at nude photographs presented to their right hemisphere whilst denying that they have seen anything is far more revealing than simply reporting how many responded and under what conditions. (The patients said they had seen nothing, and a purely quantitative approach would simply record this. However, the inclusion of the descriptive information (giggling) reveals more about the functioning of the 'speechless' right hemisphere than a simple quantitative approach could.)

Was the research ecologically valid? / Can the results be applied to real life?

In a sense this research has very little ecological validity, as Sperry's techniques artificially separate the visual and tactile information received by the individual. It is difficult to think of a situation where this would happen in real life, and as we saw in the core study, 'split-brain' patients have a number of simple strategies for coping in the real world that they were unable to use in the laboratory conditions.

On the other hand, ecologically valid research should be studying real problems, and Sperry's research is looking at a naturally occurring

variable ('split brain' as a result of surgery) and trying to understand exactly what effects this operation has on the individuals concerned.

Was the research useful?

The research was extremely useful. Sperry's work revealed facts about the lateralisation of functions between the two hemispheres that had only been suggested by previous studies.

Check your understanding

Comment on the usefulness of Sperry's work.

Comment on the ecological validity of Sperry's work.

Are there any 'real-life' tasks that 'split-brain' patients might be unable to do?

What other 'naturally-occuring variables' might psychologists be interested in investigating?

Exam Café

You should be able to explain the aim and the method of this study in some detail. Make sure you understand that Sperry did not conduct an experiment in the true sense of the word, as he had no control over the independent variable.

There are a lot of results in this study, and whilst you probably don't need to know all of them, you should be clear what each finding means and you should be able to give examples of findings that illustrate the different functions of each hemisphere.

Exam Café
Relax, refresh, result!

Relax and prepare

Hot tips

What I wish I'd known at the start of the year...

Ken

Make a poster for each of the studies. Flipchart paper is excellent for this. Each group could work on one study and when they have written as much as they can remember they pass their poster to another group, who try to add anything the first group missed out. You could make these really colourful and include images and diagrams to help you remember.

Rita

Never use full sentences in revision notes. I've wasted lots of time writing out sentences when one or two key words is all that is required. Use a highlighter pen on your class notes and handouts and then make key word summaries.

Refresh your memory

In Section B of the core studies paper you could be asked to consider changes to a study and the effects that these changes may have. The sample answer on page 93 looks at a question that could be asked, but you could prepare for this examination by completing the table below. Remember that there are a number of different answers you could give for these questions – it's up to you to justify what you have suggested.

Study	Alternative sample	Different method	Different ways of measuring	More ethical	Improvements
Dement and Kleitman					See student answer
Sperry					
Maguire et al.		Longitudinal approach	Scanning brains while the participants are engaged in a navigation task		

Get the result!

Sample answers

Exam-style question

We are going to look at a student response written under exam conditions to the following question:

Choose a study and suggest two improvements that could be made to it. Outline any effects these improvements might have. (8 marks)

Student answer

This answer refers to Dement and Kleitman.

One improvement that could be made to this study would be to have a larger sample of participants. I would suggest using a sample of about 30 people with equal numbers of male and female and of different age groups.

The effect that this improvement would have would be to allow the researchers to generalise their results to a wider population and to investigate if there are age or sex differences in REM activity.

Another improvement that I would suggest would be ask people to abstain from caffeine and alcohol for one week before the study, rather than just one day.

The effect of this improvement would be that all the participants would be in the same physiological state when doing the study and this means that the researchers have more control over this potential confounding variable. Someone who had been drinking heavily two days before the study may still be affected by this but after a week these effects should have disappeared.

Examiner says:

This is a clear suggestion. It would not have been enough to simply say 'use a larger sample', the examiner will be looking for a more specific answer. The detail that this candidate has given is appropriate.

Examiner says:

This is a good suggestion. It is focused on the procedure of the study and demonstrates that the candidate knows the study well. Again a specific improvement ('for one week') is given.

Examiner says:

Good structure here. The improvement is outlined followed by its effect and then the second improvement followed by its effect. It would be appropriate to outline both improvements and then discuss their effects, but the structure used here is clear and easy to follow.

Examiner says:

A good discussion of the effect of the second improvement. Good use of terminology 'potential confounding variable'.

Overall examiner's comment

A well planned and clearly written response, which gives the examiner precisely what was asked for.

How can this question be related to the other two studies in this approach?

Sperry

Sperry did not have access to the range of technology that psychologists can use today. It would be interesting to speculate on the use of MRI or PET scans with Sperry's participants. It would also be interesting to draw more direct comparisons between patients who had just had the operation and patients who had had the operation a longer time ago.

Maguire et al.

You could suggest that MRI scans were taken of a sample of people when they first starting their training for 'the Knowledge'. A second scan could be taken once they had been licensed taxi drivers for a number of years and their hippocampal volume could be compared.

This would allow you to investigate all sorts of things. Do some drivers have a larger hippocampal volume to start with? Do they pass 'the Knowledge' in a shorter period of time? Is there a difference between hippocampal volume before and after training? What might these results suggest in relation to the nature–nurture debate?

Social psychology

Social psychology attempts to explain our behaviour through an understanding of social processes. Whenever we are not alone we are influenced by the people around us, what they are doing, how they behave, and their characteristics. We imitate others, for example role models in the media, we conform to what others think and do in an attempt to fit in, and we sometimes make judgements about people, based on the way they look or act, and whether we identify with them because they are in the same social group.

How is social psychology studied?

It is difficult to study the influence of social processes on behaviour, because we are not usually aware of their influence. It is essential therefore that participants do not know that they are being studied, or exactly what aspect of social behaviour is being investigated. This raises several problems, not least the ethics of deceiving people.

Laboratory studies involve setting up a situation to see how participants behave, and are frequently conducted because they allow the experimenter to control extraneous variables that could affect the participants' reactions.

Field studies are more naturalistic and overcome many of the problems that can arise from the participants knowing that they are being studied: demand characteristics. Conducting studies in everyday environments makes for higher ecological validity. This makes the findings more generalisable to how social processes affect us in everyday life.

Observation is a very useful method to use when studying social psychology as social behaviour and reactions can be directly observed.

Milgram (1963)

The study by Milgram was a controlled observation investigating the nature of obedience to authority. The background to the study was an interest in the events that occurred in Nazi Germany, where soldiers obediently killed millions of people on the orders of their superiors. Milgram wanted to demonstrate the human tendency to obey orders even to the extent where personal morals and beliefs would be overridden. In this study, male participants were ordered to administer electric shocks to a level strong enough to kill. Milgram concluded that in certain conditions the average person could become a killer in the name of obedience.

Reicher and Haslam (2006)

This study put a group of men into a simulated prison environment where they were allocated to the role of either prisoner or guard. They were observed and some very antisocial behaviour was seen between the two groups. The social processes studied included identification with a group, the effect of a lack of control over the situation and the inability to change the group's status.

Piliavin, Rodin and Piliavin (1969)

This study investigated the bystander behaviour of the passengers who witnessed the feigned collapse of a 'fellow passenger'. Characteristics of the situation were varied, and included whether the collapsed person appeared drunk or ill, whether they were black or white, and whether a model got up to help first. The researchers concluded that help given by bystanders in an emergency is influenced by characteristics of the victim, which affect the judgements people make about the costs and rewards involved in helping or not helping.

Milgram (1963)

Pause for thought

◆ Who do you obey in daily life?

◆ What would society be like without obedience?

◆ Why do you think we obey people in authority?

What is this study about?

Obedience, many theorists propose, is fundamental to the structure of society. Society could not function without the majority of people toeing the line and respecting the law, so we often see loyalty, discipline and obedience as valuable qualities in a person and the fuel in the engine of a well organised and healthy society.

Blind obedience however, can get people into trouble, and it is amazing what people will do just because they are told to. The Strip Search Prank Call Scam was a series of incidents occurring between 1994 and 2004, involving a man calling a restaurant claiming to be a police detective, and persuading managers to strip-search female employees. Reports of over 70 such occurrences in 30 US states finally led to the arrest of a 37-year-old corrections officer.

A further example is the Enron scandal where, with a goal derived from the pursuit of profit, Enron employees were constantly told to break laws or perform acts that could be considered immoral. The executives of the company made millions of dollars at the electricity consumers' expense but, again, this would not have been possible without obedience on a mass scale.

Unquestioning obedience has led people to commit crimes against humanity. The best-known example is the Holocaust, where six million innocent people in Nazi Germany were slaughtered by people who were 'following orders'. Without high levels of obedience, these murders could not have happened.

In 1942, a man called Stangl began his role as commandant at Treblinka extermination camp. Stangl said that, during his time at Treblinka, he grew accustomed to the killings, even eventually regarding the Jewish prisoners as 'baggage'. His role in the mass murder of men, women and children was known and a warrant for Stangl's arrest was issued in 1961. After extradition to West Germany he was tried for the deaths of around 900,000 people. He admitted to these killings but argued that his conscience was clear, as he was only doing his duty. Stangl was found guilty in 1970 and sentenced to life imprisonment.

Milgram suggested that obedience depended on a person seeing themselves as merely an instrument to carry out someone else's wishes, and therefore as no longer responsible for their actions.

The world was stunned by these events, and psychologists wanted to explore the psychological processes involved. It was clear that Hitler had masterminded the genocide, but the question of his power, and the frightening possibility of this happening again, led to a series of theories and studies.

One theory was that the Germans were more obedient than other nationalities. This became known as the 'Germans are different' hypothesis. This was a dispositional hypothesis, as it suggested that a person's obedience depends on their character rather than the situation they are in.

Milgram favoured a situational hypothesis, and suggested the Holocaust was in fact the result of conditions at the time, specifically the existence of a powerful authority figure with charisma and powers of persuasion (Hitler), and the propaganda created by a government who controlled all the media in Germany, and who censored or eliminated views that threatened the Nazi regime.

Milgram argued that anyone, regardless of nationality, finding themselves in these conditions would obey in the same way the Germans had. He therefore designed an experiment that would allow levels of obedience in different nationalities to be compared. It was a simple experiment to test how much pain one person would inflict on another when ordered to by an experimental scientist.

Weblink

You can read more about Milgram's study of obedience (see 'Websites' on page ii).

Try this …

Read about the Holocaust and identify other features that might have led to such high levels of obedience.

Discuss other events in history that required collective obedience in order to take place, such as the Inquisition.

Practical investigation ideas

You could conduct a survey on what people think of their own levels of obedience in everyday life, or in the situation in Milgram's study.

You might find it interesting to observe obedience in everyday life, including drivers' behaviour at traffic lights or use of mobile phones while driving, or whether people put litter in bins.

Stanley Milgram

Figure 4.1 Stanley Milgram

Stanley Milgram (1933–84) was Professor of Psychology at Yale University. In 1963 he published one of six popular papers on his shock experiments on authority. Milgram was nominated for a National Book Award for *Obedience to Authority* in 1975.

Key terms

genocide deliberate and systematic destruction of a racial, political, or cultural group

dispositional hypothesis the idea that a person's characteristics determine their behaviour, e.g. personality traits

situational hypothesis the idea that conditions in a situation determine behaviour, e.g. orders from an authority figure

Links to other studies

There are strong links to the study by Reicher and Haslam (pages 104–111), who also studied the conditions in which people exhibit pathological behaviours.

Piliavin, Rodin and Piliavin's study (pages 112–119) is also relevant in that a situational hypothesis was also tested in terms of bystander behaviour.

Milgram, S. (1963)

'Behavioural study of obedience'
Journal of Abnormal and Social Psychology, 67(4), 371–8.

What was the aim of the study?

The aim of the experiment was to investigate what level of obedience participants would show when an authority figure told them to administer electric shocks to another person.

What was the methodology?

There is some debate as to the actual method used in this study; Milgram referred to it as a laboratory experiment, and it was indeed carried out under controlled conditions in a laboratory. However, the original study must be seen in the context of Milgram's initial intention to carry out the study on different nationalities, in which case the independent variable would have been the nationality of the participant.

This specific study therefore does not have an independent variable and should be considered as a controlled observation in which obedience was measured in terms of the voltage given to the victim. Milgram decided that a participant would be classed as obedient if he went all the way to 450 volts; anything less was not classed as obedient. Participants' reactions were measured by observation and interviews after the study. The sessions were also filmed and photographs taken.

The selection of participants

The participants were obtained from a newspaper advertisement and direct mailings. The respondents were 40 males aged 20–50 from the New Haven area, they included postal clerks, high-school teachers, salesmen, engineers, and labourers. They ranged in educational level from one who had not finished high school, to others who had degrees and professional qualifications. The participants were told that they would be paid $4.50 for taking part, regardless of what happened after they arrived. This type of sampling technique is called a self-selected or volunteer sample.

The location and actors in the study

The study was conducted at Yale University. An 'interaction laboratory' was used, as it was felt that this would enhance the perceived legitimacy of the study. The role of the experimenter was played by a 31-year-old Biology teacher whose manner was emotionless and appearance stern; he wore a grey technician's coat. The role of the learner/victim was played by a 47-year-old accountant, who was trained for the role and appeared likeable and mild-mannered.

The start of the study: convincing the participants of the reality of the situation

◆ The participants took part in the experiment one at a time.

◆ A 'cover story' was used to justify the procedure: participants were told that the aim of the study was to find out the effects of punishment on learning. The participants therefore were 'naïve' about the true purpose of the study.

◆ Slips of paper were drawn from a hat to determine who would play the learner (victim) and who would play the teacher. (This was fixed so that the participant always drew the part of the teacher.)

◆ The teacher and learner were taken to a room where the learner was strapped into an 'electric chair'. The experimenter explained that this was to prevent the learner escaping.

◆ Electrodes were applied to the learner's wrist and electrode paste was applied, supposedly to prevent blisters and burns.

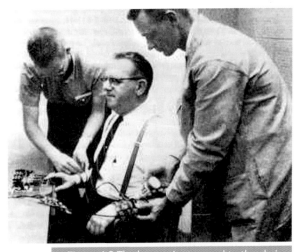

Figure 4.2 The learner is strapped to the chair

- When asked whether the shocks would be painful, the experimenter replied that no permanent tissue damage would be caused.
- Each participant was given a sample shock, this was just 45 volts from a battery wired to the generator, its purpose was to convince the participant of the generator's authenticity.

The learning task

The task involved the teacher reading a series of word pairs to the learner. The teacher then read the first word of a pair and a variety of other words, one of which had originally been paired with the first word. The learner had to indicate which of the four words had originally been paired with the first word. He communicated his answer by pressing one of four switches in front of him, which lit up one of four sections on the shock generator. This told the teacher which shock level was to be administered.

The shock generator

This instrument was produced to make sure that it looked, sounded and was perceived to be real. It had been professionally made, with the make and model printed on it, consisting of 30 switches in a horizontal line. Each switch was clearly labelled with a voltage of 15 to 450 volts. There were 15-volt increments between each switch, and each group of four switches was labelled 'slight shock', 'moderate shock', 'strong shock', 'very strong shock', 'intense shock', 'extreme intensity shock', 'danger: severe shock', and finally two switches simply marked 'XXX'.

When a switch was pressed a corresponding red light would illuminate and an electric buzzing was heard. In addition a blue light labelled 'voltage energiser' flashed and the dial on the voltage meter swung to the right whilst various clicks were heard.

Feedback from the victim

In all of the conditions the learner gave a predetermined set of responses to the word-pair test: approximately three wrong answers to one correct answer. No vocal response or other protest was heard from the learner until Shock Level 300 was reached, when the learner pounded on the wall of the room in which he was bound to the 'electric' chair. The pounding could be heard by the teacher and from this point on, the learner's answers no longer appeared on the panel. As the 315 Shock Level was administered the learner's pounding was repeated and this was the last that was heard from him.

Experimenter feedback

Only standardised feedback was given to the teacher; for example if he turned to the experimenter for guidance when no response was given from the learner, the experimenter instructed him to treat the absence of a response as a wrong answer, and to shock the learner accordingly. He advised the teacher to allow 5–10 seconds before considering no response as a wrong answer, and to increase the shock level by one step each time the learner failed to respond correctly.

Any attempt by the teacher to ask questions, seek reassurance, or refuse to go on was met by one of the following 'prods' made in sequence:

Prod 1: 'Please continue' or 'Please go on.'

Prod 2: 'The experiment requires that you continue.'

Prod 3: 'It is absolutely essential that you continue.'

Prod 4: 'You have no other choice, you *must* go on.'

If the teacher asked if the learner would suffer any permanent physical injury or expressed that the learner did not want to go on, the experimenter replied as follows, followed by the prods:

- 'Although the shock may be painful, there is no permanent tissue damage, so please go on.'
- 'Whether the learner likes it or not, you must go on until he has learned all the word pairs correctly. So please go on.'

Figure 4.3 The shock generator

After the study

After the study the participants were interviewed and given various attitude scales to ensure that they would leave in a state of well-being. A friendly reconciliation was arranged between the participant and the victim, and an effort was made to reduce any tensions arising from the study.

What were the findings?

From evidence gathered in post-study interviews, Milgram claimed that the participants had been convinced that they were giving real electric shocks, and the majority of participants rated the last few shocks given to the learner as 'extremely painful'.

Many participants showed extreme nervousness during the study, especially upon administering the more powerful shocks. Participants were observed to sweat, tremble, stutter, bite their lips, groan, and dig their fingernails into their flesh. Other signs of tension seen regularly were nervous laughing fits (14 of the 40 participants showed definite signs of nervous laughter and smiling), and seizures, in one case so violent that the study had to be stopped.

Once the study was halted, many obedient participants heaved sighs of relief, mopped their brows, and rubbed their fingers nervously over their eyes or nervously fumbled for cigarettes. Some shook their heads, apparently in regret, whilst others, who had remained calm throughout the study, displayed only minimal signs of tension from beginning to end.

No participant stopped prior to administering 300 volts, when the victim pounded on the wall and no longer answered the teacher's questions.

Figure 4.4 Signs of tension were seen in the participants

In total 14 participants were not classed as obedient:

◆ at 300 volts 5 participants refused to obey the commands of the experimenter

◆ at 315 volts 4 participants refused to obey

◆ at 330 volts 2 participants refused to obey

◆ at 345, 360 and 375 1 participant refused to obey.

Twenty-six participants were obedient until the end (450 volts – enough to have killed someone three times over!).

What did Milgram conclude?

Milgram commented on two overriding findings:

◆ the strength of the obedient tendencies

◆ the extraordinary tension generated by the procedures.

The strength of the obedience was surprising because it had been predicted that levels of obedience would be low (a survey was carried out on 14 university students, who all predicted that an insignificant minority of participants would continue to shock until the end: 3% at most).

The extreme signs of tension were also surprising, as it was expected that a participant would stop or continue as his conscience dictated. The fact that participants continued to administer shocks despite their obvious stress was observed with disbelief behind the one-way mirror.

Milgram points to various features of the conditions in the study in his explanation of the high degree of obedience observed:

1 The study took place at a very prestigious university.

2 The study seemed to be for a worthy purpose.

3 The victim had volunteered to take part in the study.

4 The participant themselves had volunteered for the study and therefore felt obliged to help the experimenter.

5 The participant had been paid to take part in the study.

6 The roles of teacher and learner were purely a chance consequence.

7 The participant was unclear about the rights of a psychologist and in turn of a participant in psychological research.

8 There was no opportunity for the participant to discuss the situation with others.

9 The participant was under the impression that the shocks would not cause any permanent damage.

10 The victim was at first 'willing to play the game'.

Milgram also points out that it was the conflict experienced by the participants that created the tension, i.e. the desire not to harm other people (the victim) and the tendency to obey those in authority (the experimenter).

Milgram concludes that his study shows that obedience can be elicited from any individual in the right situational conditions. He rejects the 'Germans are different' hypothesis, claiming that the results of his study show that obedience is not a dispositional tendency of any individual or nationality, but that the situation a person is in has the power to override conscience and morality in the name of obedience:

obedience is a deeply ingrained behavior tendency, indeed a potent impulse overriding training in ethics, sympathy, and moral conduct.

(Milgram, 1963)

Key terms

controlled observation observations of the reactions of participants in a specific situation. It differs from natural observation, where people are in their usual environments and nothing is set up by the researcher

cover story a false explanation of the aim of the study, told to participants in order to prevent demand characteristics

standardised this refers to any aspect of the procedure that is kept exactly the same for each participant. This is to control for variations in the procedure that could affect the outcome

demand characteristic a feature of a procedure (other than the independent variable) that influences the participant to respond differently

attitude scale a way of measuring a person's attitude towards something; it provides a quantitative measure

Summary of main points

1 Of the participants, 65% continued to the 450-volt shock level; 100% continued to 300 volts.

2 The conflict raised in the participants led to signs of extreme tension.

3 High levels of obedience can be brought about in any individual with the appropriate situational conditions.

Try this ...

1 Which features of the procedure were designed to convince the participants of the its reality?

2 Copy and complete the table on the right, identifying all the control measures used in the study. Explain why it was necessary to implement each control measure.

3 Draw a bar chart illustrating the levels of obedience found.

Control measures	Reason for implementation
1 Use of a 'cover story'	If the participants had known the true aim of the study they might have changed their behaviour due to demand characteristics
2	

Evaluating the study by Milgram

What were the strengths of the method used in this study?

The study was a highly controlled observation, allowing for the effects of the experimenter's commands to be observed clearly. The fact that the participants had volunteered meant they had given consent, which is more difficult to obtain in a field setting.

Another strength relates to the study's ecological validity, which has been criticised by many, but was high in terms of experimental realism. It is difficult in a laboratory study to get people to believe in the situation and to get sufficiently involved that they forget they are in a study at all. The tension shown by the participants reveals a high level of experimental realism here.

What are the weaknesses of the method used in this study?

The study has been criticised on many counts, not least in relation to ethics. The participants were deceived about the true purpose of the experiment and were made to believe they were administering real electric shocks to a naive subject. Milgram felt it was necessary to do this because any information about the true nature of the study would have brought about demand characteristics that would have rendered the findings useless.

There is debate as to whether participants were able to withdraw from the study. Despite being told that the money paid to them was theirs to keep regardless of the outcome of the study, the 'prods' given by the experimenter suggested that withdrawal was not an option. Milgram would argue though, that the participants could, and in some cases did, refuse to continue, begging the question of whether the study can be blamed for the participants' choice not to withdraw.

Many of the subjects suffered from considerable stress, conflicting with the ethical principle of protecting the participant. Again Milgram could argue that the participants could choose to leave the experiment, and post-study interviews and tests revealed that the stress caused no long-term effects. However, can Milgram be excused for putting participants into this situation in the first place?

Lack of ecological validity is one of the main criticisms of this study. Many critics have questioned the value of research carried out in controlled laboratory situations where participants are aware they are taking part in a study. Specifically, it has been argued that the social situation created in a laboratory is unique, telling us nothing about behaviour in everyday life. The combination of the 'all-knowing' experimenter and the scientist's quest for knowledge makes demands on the participant that are not found in any other situation.

Milgram would argue that the laboratory is similar to any social situation where there is a legitimate authority figure, such as a doctor's surgery or a police interview room. In this respect he would claim that the study does have ecological validity and can be generalised to many everyday situations.

A final consideration in relation to ecological validity concerns the nature of the task: the shocking of another human being. This could be criticised for being low in mundane realism, that is, the extent to which the task was a normal, everyday activity the participants might find themselves engaged in.

How representative was the sample of participants?

Milgram wanted to test the 'Germans are different' hypothesis, so he selected Americans, to see if they would be as obedient as the Germans. The levels of obedience for the American sample were so high that it was not necessary to test any other nationality; therefore the sample was deliberately ethnocentric. Other psychologists have tested subjects from many cultures and found that people generally obey figures of authority regardless of culture.

The sample included men from a range of occupations and educational backgrounds, which made it more representative, but the fact that they were a self-selected sample who had responded to an advertisement means that they may have all had similar personality types (they were extrovert enough to want to take part in research). The absence of women from the sample also restricts the generalisations that can be made from the findings.

What type of data was collected in this study?

A mixture of quantitative and qualitative data were collected in this study. The level of shocks given provided a quantitative measure of obedience, whilst the observations and interview data provided qualitative data. Collecting a mixture of data in this way can add to the validity of a study. However, measurement of obedience in terms of giving a 450-volt shock does not account for those who went part of the way, and also fails to tell us the reasons behind the level of obedience found, which is left to the speculation of the researcher.

What about the role of 'free will'?

Milgram's conclusions are deterministic and suggest that the situation we find ourselves in determines the way we behave. This paints a pessimistic view of human beings. An alternative way of explaining behaviour is that we have 'free will' – we make choices about how we behave.

How useful was this research?

'Following orders' allows individuals to abandon their emotions, separating them from feelings of duty (the 'agentic' state). As Milgram points out:

The results, as seen and felt in the laboratory, are to this author disturbing. They raise the possibility that human nature, or – more specifically – the kind of character produced in American society, cannot be counted on to insulate the citizens from brutality and inhumane treatment at the direction of malevolent authority.

(Milgram, 1963)

> ### Key terms
>
> experimental realism the extent to which the participants perceive an experimental situation to be real
>
> ethnocentric favouring one group of people
>
> mundane realism the extent to which a procedure or task relates to everyday life
>
> agentic state when individuals relinquish their personal views and act as an agent of someone else's will

> ### Check your understanding
>
> How were the participants selected?
>
> What percentage of the participants was obedient?
>
> What were Milgram's conclusions?
>
> To what extent did the study have ecological validity?

Weblinks

To read about the 'silent genocide' in Iraq, for summaries of the study, to read a participant's account of the Milgram Obedience Experiment or Derren Brown's re-enactment of the Milgram experiment, to see original film footage or a cartoon version of the Milgram experiment, see 'Websites' on page ii.

Exam Café

Remember that this study was a controlled observation carried out in a laboratory. You should be able to describe the sample and how they were selected, the procedure and all the control measures used to ensure the situation was realistic, and the fact that the participants believed the situation was real. The ethics of this study are very significant and you should make sure that you can give examples of how various ethical guidelines were broken, including the harm caused to participants. Finally, you should be able to describe the conclusions that can be drawn from this study.

Reicher and Haslam (2006)

Pause for thought

◆ Think of some groups you belong to.

◆ Think about how you behave in different situations with different groups of people.

◆ Imagine you are a player in a bottom-of-the-league football team; how would you feel?

◆ What does this show about the effect group membership can have on a person?

What is this study about?

This study is closely linked to the Stanford Prison Experiment (SPE), a study conducted by Haney, Banks and Zimbardo in 1973, which attempted to uncover the reasons for the antisocial behaviour commonly found in prisons. This study became infamous due to the severe reactions of the participants.

The SPE was stopped early, after only 6 days, due to extreme stress in the prisoners and the increasingly sadistic behaviour of the guards. The researchers' main conclusion was that the prison situation (the uniforms, status, the physical environment, together with the allocation of social roles), caused inmates and guards to behave in pathological ways. This was supported by the fact that the participants were 'normal' individuals with no criminal record or history of violence, yet in the prison they quickly became abusers and victims.

This is a deterministic view of behaviour, as it suggests that people can be excused for their actions by blaming the situation they are in.

Take for example the Abu Ghraib prison in Iraq where, beginning in 2004, abuse of prisoners by American military personnel came to public attention. Is it reasonable to take individual responsibility for such acts away from the abusers and to blame the situation they were in? You will probably agree that situations do affect behaviour, but that to ignore the role of free will is overly deterministic.

Zimbardo would suggest that these events were inevitable, given the uniforms and unequal distribution of power between the prisoners and their captors, but would everyone react in this way?

Reicher and Haslam wanted to test the situational hypothesis proposed by Zimbardo: the idea that a situation could have such a powerful influence over a person's behaviour. Reicher and Haslam wanted to get away from the idea that people had no control over their behaviour and to show that to accept that people have a natural tendency to behave in pathological ways in certain situations was to 'apologise for the inexcusable'. They wanted to show that group membership has a more powerful influence over an individual's behaviour, specifically the extent to which a person identifies with the group, or the power of group membership.

A good example is how, when individual women felt powerless to change gender inequalities in society, they identified with other women in this devalued group and acted collectively to improve its position. This became known as the Women's Movement (see Figure 4.6).

Reicher and Haslam were also interested in the conditions that can lead to changes in the behaviour of a group, including the effect of a new group member in bringing about change. For example, if a successful footballer joined a bottom-of-the-league team where morale was low, it would re-energise the other team members and might even make them hope that they could move up the league.

They also wanted to show that people are capable of reflecting before acting, and do not just follow the behaviour of others. This is a more optimistic view of people and suggests that negative behaviour is not situationally inevitable.

In variations of Milgram's study on obedience (see pages 96–103), participants were more likely to defy the experimenter when they were supported by confederates who were also disobedient. This shows that groups can serve to resist oppression, not just to perpetrate antisocial acts.

Links to other studies

The findings from the study by Milgram (pages 96–103) support a situational hypothesis of behaviour, i.e. that behaviour is determined by the situation we are in.

Try this …

The importance of group identity is also the main concept behind Social Identity Theory.

Find out about Social Identity Theory. What are the main ideas in this theory?

Key terms

situational hypothesis the idea that conditions in a situation determine behaviour, e.g. orders from an authority figure

Social Identity Theory a theory that proposes that group membership affects our identity, self-esteem and behaviour

determinism the idea that our behaviour is determined by factors beyond our control, e.g. the situation, the environment and our biology

Practical investigation ideas

You could design a questionnaire about the groups people belong to and the sense of group identity they share with other members of these groups. You could also correlate how fans of different football teams feel in relation to their team's position in the league.

Alex Haslam

Alex Haslam is Professor of Social and Organisational Psychology at the University of Exeter.

Figure 4.5 Alex Haslam

Weblinks

You can read about the original study by Reicher and Haslam in an article on the BBC Prison Study and find out more about the SPE on the SPE website. You might like to read about Abu Ghraib in an article in *The Wednesday Report* (see 'Websites' on page ii).

Figure 4.6 A group demonstration

Reicher, S. and Haslam, S. A. (2006)

'Rethinking the psychology of tyranny: the BBC prison study',
British Journal of Social Psychology, 45, 1–40

What was the aim of the study?

Given the ethical implications of the SPE, it was felt that further studies of this type would be off-limits. However, Reicher and Haslam wanted to carry out a prison study with ethical procedures that would ensure that it would not harm participants. They collaborated with the BBC, which funded the research and broadcast the findings in four one-hour documentaries.

The overall aims of the study can be summarised as follows (b is the most significant):

a   To provide data on the unfolding interactions between groups of unequal power and privilege.

b   To analyse the conditions that lead individuals to: (i) identify with their group; (ii) accept or challenge intergroup inequalities.

c   To examine the role of social, organisational and clinical factors (e.g. mood) in group behaviour.

d   To develop practical and ethical guidelines for examining social psychological issues in large-scale studies.

What was the methodology?

The study was a laboratory experiment designed to create a society in which the participants would live for 10 days. It was constructed inside a film studio in London. Prisoners lived in lockable 3-person cells off a central area that was separated from the guards' quarters by a lockable steel-mesh fence.

The independent variables

In order to achieve these aims the researchers manipulated several independent variables:

◆   Day 3: *Participants' beliefs about the permeability of group boundaries.* At the start all participants were told that the guards had been selected on the basis of their reliability, trustworthiness and initiative as measured by the pre-selection tests.

They were also told that these qualities might have been missed in some prisoners and that movement between groups was possible, i.e. prisoners with the appropriate qualities could be promoted to the position of guard. A change on day 3 meant that promotion was no longer possible.

◆   Day 6: *Participants' beliefs about the legitimacy of group divisions.* Three days after the one and only promotion took place, participants were informed that observations had revealed that there were in fact no differences in qualities between the guards and prisoners, but that it would be impractical to change the groups back. This meant that the group division that was previously thought to be based on different qualities, was now seen to be random.

◆   Day 7: *Participants' beliefs about the possibility of change, i.e. cognitive alternatives.* A new prisoner was introduced who was chosen (from the original pool of 10 participants randomly assigned to be prisoners) because of his experience as a trade-union official. This was done because it was expected that he would introduce new and alternative plans of action, based on ideas of group negotiation and equal rights (cognitive alternatives). It was also expected that he would have the skills necessary to organise the group into action that would enable the prisoners and in turn the guards to see a way of achieving more equality between the groups.

The same prisoners were used for each of these conditions, as to have different groups of prisoners in separate prisons would have been expensive. The study was therefore a repeated-measures design, and the experimental manipulations were introduced over time at predefined points in the study (a time-series approach) and their effects both within and between the groups of prisoners and guards were measured.

The dependent variable (measured)

The following features of the participants' behaviour and experience were measured:

◆ social variables: social identification, awareness of alternative plans of action, right-wing authoritarianism

◆ organisational variables: compliance with rules

◆ clinical variables: self-efficacy, depression, stress hormones.

These features were measured in a variety of ways, including:

◆ the prison was designed in such a way that participants could be video- and audio-recorded wherever they were

◆ daily psychometric testing

◆ daily swabs of saliva.

How were the participants selected?

Male participants were recruited through leaflets and advertisements in the national press. The initial pool of applicants was 332, which was reduced to 15 after three phases of screening:

1   Psychometric tests that measured both social variables (authoritarianism, social dominance, racism) and clinical variables (depression, anxiety, social isolation, paranoia, aggressiveness, demotivation, self-esteem, self-harm and drug dependence).

2   A full weekend assessment by independent clinical psychologists.

3   Medical and character references were obtained, and police checks conducted.

Sample considerations

For ethical reasons only well adjusted and pro-social people were included in the study. The researchers also wanted the participants to be representative of the population so that the results could be generalised. Only men were recruited, for comparability to the SPE, and to avoid the ethical issues of placing men and women together in cells.

The final choice of participants was made to ensure diversity of age, social class and ethnic background. The allocation of 10 participants as prisoners and 5 as guards was carefully considered with initial allocation of all participants to five groups of 3 who were closely matched on personality variables, followed by one participant from each group of 3 being randomly selected to be a guard and the remaining two to be prisoners. This was done because 'pure' random sampling does not take account of individual differences and it is possible for large differences between two groups to exist. Note: at the start of the study there were 5 guards and only 9 prisoners; the tenth was introduced later.

The induction procedure

The guards

Five participants were invited to a hotel the evening before entering the prison. On arrival, they were told they would be guards. They were shown the prison timetable, which included cleaning chores, work duties, prisoner roll calls, exercise time and a recreational hour – and were told that their responsibility was to ensure that the institution ran as smoothly as possible and that the prisoners performed all their tasks. The guards were asked to draw up a series of punishments for rule violations.

The guards were given no guidance about how they should achieve their goals. The only limits were a set of ethically determined 'basic rights' for prisoners. All participants were told that physical violence would not be tolerated; otherwise, the guards could act as they pleased.

On the morning of the study itself, the guards were taken to the prison and given a full briefing by the experimenters on the prison layout and the resources available to them. The guards' ability to enforce their authority was enhanced by: keys to all doors inside the prison, including a punishment isolation cell, access to an upper-level 'guard's station' with a surveillance system from which they could see the prisoners' cells, snacks and cigarettes to give as rewards or withhold as punishments – and the power to put prisoners on a bread and water diet.

The guards' uniform: formal trousers, shirt and tie, was superior to the prisoners', they also had superior meals, extra drinks and snacks, and superior living conditions.

The prisoners

The nine prisoners arrived one at a time; they had their heads shaved on arrival and were given a uniform: a t-shirt printed with a 3-digit number, loose trousers and flimsy sandals.

The prisoners were given no information apart from the prison rules, a list of prisoners' rights that was posted in their cells and a brief loudspeaker announcement from the experimenters, explaining the possibility of promotion from prisoner to guard and telling them that violence was not allowed.

Try this ...

Explain why a trade-union official was chosen as the latecomer.

Read through the procedure and details of the sample, then list all the control measures included in the design of the study (measures taken to ensure the study was valid).

How did the researchers safeguard against harming the participants?

◆ Prior to the study a plan of the research was submitted to the BPS ethics committee.

◆ There was a three-phase clinical, medical and background screening.

◆ There was a comprehensive consent form.

◆ Two independent clinical psychologists monitored the study throughout.

◆ A paramedic was on constant standby.

◆ There were on-site security guards.

◆ There was a round-the-clock independent ethics committee.

What were the findings?

The prisoners behaved more or less as predicted. At first they were compliant and worked hard to improve their situation. This, the researchers felt, was due to the possibility of promotion, i.e. permeable group boundaries.

When opportunities for promotion were eliminated on day 3, the prisoners started to see themselves as a group and became uncooperative with the guards. This was put down to the realisation that they would remain prisoners. This shared identity led to improved organisation, effectiveness and mental well-being. As the study progressed, the prisoners became more positive and empowered.

The guards behaved in a way that was not predicted. Some were troubled by the idea that groups and power are dangerous, and were reluctant to exercise control. They disagreed with colleagues as to how their role should be interpreted, and never developed a shared identity. As a result there was a lack of organisation among them and they became despondent. As the study progressed their administration became weaker.

Figure 4.7 shows the strength of the identification the prisoners and guards felt with their group as the study progressed. It can be seen that the guards started off feeling quite a strong identity with their group, but this tailed off after the second day as they failed to reach a common agreement about their role. The prisoners, on the other hand, had an increasing sense of shared identity, especially after the possibility of promotion from prisoner to guard was eliminated

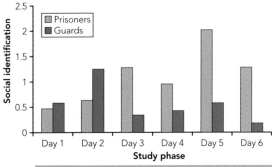

Figure 4.7 Social identification as a function of assigned group and time

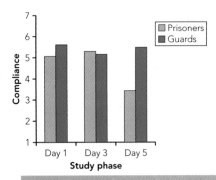

Figure 4.8 Compliance with prison rules as a function of assigned group and time

on day 3 and they realised they were going to remain prisoners.

Figure 4.8 shows how the prisoners' compliance with prison rules diminished once the possibility of promotion from prisoner to guard was eliminated after day 3. The introduction of alternative plans of action by the new prisoner on day 5 also led to a marked decrease in compliance with prison rules.

Following the introduction of the new group member, the prisoners collaborated to challenge the fragmented guards, leading to an organised breakout and the collapse of the prisoner–guard structure. After the complete breakdown of the system, prisoners and guards established 'a self-governing, self-disciplining commune'. The introduction of a new group member had given them an alternative plan of action.

However, some supporters of the commune started losing faith in their ability to make it work. In response, a number of former prisoners and guards decided to become the 'new' guards. They asked for black berets and dark glasses as symbols of a new authoritarian management that they wanted to impose.

The researchers expected those who had supported the commune to defend it, but instead they did nothing. They lacked the individual and collective will to make a stand against the new regime, assumed to be due to the lack of shared identity and a lack of cognitive alternatives.

The new regime never occurred. For ethical reasons the experimenters could not risk the type of force witnessed in the SPE, and the study was stopped on the eighth day.

What did Reicher and Haslam conclude?

The researchers claim that although the outcome resembled that of the SPE, the path the participants took to reach that point was very different. They claim that events were not determined by the participants being in groups, or their social roles, but by the failure of those groups.

The guards failed to develop a shared identity, the failure of the commune thwarted any possibility of positive change, there were no cognitive alternatives left for the participants, hence the acceptance of a proposed authoritarian regime.

The researchers agree with earlier studies such as the SPE that tyranny is a product of group processes and not due to an individual deviancy. But they disagree about the nature of group processes, in that people do not lose their minds in groups, do not helplessly conform to their roles, and do not automatically abuse power when in a group.

Instead, individuals identify with groups only when it makes sense to do so, and consciously attempt to implement the group's values. Groups give people choice and the ability to exercise it, but when groups fail and have no hope of change, problems arise and tyranny can result.

Summary of main points

1   At first the prisoners tried to improve their position.

2   When this was not possible they identified with each other and formed a strong group.

3   With the new prisoner's introduction of ways to confront the inequalities, a commune was established.

4   Once this broke down an authoritarian regime was planned, against which nobody acted.

Key terms

self-efficacy belief in one's ability to bring about change

repeated-measures design where the same participants experience each condition of the independent variable

time-series approach a study that introduces changes to the independent variable over time

psychometric testing tests that attempt to measure psychological characteristics such as mood and self-esteem. These normally produce a quantitative score

commune a democratically-run society whose members all have a say in its organisation

Evaluating the study by Reicher and Haslam

What were the strengths and weaknesses of the method used?

The ecological validity of the study could be both a strength and a weakness. One strength was that the participants got sufficiently involved to react naturally; this is called experimental realism and is an important part of achieving ecological validity. It can be seen in reality TV shows like *Big Brother*, which last long enough and are intense enough for participants to forget that they are being watched and show their true emotions. Some extracts from conversations between prisoners and guards suggest that they did get genuinely involved in the situation.

However, the prison was not real and the participants were not real prisoners or guards. In fact, the possibility of being shown on national television could mean that the participants were faking their behaviours for the cameras; Zimbardo even criticised the study for being reality TV.

The researchers defend their study by suggesting that acting would have been difficult to sustain for nearly 9 days. They also argue that surveillance is becoming a common feature of our lives and would not necessarily cause unnatural behaviour. It would also have been hard, they say, to fake the psychometric and physiological data that were gathered on a regular basis.

The ethical implications of the study were much reduced by the many steps taken to avoid harming the participants. It is widely accepted that the study was stopped before things turned nasty. On the whole, the study avoided many of the ethical problems of the SPE, but as Alex Holmes, BBC executive producer on *The Experiment*, commented: 'There was a lot of aggression, there was a lot of tension, this is a tough environment.' Who knows what damage was done to the participants, but the ethical committee's report concluded that the study showed that it is possible to conduct dynamic field studies that are also ethical.

The laboratory-based experimental method allowed the researchers to control many variables in the study, for example the selection procedure and the prison environment. A high degree of control allows cause and effect to be established (in this study to see the effect of manipulating the group conditions on social behaviour). The weakness of so much control can be the artificiality it brings with it, which can affect the ecological validity of the study.

How representative was the sample of participants?

The sample was chosen to reflect a wide variety of variables including age, social class and ethnic background. However the participants were all male and had volunteered, which suggests they may all have had similar personalities, making the sample less representative.

What type of data was collected in this study?

The data collected in the study were a mixture of quantitative and qualitative data, collected via a range of techniques including observation, psychometric testing and physiological measures. This variety of measures can increase the validity of the study, since the weaknesses of individual measuring systems can be overcome.

One weakness could be the lack of qualitative self-reports: it would have been useful to ask the participants how they felt and what they were thinking rather than just giving them tests and scales, which can be reductionist.

> **Try this …**
>
> Compare the different methods used to collect data and evaluate the strengths and weaknesses of each.

Key terms

reductionist any explanation or method that simplifies behaviour and experience in such a way that the complexity of the human condition may be lost or underestimated

U1
4

Reicher and Haslam (2006)

How useful was this research?

The results of this study have challenged earlier ideas about the inevitability of antisocial behaviours in groups. Reicher and Haslam point out that the conditions and prevalent values of the group determine collective action. The values of a group are often dictated by influential or powerful individuals, especially when collective attempts to bring about democracy and positive conditions fail.

There is no doubt that groups can be powerful, but they can behave in pro-social as well as anti-social ways. If group boundaries are impermeable, individuals can join together to take collective action, but if this fails, individuals identify less with their group and succumb to more authoritarian regimes.

Groups can commit atrocities, but not all groups are brutal. Two main circumstances can lead to tyrannical groups:

◆ the success of groups that have oppressive values (often given to them by their leaders)

◆ the failure of efforts to bring about democratic and humane social values, making a rigid and hierarchical order more attractive (e.g. the re-emergence of anti-democratic forces in Iraq, and the fall of the Weimar republic and the emergence of Nazism in 1930s Germany).

A less deterministic theory of group dynamics brings about the possibility of change, whereas a fatalistic picture of groups renders us victims of the situation we find ourselves in.

Weblinks

To read articles on *The Experiment* or the British Psychological Society discussion of the prison experiment, see 'Websites' on page ii.

Check your understanding

What were the aims of the study?

Why was there a rigorous selection procedure?

What factors led to the establishment of the commune?

What factors led to the breakdown of the commune?

Why did the participants go along with the 'new guards' and their planned authoritarian regime?

Exam Café

This study was a laboratory experiment and you need to know the independent variables that were manipulated and the effects on behaviour that were measured (dependent variable).

The study was filmed for television viewing and you should be able to explain how this may have caused demand characteristics in the participants.

The participants went through a rigorous selection procedure before being allocated to their roles and you need to be aware of why this was important. The fact that the prison was created for the study has important implications in terms of ecological validity and you should be able to explain this.

You should also be able to describe the conclusions that can be drawn from this study and the strengths and weaknesses of the method and procedure used.

Reicher and Haslam (2006)

Figure 4.9 Nazi soldiers: where did their values come from?

Piliavin, Rodin and Piliavin (1969)

Pause for thought

◆ Have you ever helped a stranger?

◆ What factors would put you off helping?

◆ What type of person would you be most likely to help?

What is this study about?

It is sad that some people become famous for the way they die. One such person was Kitty Genovese, who was stabbed to death near her home in the Queen's area of New York in 1964. The circumstances of her murder and the apparent reaction of her neighbours were reported by a newspaper article published two weeks later, and prompted investigation into the psychological phenomenon that became known as the 'bystander effect' or the 'Genovese syndrome.'

Kitty Genovese was stabbed to death whilst several people witnessed her cries for help; some even saw her staggering about. The attack lasted approximately half an hour, and whilst some witnesses did call the police and shout out, no one actually went to help her. An article in the *New York Times* claimed that the attack was witnessed by 38 people; this was actually an exaggeration as it turned out to be no more than 12, none of whom could have seen or been aware of the entire incident.

The supposed callousness of the witnesses in this case sparked debate about the so-called apathy towards people in need of help, not just in urban America but of humanity in general. Several studies of bystander behaviour followed, the present study being one of the best-known.

Studies had been conducted in laboratory settings, for example by Darley and Latane who carried out several experiments, most significantly on the effect of the presence of other witnesses on a individual's willingness to help. They reported that under certain circumstances there is not 'safety in numbers', but rather what they call a 'diffusion of responsibility', where people are less likely to offer assistance if they believe other witnesses are present. Also, Bryan and Test conducted a study on the effects of observing others help, and concluded that a

Figure 4.10 The Kew Gardens district in New York

person would be more likely to help if they had just observed another individual performing a helpful act: the 'modelling effect'.

These studies had the drawbacks associated with laboratory research, and Piliavin, Rodin and Piliavin wanted to carry out research in a field setting with the advantage of greater reality. They wanted to identify some of the variables that affect whether bystanders help (bystander intervention) in an emergency or whether they ignore a person's need for help (bystander apathy), even in a situation that is clearly an emergency. They specifically wanted to test the effects of diffusion of responsibility and modelling found in earlier studies.

Piliavin, Rodin and Piliavin believed that it is characteristics of the emergency situation (situational hypothesis) as opposed to characteristics of the bystanders themselves (dispositional hypothesis) that determine whether help is given in an emergency. Referring back to the example of Kitty Genovese, a situational hypothesis would focus on features of that situation to explain the lack of help given, rather than the selfish, uncaring disposition or personality of the witnesses.

A wider question addressed by this study is whether altruism (acts of kindness towards others with no thought of personal gain) exists. Do you think it does?

Links to other studies

We have seen a situational explanation in the study by Milgram (pages 96–103), where he suggests that in certain conditions any individual can be obedient to a destructive degree.

Try this ...

Read about the case of Kitty Genovese on the Internet and identify features of the situation that you feel may have influenced the witnesses not to help.

Find examples of emergency situations in newspapers and identify features of the situation that you feel may have influenced bystanders not to help.

Practical investigation ideas

You could devise a questionnaire asking people about the types of situations in which they would/would not offer help. You could ask about features such as the age of the victim, the gender of the victim, the time of day, the nature of the emergency etc.

Irving Piliavin

Figure 4.11 Irving Piliavin

Irving Piliavin is Emeritus Professor of Social Work and Sociology at the Institute for Research on Poverty, University of Wisconsin-Madison, USA. He specialises in criminology and correctional programming, organisation and delivery of welfare services, and social-service program evaluation. He has been consulting editor for the *Journal of Personality and Social Psychology*, the *American Sociological Review*, and *Social Psychology Quarterly*. His research interests include evaluation of welfare reform programs, foster-care programs, and homelessness.

Weblink

To read a summary of the study, an analysis of the *New York Times* article on Kitty Genovese and an article from *Time* magazine 1970, see 'Websites' on page ii.

Key term

bystander behaviour the reactions of those who witness an emergency

Piliavin, I. M., Rodin, J. and Piliavin, J. A. (1969)

'Good Samaritanism: an underground phenomenon?'
Journal of Personality and Social Psychology, 13(4), 289–99

What was the aim of the study?

The researchers wanted to investigate the effect of several variables on helping behaviour using express trains of the New York Eighth Avenue Independent Subway as a 'laboratory on wheels'.

The study had four areas of focus:

1 Responsibility of the victim.

2 Race of the victim.

3 Effect of modelling.

4 Effect of size of group.

The researchers predicted that a person who was drunk (and therefore responsible for their condition) would receive less help than someone who was ill (and therefore not responsible for their need for help). It was suggested that this would be due to the possible cost of helping someone whose behaviour was unpredictable.

The race of the victim was predicted to affect the rate of helping. It was predicted that more help would be given to a person of the same race as the bystander: same-race helping. This prediction was based on previous findings concerning similarity and liking.

In addition, the study aimed to examine the impact of modelling in emergency situations, since previous research had suggested that seeing another person help would lead others in that situation to behave in a similar way. Finally, it was intended that the study would examine the relationship between size of group and helping response, specifically to test the 'diffusion of responsibility' found in earlier studies: the idea that the more who were people present, the less help would be given.

Piliavin, Rodin and Piliavin thought it would be useful to be able to predict the conditions under which bystanders would or would not offer help in an emergency. Such a model is known as a heuristic device, a framework that can predict behaviour.

Key terms

modelling how our behaviours can be changed by observational learning, when participants in a study base their behaviour on that of the model

heuristic device a framework that can be used to predict behaviour

What was the methodology?

The study was a field experiment. The independent variables were:

1 The type of victim (drunk or ill).

2 The race of the victim (black or white).

3 The presence or a model (early or late).

4 The number of bystanders present (varied naturally).

The dependent variable was helping, of which various measures were taken:

◆ the time taken for the first passenger to offer help

◆ the total number of passengers who helped

◆ the gender, race and location of every helper

◆ the time taken for the first passenger to offer help after the model had assisted.

Figure 4.12 Passengers read their morning newspapers en route to work, New York 1963

Several other measures were taken, including:

◆ the movement of any passengers out of the critical area

◆ the gender, race and location of every passenger in the critical area

◆ spontaneous comments made by passengers.

The location

The study was carried out on the A and D trains of the 8th Avenue IND in New York City. These were selected because they make no stops between 59th Street and 125th Street, and so for about 7½ minutes there was a captive audience who, after the first 70 seconds of their journey, became bystanders to an emergency situation.

In total, 103 trials of the experiment were conducted. The designated experimental or 'critical' area was at the end of the carriage where the doors to the next carriage were. There were 13 seats and some standing room in this area on all trains.

The participants

About 4450 men and women who used these trains on weekdays between the hours of 11.00am and 3.00pm, during the period 15 April to 26 June 1968, were the unsolicited participants in this study. The racial composition of a typical train was about 45% black and 55% white. The mean number of people per carriage during these hours was 43. The mean number of people in the 'critical area' where the staged incident took place was 8.

The confederates

On each trial a team of four Columbia General Studies Students, two males and two females, acted out the emergency. There were four teams, whose members always worked together. The female confederates observed and recorded data, while the males played the roles of model and victim.

The four victims, one in each team, were males aged 26–35. Three were white and one was black. All were identically dressed in jackets, old trousers and no tie. The four models were aged between 24 and 29. They wore informal clothes, although they were not dressed identically.

The emergency

The team of two males and two females boarded the train using different doors. The location of the experimental car, where the emergency took place, was varied from trial to trial. The female confederates took seats outside the critical area and recorded data as unobtrusively as possible for the duration of the journey. The victim always stood next to a pole in the centre of the critical area.

As the train passed the first station, approximately 70 seconds after departing, the victim staggered forward and collapsed. He lay on the floor looking at the ceiling until receiving help.

If the victim received no help by the time the train slowed to a stop, the model helped him to his feet. At the stop the team got off the train and waited separately until the other passengers had left the station. They then proceeded to another platform to board a train going in the opposite direction to repeat the experiment. Six to eight trials were run on any given day, all of which were of the same 'victim condition'.

When the model provided assistance, he raised the victim to a sitting position and stayed with him for the remainder of the trial. An equal number of no-model conditions were randomly assigned to each team.

Victim and model conditions

Drunk victim condition: on 38 trials the victims smelt of alcohol and carried a brown bag.

Cane victim condition: on 65 trials the victim appeared sober and carried a black cane.

Early model /critical area: the model stood in the critical area and waited until passing the fourth station to offer help (70 seconds after the collapse).

Late model/critical area: the model stood in the critical area and waited until passing the sixth station to offer help (150 seconds after the collapse).

Early model/adjacent area: the model stood in the area adjacent to the critical area and waited until passing the fourth station to offer help.

Late model/adjacent area: the model stood in the area adjacent to the critical area and waited until passing the sixth station to offer help.

The observations recorded

On each trial one of the observers noted the race, sex and location of every passenger seated or standing in the critical area. She also noted the total number in the carriage, the total who came to help the victim and the race, sex and location of every helper.

The second observer coded the race, sex and location of every person in the adjacent area, along with the time taken for the first help to be given after the model had arrived.

Both observers recorded comments made spontaneously by nearby passengers and attempted to elicit comments from a passenger sitting next to them.

What were the findings?

◆ An individual who appeared to be ill was more likely to receive aid than one who appeared to be drunk, even when the immediate help needed was of the same kind. The 'cane victim' received spontaneous help 95% of the time compared to 50% for the 'drunk victim'. This pattern was the same for black and white victims.

◆ Of the spontaneous first helpers, 90% were male.

◆ There was some tendency for same-race helping to be more frequent; this was increased when the victim was 'drunk' compared to 'ill'.

◆ There was no strong relationship between the number of bystanders and speed of helping; the expected increased 'diffusion of responsibility' with a greater number of bystanders was not obtained for groups of these sizes.

◆ The longer the emergency continued without help being offered:

◇ the less impact a model had on the helping behaviour of observers

◇ the more likely it was that individuals left the immediate area to avoid the situation

◇ the more likely it was that observers discussed the incident and its implications for their behaviour.

Spontaneous comments

Far more comments were obtained in the drunk trials than on the cane trials. Similarly, most of the comments were obtained in trials in which no one helped until after 70 seconds. The discomfort observers felt in sitting inactive in the presence of the victim may have led them to talk about the incident, perhaps hoping others would confirm the fact that inaction was appropriate.

What did Piliavin, Rodin and Piliavin conclude?

From these findings, Piliavin, Rodin and Piliavin suggested a situational explanation of bystander behaviour had been supported. They proposed a model of response to emergency situations: the Arousal Cost-Reward Model, a heuristic device that could be used to predict helping behaviour in any given emergency:

◆ observation of an emergency creates emotional arousal in the bystander

◆ this arousal state is higher:

◇ the more one can empathise with the victim, i.e. see themselves in his situation

Trials	White victims		Black victims	
	Cane	Drunk	Cane	Drunk
No model	100%	100%	100%	73%
Number of trials run	54	11	8	11
Model trials	100%	77	-	67%
Number of trials run	3	13	0	3
Total number of trials	57	24	8	14

Table 4.1 Percentage of trials in which help was given by race and condition of victim, and total number of trials run in each condition

1   Re-create the subway carriage in your classroom and act out the emergency.

Allocate the confederate roles of victim, model, two observers and all the passengers. You will need to take into account all of the variations, including race and type of victim and early or late model. You could record this on video and watch it.

You could perhaps interview passengers to find out what they thought of the emergency.

Don't forget to think about what props you will need!

2   Complete a cost-reward matrix for each of the conditions in the experiment.

	Costs	Rewards
Helping	e.g. effort, embarrassment, possible disgusting or distasteful experiences, possible physical harm	e.g. praise from self, victim, and others
Not helping	e.g. self-blame, judgement by others, guilt	e.g. less effort, continuation of other activities, avoidance of physical harm and unpleasant experiences

Table 4.2 Cost-reward matrix

◇   the closer one is to the emergency

◇   the longer the emergency continues without help being given

◆   arousal can be reduced by:

◇   helping directly

◇   going to get help

◇   leaving the scene of the emergency

◇   rejecting the victim as undeserving of help.

Piliavin, Rodin and Piliavin go on to suggest that the bystanders' responses are determined by weighing up the costs and rewards of helping or not helping, and are shown in Table 4.2.

They went on to explain the findings from the subway study in terms of the Arousal Cost-Reward Model: for example, the drunk is helped less because costs for helping are higher (e.g. greater disgust) and costs for not helping are lower (e.g. less self-blame and censure because he is responsible for his own victimisation). The lack of diffusion of responsibility was explained by the fact that the passengers could not escape the emergency situation. It must be noted that the researchers point out:

The major motivation implied in the model is not a positive 'altruistic' one, but rather a selfish desire to rid oneself of an unpleasant emotional state.

(Piliavin, Rodin and Piliavin, page 298)

Key terms

unsolicited participants people who are not aware that they are taking part in a study

trial each time an experiment is carried out

confederates actors who take part in experiments

Summary of main points

1   Characteristics of a victim do affect whether or not help is offered, including the perceived reasons for the victim's situation, i.e. whether they are drunk.

2   The tendency for same-race helping only occurred in the 'drunk' condition.

3   Diffusion of responsibility did not occur in this study.

4   The bystander makes the decision to help or not, based on the costs and rewards involved.

5   A model of response to emergency situations is offered in the form of the Arousal Cost-Reward Model. This can be used as a heuristic device to predict when help will be given.

U1

4

Piliavin, Rodin and Piliavin (1969)

What were the strengths and weaknesses of the method used?

The study was a field experiment and so was high in ecological validity, given that it was an everyday situation for the passengers, who did not know that they were taking part in a study.

Having naïve participants reduced possible demand characteristics and avoided the inevitable pro-social behaviour that would have arisen from their wanting to look helpful had they known that their behaviour was being observed (social desirability effect).

Several control measures were put in place to ensure that the study was valid:

◆ the victims all collapsed in the same way and wore the same clothes, since variations could have affected whether help was given (standardised procedure)

◆ the female confederates observed as 'unobtrusively' as possible, that is, from behind newspapers and without drawing attention to what they were doing.

One disadvantage of the field experiment, however, is the experimenters' lack of control over the situation. For example it was not possible to control which passengers boarded the train, or how many. There was always the danger of the same passengers seeing the emergency and suspecting it of being a hoax. Indeed, any passenger could have called the emergency services on leaving the train, or pulled the emergency stop cord, which would have been embarrassing for the researchers.

A further disadvantage relates to the ethics of the study. The participants were not aware that they were taking part, so had not given their consent. The acting on the part of the victim constitutes deception, and the fact that the passengers could not get off the train during the emergency also means that they could not withdraw from the study.

In addition, since the passengers went on their way on leaving the train, it was not possible to

debrief them after the study, and so they were left believing that the emergency situation was real. They may have felt guilt or worry because of the situation, which raises issues about protecting participants from physical or psychological harm.

There is no doubt, in view of all the guidelines breached, that the study was unethical, but there is debate as to when unethical research can be justified. Some psychologists argue that if the knowledge gained from research outweighs the ethical implications, then it can be justified, but who is to decide which research is important and which is not? If the study was proposed today it would probably not be permitted.

One final criticism of the study is the uneven number of trials carried out in each condition. There were more cane trials than drunk trials, and they were distributed unevenly across black and white victims.

The reason given for this was that Teams 1 and 2 (both white victims) started the first day in the cane condition. Teams 3 (black victim) and 4 (white victim) began in the drunk condition. Teams were told to alternate the conditions across days, but on the fourth day, Team 2 violated the instruction and ran cane trials when they should have run drunk trials, because the victim did not like playing the drunk. Then there was a Columbia student strike, the teams disbanded, and the study was over. This anomaly in the number of trials carried out makes the results in each condition less comparable.

How representative was the sample of participants?

The sample consisted of the 4450 passengers using that particular train, 45 per cent of whom were black and 55 per cent white. This sample is likely to be fairly representative of the American public, however it is restricted to the people who were using that train at that time and since it was during office hours the sample may have been biased towards people not in work or school.

What type of data was collected in this study?

The data gathered were both quantitative and qualitative. The quantitative data included the number and type of passengers who helped as well as the time taken to offer assistance. The qualitative data came from the spontaneous comments made by the passengers.

Both types of data are valuable in building up a full picture of what happened. The quantitative data allowed for comparisons and statistical analysis and the qualitative data provided some of the thoughts and feelings of those involved, perhaps providing explanations for why they did or did not help.

How useful was this research?

We see examples every day of heroes who risk their lives to save other people, but we also see extreme examples of selfish behaviour such as adults trampling over children to escape emergency situations. The question of why this happens is one which is worth investigating as this study attempts to do.

Piliavin, Rodin and Piliavin suggest a way of predicting how people will behave in emergency situations by proposing their Arousal Cost-Reward Model, which seems a useful tool in planning for emergencies.

However, some psychologists would argue that this model paints a very deterministic view of humanity: is behaviour so predictable? Are humans so selfish?

If Piliavin, Rodin and Piliavin's views are accepted then we are forced to view humans in this way. An alternative view is that people make active choices that are less predetermined, or perhaps the role of personality or disposition plays a greater part in how individuals behave.

With regard to the existence of altruism, the model in this study would suggest that our behaviour is calculated more in terms of personal gain than any act of selflessness, again rather a pessimistic view of the human race.

Check your understanding

What were the dependent and independent variables in this study?

In what ways was the procedure for the emergency standardised?

What explanations are there for the lack of diffusion of responsibility found in this study?

What are the problems of conducting field studies?

Exam Café

Make sure you are able to explain the aim and the method of this study. It was a field experiment and the strengths and weaknesses of this research method need to be clearly understood.

Observation was used to record data and again there are limitations to the type of data recorded.

The ethical implications of deceiving members of the public should also be addressed.

You should be aware of the sample used in this study and the extent to which the results can be generalised to a wider population.

You should also be able to describe the conclusions that can be drawn from this study.

Exam Café

Relax, refresh, result!

Relax and prepare

What I wish I'd known at the start of the year...

Maya

Use some index cards to make very brief revision notes on each study. You could write about a study on the front of each card and evaluation issues on the back.

Use colour as well – a different colour for each approach, or a different colour for each point, e.g. sample always in red, method always in blue.

Refresh your memory

A common question in the examination asks you to consider possible changes to the core study and the effects that these changes might have. To help you think about this, copy and complete the table below: for each of the three studies, think about how changes would affect the results.

Study	Alternative sample	Different method	Different ways of measuring	More ethical	Improvements
Milgram	Females		Alternative to shock generator		
Reicher and Haslam					
Piliavin, Rodin and Piliavin		Lab study		See student answer	

Exam-style question

We are going to look at a student response written under exam conditions to the following question:

Choose a study and suggest two ethical improvements to it. Outline any methodological implications that this alternative may have. (8 marks)

Student answer

One ethical improvement that could be made to the study by Piliavin, Rodin and Piliavin would be to get general consent from the participants before the experiment; this would make the study more ethical in that the participants would know that they were taking part in a study. However a negative effect of this would be that the participants may not behave naturally as they would know that they were being observed and this may change their behaviour, specifically they may want to look like 'good' people and help more than they would have done normally. This is called the 'social desirability effect'.

A second ethical improvement would be to debrief the participants after the study has taken place. In the study participants were not told that they had taken part in a study and were left to get off the train with any distress or concern they may have experienced for the victim. By debriefing the participants they would be less likely to experience any after-effects of witnessing the victim collapse such as guilt or worry and this would protect them from any harm caused by the experiment.

Examiner says:

A very clear answer. The core study by Piliavin, Rodin and Piliavin raises lots of ethical issues and this student has selected two important ones. In this answer the student has given the first ethical improvement followed by its effect and then has done the same with the second improvement. It would also be fine to write about both ethical improvements in the first paragraph and discuss their effects in the second paragraph.

How can this question be related to the other two studies in this approach?

Milgram

The problem with choosing Milgram for this question would be knowing when to stop writing.

There are several serious ethical issues that could be discussed here and you should consider carefully how this study could be made more ethical. If you gave participants fully informed consent they would know that the study was a 'set-up' and this would inevitably make their behaviour very different.

One way that psychologists sometimes deal with this kind of problem is to ask informed participants to role-play the part of naïve participants. Do you think that this would work in this study?

Reicher and Haslam

There are several ethical improvements that could be made to the Reicher and Haslam study, for example the study was done on volunteers rather than real prisoners and guards, and the situation affected some of them in a negative way.

What would be the effect of using real prisoners and guards? You could explore the strengths and weaknesses of this.

Further areas to focus on could be gaining fully informed consent and avoiding the use of deception, but again you would need to discuss the implications of these changes.

Individual differences

Why 'individual psychology'?

Although most of us are aware that we are unique individuals, it is important at times for psychologists to disregard this and to consider the 'average person'. This may make some sense if we consider, for example, a psychologist working within a school to develop a new way of teaching geography. It would be unwise to try this on one student, as the findings would only relate to them, so a group of students needs to be selected. Before the new teaching programme begins, the psychologist could measure academic achievement or student engagement for a group of students. This group could now be split into two, with one group being taught in the new way and the other the same way as before. After a period of time the measurements could be taken again and the results for both groups compared.

Most psychologists would regard the use of statistical analysis as the only appropriate and valid way to compare these two groups, and to do this large data sets are required. The head teacher is unlikely to start a new scheme that has only been trialled on only one student. Consequently the psychologist and the headteacher will only be concerned with the average results of the whole group. If the new teaching method is seen to improve achievement and engagement, then it is likely that all teachers will adopt it.

What is of interest here to the individual psychologist is that we are not all average and there will be many students who may have performed better or worse than before. These are the people that the individual psychologist is interested in, as we can learn a lot about human behaviour by considering all behaviours, not just the average ones. Psychologists have the dilemma of trying to investigate the features that we all share, while at the same time acknowledging that differences between individuals exist.

Rosenhan (1973)

This study certainly challenges the normal/abnormal debate, as Rosenhan and colleagues highlight how difficult it is for the medical profession to accurately distinguish between the sane and the insane. Here sane people are admitted to a mental hospital as schizophrenic, despite not showing the correct symptoms, and once admitted find it difficult to be discharged despite their 'normal' behaviour.

Thigpen and Cleckley (1954)

This is a case study of an extremely rare condition known as multiple personality disorder. This is clearly an example of human behaviour that is beyond the experience of most people, and Thigpen and Cleckley suggest that the case study can provide more valuable information on this condition. There is still some debate as to whether the findings are reliable, as they refer to only one patient and two therapists. What it does provide is a fascinating insight and also information for suitable treatment. Interestingly, Thigpen and Cleckley are not entirely sure of the correct treatment and consider the ethical issue of 'killing off' one of the personalities.

Griffiths (1994)

Griffiths provides a detailed insight into the thought processes of gamblers addicted to playing fruit machines and suggests that the addictive behaviours they display are similar in origin to those with alcohol or drug addictions. The regular gamblers were shown to have a particularly irrational set of beliefs about their own ability and understanding of how they played the fruit machine. What Griffiths went on to show was that if gamblers could hear their own 'thought processes', this could be used therapeutically to help them change their gambling behaviour.

Rosenhan (1973)

Pause for thought

◆ Increasingly large numbers of people are being diagnosed with mental illnesses. Why do you think this may be?

◆ What mental illnesses have you heard of? Do you know what the symptoms of these conditions are?

What is this study about?

Rosenhan's investigation is centred on the diversity of human behaviour. It provides an important focus as to how psychologists both study and consider individual differences. Central to this is the idea that some differences are so distinct that we can regard them as abnormal.

What Rosenhan set out to do was to question whether abnormal behaviour was a feature of an individual or due instead to how others perceive this behaviour. This is a difficult task, as we all have views on the 'rightness' of human behaviour and these have been framed by our particular social, cultural and even historical backgrounds.

How do we identify 'abnormal' behaviour?

One of the wonderful things about the human condition is how we are all different and can all have a positive impact on those around us. But from early times some differences were considered to be too great to have a positive effect on society and became regarded as a mental illness. Hippocrates, who lived in the fourth century BC, identified abnormalities such as manias, paranoia and even epilepsy.

The difficulty about mental illness is to be able to identify what behaviour is acceptable or unacceptable. For example, the shaman of the past who heard voices and communicated with spirits was regarded as an important person, whereas today they might be sectioned under a Mental Health Act.

This issue is fundamental to Rosenhan as he considers that the different contexts in which we see a behaviour have an impact on how we value them. Our outlandish behaviour at a party would have us removed from a classroom and equally if we transferred our 'classroom behaviour' to the party we would no doubt be ostracised. Therefore it is of paramount importance that a mental illness can be clearly identified and hopefully treated.

Try this ...

Watch an 'old' film like *Brief Encounter*.

Try to identify behaviours that would seem strange if you saw them now.

Or try to look at it the other way round and transform one of the characters into the modern day. How do you think the rest of the characters would react?

It does often seem that our behaviour only makes sense in the right context.

Watch some scenes from the film *One Flew over the Cuckoo's Nest.*

The two main characters are Randle McMurphy, who is only pretending to be insane, and Nurse Ratched, who likes to control her patients.

How easy is it to distinguish between the sane and the insane?

Categorising and treating mental illness

An individual can be considered as having a mental illness if their behaviour is sufficiently abnormal compared with the rest of the population and may cause harm to the individual or others.

Since the early 1900s such an illness has been regarded in the same way as any other physical illness, and one of the effects of this is that mental illness is subject to the principles of the 'medical model'.

The medical model assumes that it is possible to identify characteristics of illnesses and to group them into categories. Once an illness has been identified it can be studied; hopefully the cause can be discovered and a treatment can be developed.

The advantage of classifying illnesses into identifiable groups is that doctors can communicate with each other and be confident that they are talking about the same illness.

The problem with a mental disorder is that the symptoms are not quite as clear as the symptoms of a physical illness. We know when we have a cold because the symptoms are readily identifiable (we cough, make too much mucus and sneeze a lot), but the symptoms of mental illness are based on our behaviour and how we think.

The symptoms of a mental illness are more subjective and less objective than those of a physical illness, which increases the possibility of

an inaccurate diagnosis. The most widely used system for classifying mental health problems is the *Diagnostic and Statistical Manual of Mental Disorders* (now in its fourth edition, the *DSM-IV*). Despite its widespread use, the third edition only provided a 70% agreement on diagnosis among those clinicians who used it (Kirk and Kutchins, 1992).

This background provides the rationale for Rosenhan's impressive investigation.

◆ Can we distinguish the sane from the insane?

◆ Is diagnosis dependent on the features presented by an individual or is it influenced by the context and environment?

Links to other studies

The study by Reicher and Haslam (see pages 104–111) also discusses how context can influence behaviour.

Weblink

The information page for MIND (National Association for Mental Health) contains much accessible and useful information, including information on schizophrenia (see 'Websites' on page ii).

David Rosenhan

Figure 5.1 David Rosenhan

David Rosenhan is Emeritus Professor of Law and Psychology at Stanford University. He has pioneered the application of psychology to the process of law including jury selection and consultation. He recently appeared in a BBC documentary, *The Trap*, which discussed human freedom.

Rosenhan, D. L. (1973)

On being sane in insane places. *Science* 179, 250–258.

What was the aim of the study?

This study aimed to test the hypothesis that the classification system (DSM) used by psychiatrists to diagnose whether someone was sane or insane was not reliable. If psychiatrists could not reliably diagnose conditions such as schizophrenia the DSM would not be valid.

Rosenhan was not seeking to disprove the existence of abnormal behaviours that can cause mental illness. The issue was about how useful such a diagnosis could be if, as he suspected, such decisions were heavily influenced by the context in which they were made. The experiment was in fact comparing the influence of disposition (individual's character) and situation (psychiatric hospitals).

Study 1

What was the methodology?

Aim:

To see if sane individuals can be diagnosed as insane and admitted to a psychiatric hospital.

Procedure:

The sane individuals were 'pseudopatients', or false patients. These were people who had no history of mental illness but for this experiment they were going to fake abnormal behaviour.

Eight such pseudopatients were used: 5 males and 3 females of various ages and occupations; one of the males was Rosenhan himself. In order to obtain a sample that generalisations could be made from, the psychiatric hospitals used were selected from different locations across America and represented different types of hospital. Twelve in total were used, including modern, old, well staffed and poorly staffed institutions.

Each pseudopatient contacted a hospital for an appointment and on arrival they reported that they were hearing voices and although these were unclear, words like 'empty', 'hollow' and 'thud' could be recalled (this is the independent variable). The words were carefully chosen as they were considered to represent an existential crisis concerned about the meaningfulness of one's life and as yet had not been reported in academic literature.

The pseudopatients provided accurate details of their lives, apart from changing their names and also their occupation if this was related to psychology. If they were diagnosed as insane and admitted (the dependent variable) to a ward, they were to behave normally and report that they were no longer hearing voices. Each pseudopatient would remain in hospital until they were discharged.

What were the findings?

All of the pseudopatients were admitted. Eleven were diagnosed with schizophrenia and one with manic depression (now called bi-polar disorder). The pseudopatients spent between 7 and 52 days in hospital before they were discharged. When they were discharged they were diagnosed as being 'in remission' and therefore still insane although not presenting the characteristics of their illness.

Rosenhan interpreted this inability to detect the pseudopatients as a feature of the diagnosis procedure. The doctors were more likely to diagnose a sane person as being insane, as it is 'safer' to misdiagnose an illness. The consequences of not admitting an insane person are potentially more serious than admitting a sane person incorrectly. Making a false positive choice (misdiagnosing a sane person) is known as a *type 2 error*. To make a false negative choice (not admit an insane person) is known as a *type 1 error*.

The failure to detect the insane is not thought to be due to the settings, as the hospitals were all different and yet they all admitted the pseudopatients. It is also worth noting that many of the real patients seemed to be aware that the pseudopatients were not insane and made comments such as 'You're not crazy. You're checking on the hospital.'

What was the methodology?

Aim:

To see if the insane can be diagnosed as sane.

Procedure:

Rosenhan sited the next study in a psychiatric teaching and research hospital that was aware of the findings from study 1. The staff in this hospital doubted that such an error could occur in their hospital. They were informed that over the next 3 months one or more pseudopatients would try to get admitted to their hospital. Each member of staff was asked to rate the likelihood that the patients who sought to be admitted were pseudopatients.

In reality no pseudopatients would attempt to be admitted.

What were the findings?

During the 3-month period 193 patients were admitted.

19 were thought by a psychiatrist and one other member of staff to be pseudopatients.

23 were thought by at least one psychiatrist to be pseudopatients.

41 were thought by at least two members of staff to be pseudopatients.

It now appears that more insane people are being diagnosed as sane. This is a false negative, a *type 1 error*, and suggests that the staff are now trying to avoid the *type 2 error* highlighted in study 1. For Rosenhan this indicates that the process of diagnosis is open to many errors.

Other findings

There are qualitative findings to this study that resulted from the pseudopatients being participant observers and making written notes of their experiences.

The 'stickiness' of psychodiagnostic labels

Rosenhan highlights how once a patient is diagnosed, in this case as schizophrenic, this label 'sticks' and profoundly influences how others perceive them. The label acts like a powerful personality trait that even influences how normal behaviour is viewed.

Examples are given of a pseudopatient who recounts a fairly typical family life and yet this is written up in a report that aligns his experience to what would be expected for a schizophrenic – the writer of the report is swayed by his psychodiagnostic label and perceives that it must have happened. Queuing for lunch is interpreted as an oral-acquisitive pathological behaviour. Even when the pseudopatients were observed writing notes, nurses recorded this as pathological 'writing behaviour'.

The effect of the psychodiagnostic label is to suggest that an insane person is always insane, or indeed that a sane person is always sane. This clearly is not the case, as once the pseudopatients were admitted they behaved normally. Rosenhan regards it as much more useful to focus on behaviours and what stimulus may be causing this.

The experience of psychiatric hospitalisation

Diagnosing mental illness and offering humane treatment would appear to be better than dismissing people as being crazy or even witches. Yet the experience recorded by the pseudopatients does not seem to be a particularly caring one. The effect of labelling has already been discussed and study 1 also indicates that even within the medical community, individuals are always seen as being insane, since they are discharged not as being better, but in remission.

For almost 90% of the time in the ward the patients were left alone as the staff spent most of their time in glassed offices that separated them from the ward. Rarely were psychiatrists recorded entering the ward!

In four of the hospitals the pseudopatients approached members of staff to ask an appropriate question such as, 'Pardon me, Mr/Dr/Mrs X, could you tell me when I will be presented at a staff meeting'. This approach was made when the member of staff was not busy. The reply was normally brief with little or no eye contact, and only 4% of psychiatrists stopped to talk. When a similar question was asked on a non-medical campus 100% of those approached stopped and talked, no matter how busy (see Table 5.1.

Powerlessness and depersonalisation

The pseudopatients noted that little respect was shown towards the patients. We can see from the above that there were very few social interactions; there were also examples of punishment.

A lack of personal space in toilets and bathrooms only served to highlight the lack of attention given towards personal choice.

Crucially, Rosenhan questions the effect of seemingly poor diagnosis procedures along with uncaring and depersonalising psychiatric hospital wards and asks how many people have been needlessly stripped of their privileges of citizenship. And of course how many patients would be regarded as sane outside of the hospital environment?

Interestingly, Rosenhan did not criticise the staff. He regarded them as caring and intelligent and any failures on their part were in fact due to the attributes of the environment they were working in, particularly one that relies heavily on diagnosis.

What did Rosenhan conclude?

It is not possible to distinguish the sane from the insane in psychiatric hospitals. The hospital and the labels provided influence perceptions of behaviour, which is more likely to be interpreted as insane. Individuals with mental-health problems may be better served by:

◆ community programmes, intervention centres and the use of behaviour therapies

◆ more sensitive mental-health workers

◆ a focus on behaviours, not 'global' diagnoses.

Summary of the main points

1 The diagnosis of mental illness is influenced by the context in which the behaviours are observed and the expectation of others.

2 Once a patient has been labelled with a mental illness it is hard to remove the label.

3 Type 2 errors appear to be common in medical diagnosis.

4 It is more useful to focus on individual behaviours than overarching diagnosis.

5 Patients may benefit more from community health care than from being institutionalised.

Interaction	Response rates
Responses to requests made to psychiatrist	13 responses to a total of 185 requests = 7%
Responses to requests made to nurses and attendants	47 responses to a total of 1283 requests = 3.6%
Amount of time spent with psychologists, psychiatrists etc.	Average = less than 7 minutes per day

Table 5.1 Interactions between medical staff and pseudopatients

Evaluating the study by Rosenhan

What are the strengths of the methods used in this study?

A great strength of the study is the creative experimental design and how Rosenhan used this to test the reliability of identifying both sane and insane people. Study 1 and the carefully selected symptoms are clever, but the deception in study 2 is a stroke of genius.

By using pseudopatients as participant observers, Rosenhan is able to gain an insight into the experience of being in a psychiatric hospital. It could be argued that as the pseudopatients are not really insane, their experiences do not reflect those of regular patients. But the process of being admitted as insane and not being discharged until diagnosed as sane, which for some lasted 52 days, in this context is arguably as close to an ecologically valid study as is possible.

What are the weaknesses of the methods used in this study?

There was much backlash after this study was published and it is easy to imagine how the psychiatric community felt defensive about the findings. Particular emphasis has been placed on the use of pseudopatients and the effect of their pretending to be insane.

Pretending to be unwell is not difficult. We should expect the pseudopatients to be admitted as they are effective in their deception, but we should also remind ourselves that the symptoms were not part of any previous diagnosis system, and this is a methodological strength.

Spritzer (1976) argued that the psychiatrists' diagnoses were perfectly correct when the pseudopatients were admitted and also when discharged.

We can question the admission diagnosis, as the symptoms presented were not part of those normally used to identify schizophrenia, in other

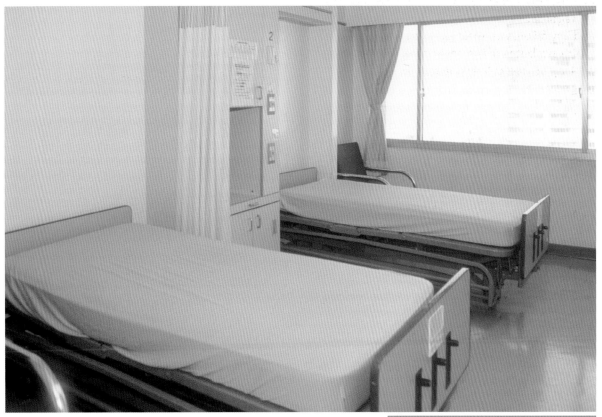

Figure 5.2 Inside a psychiatric hospital

words the psychiatrist got this wrong. But the discharge diagnosis of schizophrenia in remission is more plausible, as schizophrenia is usually a long-term illness.

Therefore to be discharged with schizophrenia 'in remission' is extremely rare, but in this study it could be regarded as accurate since the symptoms were not apparent after admission and typical experience of the illness would suggest that the symptoms could return.

How representative was the sample of participants?

There were two samples in this study: the pseudopatients and the hospitals. The selection of hospitals provides an opportunity to generalise the findings, as a wide variety of hospitals were used from the east and west coasts of the United States.

It is worth questioning whether the process of diagnosing and treating the mentally ill in US hospitals is applicable to other countries, as not all countries use the same diagnostic characteristics to identify mental illness.

Only 8 pseudopatients were used; at least 6 of these had psychological backgrounds and we only know that the other two were a painter and a housewife. The sample therefore appears to be small and biased towards those who have an understanding of psychological issues. Although this bias could be usefully employed in making insightful notes within the hospitals, it may also have had an impact on their own behaviour within the wards.

What type of data was collected in this study?

This study provides both qualitative and quantitative data. The quantitative data include the numbers admitted and discharged in study 1 as well as the social interaction data from study 2. These data are useful as they provide 'harder' evidence for the qualitative findings related to the experience of being in hospital; the stickiness of psychodiagnosis and the feelings of powerlessness and depersonalisation.

It could be argued that the descriptions selected by Rosenhan from the 8 pseudopatients in 12 hospitals are only those that support his hypothesis, or indeed that he only used qualitative data that supported the numerical findings. What is useful is that he uses both types.

How useful was this research?

Rosenhan's study highlighted the difficulty of applying a medical model of diagnosis to mental health and has been the focus of much debate about what can be regarded as normal or abnormal behaviour. The most direct applications are related to highlighting an awareness of the long-term impact of psychodiagnostic labels and how to improve practice in mental-health institutions.

Try this ...

Ask your teacher to record a sports programme like 'Match of the Day'. Observe how the players and the fans behave. Can you identify different explanations for the behaviour you record? Do the home and away players or fans provide different explanations?

(Hint: Think about the dispositions of the individuals and the situation they are in. How do home fans and away fans respond to a foul?)

This is the time to 'come clean'. Have you ever convinced someone that you are ill, in order to avoid a task?

What did you do and why was it successful? Is it easy to convince others that we are not well?

How easy do you think it would be to convince others of a mental illness? Refer back to *One Flew Over the Cuckoo's Nest* if that helps.

Check your understanding

What was the overall aim for this investigation?

Why was it necessary to have two studies?

What did the pseudopatients have to do in order to be admitted and then later discharged?

Explain the type 1 and type 2 errors.

How was this study useful for the psychiatric community?

Exam Café

The 'stickiness' of labels is a common focus for an exam question. Make sure that you can explain this 'stickiness' in terms of people's expectations.

Also be clear that this refers particularly to psychodiagnostic labels, as these seem to be attached to individuals for long periods of time.

This is set in a clinical setting, so suggesting that other labels will be equally sticky may not be appropriate – a label acquired in a PE lesson won't necessarily stick or affect a person's academic achievement.

U1

5

Rosenhan (1973)

Thigpen and Cleckley (1954)

What is this study about?

Some things are so rare or unusual that they are almost unbelievable. When drawings of a duck-billed platypus first came back from Australia, many people thought it was a hoax, as it was beyond the experience of most Europeans. All around the globe there are stories of unlikely beasts: Yetis, giant snakes and the Loch Ness monster. Thigpen and Cleckley provided a case study about a barely believable psychological condition known as multiple personality disorder (MPD). This condition had been talked and written about for many years, yet it was so rare that few clinicians had experience of it and many were beginning to doubt its existence. Then Thigpen and Cleckley, who were practising psychiatrists, came across an individual who they considered to show the symptoms of MPD. Their case study is one of the few documented studies of this condition and provides an opportunity to decide whether it is myth or reality.

Try this ...

What is the most unlikely thing that you have seen? Embellish the story a bit and tell it to a friend who is not studying psychology. Do they believe you? If not, ask them why not.

Does this give you any insight into why MPD was regarded by many as not existing?

What is MPD?

It is first worth considering what MPD is not. The study by Rosenhan (pages 124–131) highlights the problems of reliable diagnosis and in particular the impact of labelling someone with schizophrenia. Schizophrenia is comparatively common and often has an impact on how we perceive all mental illnesses, as it is one that we know much about. In the Rosenhan study, despite not showing the correct symptoms, the pseudopatients were admitted to hospital. There is a common misconception that schizophrenia means having a 'split personality'. But a person diagnosed with schizophrenia is considered by the medical profession to be having problems relating to reality, which is a psychosis. They may have delusional thoughts, hallucinations or disorganised speech, or lack emotions.

MPD is difficult to diagnose, due to its rarity, and is distinguished from schizophrenia as it is regarded as a neurosis. This is because the individual is still in touch with reality, even though they suffer from psychological problems related to anxiety.

Key terms

neurosis a mental illness in which the individual remains in touch with reality but suffers psychological problems related to anxiety

psychosis a mental illness in which the individual has difficulty relating to reality, and their intellect and emotions are often divorced

As the name suggests, one of the diagnostic features for MPD is the existence of more than one personality in one individual. The US-based publication *Diagnostic and Statistical Manual of Mental Disorders*, 4th edition (DSM-IV) calls MPD dissociative identity disorder (DID), which provides clues for another diagnostic feature. Not only is there more than one personality, but these personalities can appear totally separate from, and may be unaware of, one another. The disturbance in personality is complete, unlike schizophrenia. Each personality will have different memories, perceptions and intellectual abilities, and may even use spectacles of different strengths. When one of the personalities is 'in control' all of their characteristics are engaged and all the other personalities disappear. Although not entirely accurate, one of the most useful ways to think about this is to remind yourself of the story 'Dr Jekyll and Mr Hyde': the character is only ever Jekyll or Hyde, never a bit of both.

Another strange feature of MPD is a kind of amnesia known as a fugue. This is when significant information can be forgotten, such as leaving home and not remembering why. The individual may not feel confused or disorientated as the 'other' personality is completely in control.

Key term

fugue a state of mind in which an individual forgets who they are, characterised by loss of their memory and personality

Links to other studies

Freud (pages 56–62) provides an interesting link as his study of Little Hans also tries to understand unusual behaviour using hypnosis and past memories. The study by Loftus and Palmer (pages 12–19) could provide some insight into the impact of leading questions on the patient's responses.

Corbett Thigpen

Corbett Thigpen was a clinical professor of psychiatry at the Medical College of Georgia until he retired in 1987.

Figure 5.3 Corbett Thigpen

Try this …

MPD is a serious and rare psychiatric condition and we should not make light of it. However, there are times when we all feel as though we are many different people. Discuss with a small group how you behave: at school with different teachers; at a party; at your grandparents' home; or alone with your best friend. Is there only one you?

Weblinks

You may find the *Psychology Today* website useful to find out more about MPD/DID and you can read the full story of the 'piano man' in a news article (see 'Websites' on page ii).

Try this …

The 'piano man' was found on the Isle of Sheppey, off the northern coast of Kent. He was wet and confused and was taken to a hospital but could provide no idea of his identity. He drew a piano and played the one in the hospital chapel well. Even after a couple of weeks at the hospital he had not said a word, but loved to play the piano.

What insight does this give into fugue states? How do you think this man should be cared for?

Figure 5.4 The type of piano drawn by the 'piano man'

U1

5

Thigpen and Cleckley (1954)

Thigpen, H. C. and Cleckley, H. (1954)

'A case of multiple personality',
Journal of Abnormal and Social Psychology, 49, 135–51.

What was the aim of the study?

The aim of this study was to provide an account of the case of an individual considered to have MPD. This was seen as significant as, despite the condition being well known, little had been written about it for many years and MPD was being either forgotten or rejected by the psychological community. This account is based on the psychotherapeutic treatment of a 25-year-old patient known as Eve White, who had been referred to Thigpen because she was experiencing severe blinding headaches.

What was the methodology?

The treatment of 'Eve' involved psychotherapeutic interviews and occasional hypnosis with Thigpen and Cleckely. Family members were interviewed to obtain background information and to corroborate some of 'Eve's' stories.

'Eve' also undertook a number of psychological tests including psychometric tests to measure IQ and memory ability. Two projective tests were carried out, supposedly to gain some insight into unconscious feelings and wishes: the tests were drawings of human figures and the Rorschach ink blot test. The therapists would use the emphasis placed in the drawings and 'Eve's' interpretation of the ink blots to suggest what unconscious motives might be causing the behaviours they were observing. When a third personality appeared an electroencephalogram (EEG) was used to measure and compare the brain activity of each of the personalities.

What were the findings?

Eve White

Eve White (EW) had been in therapy (with Thigpen) to discuss severe headaches and the blackouts, which did not result in a loss of consciousness, that often followed them.

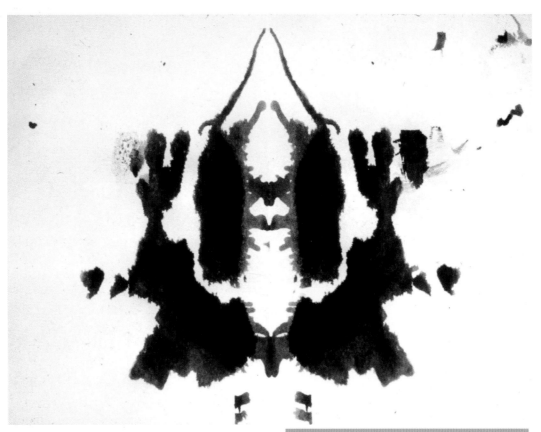

Figure 5.5 An example of a Rorschach ink blot

She talked about marital and relationship difficulties but this did not seen unusual and she herself came across as 'a circumspect, matter of fact person, meticulously truthful and consistently sober and serious about her grave troubles' (Thigpen and Cleckley, 1954, page 137). Thigpen and Cleckley were puzzled by a trip that EW had taken but had no memory of, so – as was normal medical practice – they hypnotised her and the memory loss was recovered. The events that followed suggested something more unusual and initiated the detailed case study.

A few days after the hypnosis, Thigpen and Cleckley received a letter that had all the appearance of being written by EW apart from the final paragraph, which appeared to be the work of a child and not the sober author earlier in the letter. In the next therapy session EW was questioned about the letter. She denied sending it but could remember starting a letter but then having destroyed it. During this discussion the self-controlled EW became agitated and distressed. She eventually questioned whether occasionally hearing imaginary voices indicated that she was insane. The therapists were surprised by this comment as hearing voices would suggest schizophrenia and yet EW was clearly acutely embarrassed by asking this question. If EW was schizophrenic she would not be embarrassed by the question as she would be unable to relate to the reality of the situation she was in and would therefore not be emotionally affected by it. After a few moments EW appeared to be seized by pain, dropped her hands down to her sides and then smiled and in a bright voice said 'Hi there, Doc!' (page 137).

EW had been transformed into a different person. The woman who now sat in front of the therapists was more playful, sexually attractive and free of the signs of distress familiar in EW. She even spoke about EW and her problems, referring to EW as 'her' and 'she' as if she was another person. When she was asked her own name she replied, 'Oh I'm Eve Black' (page 137).

From this time on Thigpen and Cleckley conducted over 100 hours of interviews over a 14-month period to find out more about Eve White and Eve Black (EB).

Eve White/Eve Black

After the initial appearance of EB it was necessary to hypnotise EW in order for EB to 'come out', and as this process continued more regularly it became possible for EB to be 'called out' just by the therapists using her name. This had an impact on EW's life as EB was now finding it easier to 'pop out' more frequently.

Considerable evidence suggested that EB had had an independent life since early childhood, yet it was not until this first appearance of EB during therapy that EW had become aware of her existence. The relationship between the two 'Eves' was not straightforward: they shared the same body, yet were not equally aware of each other. It seems that when EB was 'out', that is, when this personality took over, EW had no awareness of what EB did. Yet when EB was not 'out' she was aware of what EW did but did not share her thoughts and feelings.

It may be easier to understand the relationship between EW and EB by considering EW's family. EW was troubled about her unhappy marriage, but EB thought this level of distress was silly and despised the husband. EW had a loving relationship with her only daughter but EB described this as 'something pretty corny' (page 138). Thigpen and Cleckley described EW as having a 'quiet dignity about personal sorrow' (page 138) and EB as being 'immune to major affective events in human relations' (page 138), but not in a cruel way: she just seemed unable to comprehend such things.

Eve Black: the mischievous years

During the therapy it became clear that EB had enjoyed an independent life since early in EW's life, but EW's parents (and later her husband) were unaware of EB, as she never made herself known to them. When she did 'come out' she could imitate EW and not be recognised. However, as a result of undergoing therapy, when EB first appeared to the therapists they were immediately aware of a different individual, as 'Eve's' voice and body language completely changed since EB did not hide herself from the therapists. Some examples may make this a little clearer.

EB appeared to have a mischievous streak. EW had a childhood memory of being punished for going into a nearby wood despite denying that she had been there. During therapy EB admitted to being in the wood but 'went back inside' in time for EW to receive the punishment. EW's parents confirmed this story and indicated that on many other occasions there had been unaccountable changes in EW's behaviour.

EW was beaten by her husband for going out and spending so much on clothing that the family was plunged into debt. She denied all knowledge of the purchases, even when they were found in her house. EB confirmed that she had indeed bought and hidden the clothes and was unmoved by the impact this had on the relationship between EW and her husband. EB even went out drinking and left EW to suffer the hangover in the morning.

Psychological differences

EW is described as being demure, careful and dignified, often looking sad, being hard working, not spontaneous and dressing simply. Her IQ was 110 and her memory ability was above that of someone with her IQ. The projective tests were interpreted to suggest that she had a repressive personality that resulted from her not being able to cope with the conflicts of being a wife and mother.

In contrast, EB is described as a vain party girl, spontaneous, mischievous, never serious, talking in slang and dressing provocatively. Her IQ was lower than EW's at 104, and she had a memory ability that corresponded to this. (The difference in IQ shows the extent to which they were two different people in the same body.) The projective tests indicated a regressive personality, that is, a wish to return to early life experiences, and interestingly Eve Black was Eve White's maiden name.

Therapy

The goal of the therapy was to enable 'Eve' to have one personality. This process was difficult because EB could not be hypnotised, had no sympathy for EW and did not co-operate with the therapists. EB did admit to causing the headaches and the imaginary voices, as well as having the ability to erase EW's memory.

EW became increasingly aware of EB and was more able to prevent her 'getting out' and

causing trouble. She began to do well at work and also left her husband. The headaches, voices and blackouts disappeared and all seemed to be going well.

Then, after about 8 months, the headaches and blackouts returned, this time for EW *and* EB. During a session of hypnosis 'Eve's' voice and manner changed again and a husky voice asked the therapist, 'Who are you?' As a result of the therapeutic process a new personality had appeared: this was Jane, who was more responsible than EB and more interesting than EW. The therapists hoped that Jane could be 'far more of a woman' (page 145) than either of the 'Eves'. EEGs showed that Jane and EW were similar and both could be distinguished from EB.

Jane

Jane was aware of EW and EB, had some control over EW and had even begun taking over many of EW's tasks. Jane could not displace EB but she could determine when EB was lying. It was anticipated that Jane would be the most likely fully to integrate three personalities and provide an appropriate solution to the therapy.

What did Thigpen and Cleckley conclude?

Thigpen and Cleckley offer no explanation, simply their observations and a request for further research into MPD.

Summary of main points

1 Eve White was a woman who suffered from headaches and blackouts.

2 Eve Black 'emerged' during therapy as a person, in Eve White's body, who looked and behaved differently from Eve White.

3 Eve White did not know about Eve Black until the therapy.

4 Eve Black had known about Eve White since early childhood.

5 A third, more reasonable, person emerged, called Jane, who seemed to offer a solution to therapy.

Evaluating the study by Thigpen and Cleckley

What are the strengths of the method used in this study?

This case study sets out to provide an account of the psychotherapeutic experience of an individual who is thought to have MPD, and one of the evident strengths of the methodology is the detailed information this process provides. The therapists spent over 100 hours with Eve, and supplemented this by interviewing her parents and husband. This enabled them to check the stories that the multiple personalities were presenting during therapy and consider these in the light of Eve's early childhood experience and present home life.

A number of psychological tests were used to obtain more information about the personalities. Apart from the projective tests, the psychometric tests were all quantitative and intended to provide objective numerical data. Independent witnesses either carried out these tests or interpreted the results, as they would be more likely to take an objective stance.

Thigpen and Cleckley were concerned that they were being fooled by a good actress, but they found the evidence from the independent witnesses and the behaviour of EW, EB and Jane to be too consistent for too long to consider this a possibility.

What are the weaknesses of the method used in this study?

This case study only provides evidence from one individual thought to have MPD and two psychotherapists working with her. It is therefore difficult to generalise across the population. This also produces problems with the use of

Figure 5.6 Is Gollum/Sméagol showing features of MPD as he switches between the good Sméagol and the bad Gollum in *The Lord of the Rings*?

psychometric tests, as these are developed for use in normal populations, while this study involved only one individual with an extremely rare psychological condition.

Thigpen and Cleckley's findings could be biased as a result of believing they had come across a case of MPD. They would be more willing to interpret what could be typical behavioural changes for a patient with psychological difficulties as being evidence for a different personality.

It is also possible that the independent witnesses were not as objective as Thigpen and Cleckley originally thought, as normal experience would suggest that different sets of data would come from different people – and MPD is extremely rare. Therefore, there is an existing bias to perceive different data as representing separate individuals and it is unlikely that the witnesses were looking for similarities between EW, EB and Jane.

The case raises interesting ethical problems, due to the existence of more than one personality in one physical body. If there are three personalities, who is giving consent and what right do the therapists have to suggest that Jane is a more suitable personality for the body she has come from? They very 'discovery' of a suspected case of MPD creates problems about regarding 'Eve' as a patient, a subject or perhaps as a means to two young therapists making themselves famous.

How representative was the sample of participants?

As discussed earlier, the sample was not very representative. Due to the extraordinary nature of MPD it could be that no matter how many case studies there are, it may not be possible to describe a typical example. However, it is worth noting that *Diagnostic and Statistical Manual of*

Figure 5.7 The classic *Three Faces of Eve* was based on this case study

Mental Disorders, 3rd edition (DSM-III) includes MPD, suggesting that, in the USA at least, the condition is thought to be possible.

What type of data was collected in this study?

The data were mainly qualitative and were gathered during psychotherapeutic interviews and projective tests. Supporting quantitative data were collected from psychometric tests and EEG recordings.

How useful was this research?

If MPD does exist, it is vital to have accounts such as this so that effective diagnoses can be made and suitable treatment can be developed. It appears that despite the 50 years since the study was published, the debate on MPD still rages and very few cases have been documented outside the USA. This would seem to suggest that even within the psychiatric profession there is still little agreement about this condition. It is, of course, possible that MPD is better known in the USA, due to the publicity created in the 1957 film, *The Three Faces of Eve*, which was based on this case. As a result individuals with psychological problems may know enough to mimic the symptoms, or clinicians may be better informed and so diagnose the condition more frequently.

The story of EW and EB provides some explanation for fugue states. A surprising number of people have such experiences, which may range from forgetting why they are shopping in a different town to going missing for many months.

Check your understanding

Why did Eve White seek psychotherapy?

Describe the qualitative differences between Eve White and Eve Black.

Describe the quantitative differences between Eve White and Eve Black.

Why did the therapists interview Eve White's parents and husband?

Give an example of how Eve Black may have been responsible for Eve White's fugues.

Why was Jane seen as a 'better' character?

Exam Café

What evidence is there to suggest that Eve White had MPD and was not just a good actor?

Much of the evidence will be linked to the psychological tests and to the fact that Thigpen and Cleckley spent so much time with Eve and were persuaded that she suffered from MPD. When you select the data from the psychological tests, make sure you explain why they show a difference in personality between Eve White, Eve Black and Jane. This is central to the study. The best way to do this is to use a wide range of findings and to present a summary of what Eve White and Eve Black were like (note: we are given fewer details about Jane). Just noting a difference in IQ is not overly convincing, but to link IQ to memory and the projective tests to the therapists' descriptions would provide a compelling answer.

Griffiths (1994)

What is this study about?

It could be argued that individuals become 'problem gamblers' due to personality disorders or due to shortcomings related to their educational or social background. This study adds to this debate and builds on previous research (Wagenaar, 1988) that suggests that problem gambling behaviour may be associated with how gamblers process information. In other words, it seeks to investigate the cognitive processes used by gamblers and how these may lead to addictive gambling behaviours.

Why study fruit-machine gambling?

The behaviours related to fruit-machine gambling provide a useful area for psychological research into individual differences. Fruit-machine gamblers may spend many hours inside a dark, noisy building trying to 'hit the jackpot', instead of enjoying natural sunlight and the conversation of real people. This is even more common among adolescents: Griffiths (2002) claims that twice as many young people, compared to adults, have gambling problems with fruit machines. Despite this, it can still be regarded as a hidden addiction and one that is not taken as seriously as drug or alcohol dependency.

Griffiths argues that being addicted to playing fruit machines is an addiction to certain types of behaviours. Playing the machines involves behaviours that produce rewards and if these behaviours and their rewards are denied, withdrawal symptoms are experienced. The personal cost of gambling can be to cause mood swings and affect relationships, and problems at work or school can have a wider impact on society.

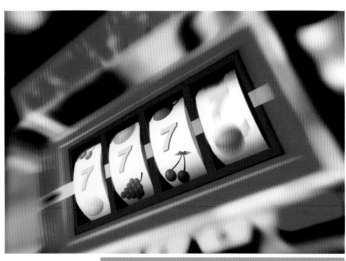

Figure 5.8 A winning line on a fruit machine

Why are psychologists interested in cognitive bias?

To put it simply, if psychologists are to help those addicted to fruit-machine gambling it is essential they know as much as possible about how gamblers think. One view, called normative decision theory, suggests that gamblers make rational and predictable decisions about the choices that face them. This theory is not very useful, as gamblers are essentially irrational. Why otherwise would they even start gambling?

Key terms

heuristics common-sense sets of rules that are used to solve problems

pathological a behaviour that is unusual and interferes with everyday life

Another theory is based on the heuristics and biases used by gamblers. Heuristics are a little like intelligent guesswork that is used to help us to understand a situation. One idea about gambling behaviour is that gamblers may be using the wrong heuristic in a given situation and that the way they are thinking is slightly distorted. Gamblers can be seen to use many heuristics, including:

◆ the *illusion of control*: gamblers think they have a greater chance of winning than probability would suggest, and also that their skill influences their chance of winning

◆ *flexible attributions*: gamblers consider that success is due to their own skill and that failure results from external influences such as a malfunctioning fruit machine.

The link in the gambler's mind between perceived skill and winning is central to this study. Griffiths suggests that pathological gamblers apply the 'illusion of control' heuristic to a greater extent than casual gamblers, and perceive themselves to have sufficient skills to beat the fruit machines. Modern fruit machines have so many buttons and features that allow the gambler to have some input that this inflated view of ability could be entirely expected. Griffiths set out to investigate what heuristics were being used by gamblers as they attempted to win more money or extend the amount of time they spent playing on a machine.

Try this …

Try to explain to someone what decisions you are making when you cycle, skateboard or even walk up the stairs.

If you have just started driving, reflect back on how hard it first seemed to control the clutch or reverse around a corner.

Mark Griffiths

Figure 5.9 Mark Griffiths

Mark Griffiths is Professor of Gambling Studies at Nottingham Trent University. He is internationally renowned for his knowledge on gambling and addictive behaviours. He is one of the most published psychologists of recent years and has received numerous prestigious awards for his work.

Try this …

Number 20 pieces of paper from 1 to 20 and put them in a bag. Pull out five pieces of paper and record their numbers. Repeat this 10 times and keep a tally of the numbers that you pull out. Continue for another 10 goes but this time predict the numbers that will come out. How successful were you? What heuristics did you use? Is there any point in trying to guess what numbers are coming out next?

Figure 5.10 Try to guess the number sequence

U1

5

Griffiths (1994)

Griffiths, M. D. (1994)

'The role of cognitive bias and skill in fruit machine gambling',
British Journal of Psychology, 85, 351–69.

What was the aim of the study?

The aim of this study was to examine the factors and variables relating to cognition and the gambling process. The investigation aimed to examine whether the skills involved in fruit-machine gambling are 'actual' or 'perceived', by comparing the success of regular and non-regular gamblers.

A technique called 'thinking aloud' was used to monitor cognitive activity during gambling. No independent variables were manipulated and the dependent variables were the behaviours and verbalisations of the gamblers.

Four hypotheses were developed:

1 There would be no difference between the skill levels of regular and non-regular fruit machine gamblers.

2 Regular gamblers would produce more irrational verbalisations (those that defy reason) than non-regular gamblers.

3 Regular gamblers would report themselves as being more skills orientated than non-regular gamblers.

4 'Thinking aloud' participants would take longer to complete the task than 'non-thinking aloud' participants.

Figure 5.11 Rational or irrational verbalisation?

What was the methodology?

To enhance the ecological validity, the experiment took place in a real amusement arcade and as no independent variables were manipulated it can be regarded as a quasi-experiment. The participants were recruited from a poster placed in the local university and college (see Table 5.2).

Each participant had to have played on a fruit machine at least once in their lives. Regular players were regarded as those who gambled on fruit machines at least once a week and non-regular players were defined as those who played once a

	Males	Females	'Thinking aloud' participants	'Non-thinking aloud' participants	Total	Mean age
Whole sample	44	16	30	30	60	23 years 4 months
Regular gamblers	29	1	15	15	30	21 years 6 months
Non-regular gamblers	15	15	15	15	30	25 years 3 months

Table 5.2 Number and distribution of participants

month or less. All the participants were randomly divided into two groups: 'thinking aloud' and 'non-thinking aloud'. In the 'thinking aloud' condition the participants were asked to say whatever was going through their mind while they were playing. All verbalisations made by the participants were recorded and transcribed within 24 hours.

Each participant was given £3.00, which was the equivalent of 30 'free gambles', and asked to stay on a machine for 60 gambles. This required them to break even and win back the £3.00. If the participants reached the 60 gambles they had the option of continuing with the gambling or keeping the money. This option was considered exciting enough to motivate the regular fruit-machine gamblers. The gambling behaviours (dependent variables) that were recorded included those shown in Table 5.3.

Total play	total number of plays in a session
Total time	total time in minutes of play during one session
Play rate	total number of plays per minute during one session
End stake	total winnings in number of 10 pence pieces after the playing session
Wins	total number of wins
Win rate (time)	total number of minutes between each win during a playing session
Win rate (plays)	total number of plays between each win during a playing session

Table 5.3 Gambling behaviours recorded

What were the findings?

Analysis of behavioural data

Within the seven possible gambling behaviours only two significant differences were found.

1 Regular gamblers had a higher playing rate of 8 gambles per minute. Non-regular gamblers had a playing rate of 6 gambles per minute.

2 Regular gamblers who thought aloud had a lower win rate (in plays – see Table 5.2) and therefore made fewer gambles between each win than the other groups.

Two interesting but not significant findings were as follows:

1 Regular gamblers were seen to spend more time on the fruit machine by having more gambles using the same initial stake.

2 There were no significant differences in the amount of total winnings between those who thought aloud and those who did not.

As there are only two significant differences out of a possible seven, these findings support the first (null) hypothesis that there would be no difference in the skill levels between regular and non-regular fruit-machine gamblers. Regular gamblers did spend more time on the fruit machines. Even though this is not significant it may suggest that some skill is involved in playing on these machines. Griffiths suggests that regular gamblers know they will lose their money, but by using familiar machines and having some level of skill they are able to maximise the playing time. Playing the machine offers its own rewards and it can be argued that gamblers are playing *with* money and not for it. There is also some support for the hypothesis that thinking aloud causes gamblers to take longer to gamble.

Analysis of the verbalisations

The verbalisations were recorded for 30 gamblers (15 regular and 15 non-regular). Griffiths carried out a content analysis on all the scripts and from these he intuitively identified 30 different categories of utterance. Of these 30, four were regarded as representing irrational cognition and the remainder were considered rational.

Irrational verbalisations included:

◆ personification of the fruit machine – 'The machine likes me'

◆ explaining away losses – 'I lost there because I wasn't concentrating'.

Rational verbalisations included:

◆ general swearing/cursing – 'damn' etc.

◆ reference to winning – 'I won forty pence I think'.

Each utterance was tallied and given a weighting in percentages that reflected the total number of utterances. The categories were then compared between regular and non-regular gamblers. Table 5.4 shows the most frequent utterances for each group.

Non-regular gamblers were also reported to comment on 'their minds going blank' and how 'frustrated' they felt (Griffiths, page 360). Neither of these utterances was recorded for regular gamblers. Regular gamblers also stopped speaking more often.

The number of irrational compared to rational verbalisations differed significantly between the regular and non-regular gamblers, with 14 per cent of the regular gamblers and only 2.5 per cent of the non-regular gamblers using irrational utterances.

Gamblers did use a variety of heuristics but not widely; when they were used they often explained away losses. The 'hindsight bias' was used to predict events after they had happened, for example: 'I had a feeling it wasn't going to pay very much after it had just given me a "feature" [features are 'nudges' and gamble buttons]' (page 360). 'Flexible attributions' were used to blame an external influence, for example: '… two nudges, gotta be … oh … you [the machine] changed them! You snatched the win' (page 360).

These findings support the hypothesis that regular gamblers will produce more irrational verbalisations that may well result from cognitive bias and the use of heuristics. The difference in use of heuristics could be due to intrinsic factors such as mood and extrinsic factors including gambling history. The reported confusion experienced by non-regular gamblers comes as no surprise. Interestingly, regular gamblers were more likely to stop speaking when 'thinking aloud'. Griffiths proposes that this may be due to being so familiar with the game that it is played automatically and that these gamblers are not aware of what they are doing. (Remember how difficult it is to try to explain how to ride a bike or balance on a skateboard – you can do it but cannot explain how.)

Analysis of skill variables

These findings resulted from post-experiment semi-structured interviews. When asked if any skill was involved in playing a fruit machine, most non-regular gamblers considered that

Type of fruit-machine gambler	Most frequent utterances	
	Irrational verbalisations	Rational verbalisations
Regular	Personification of the machine* Explaining away losses+ Swearing at the machine+	Reference to the number system – 'I've got a "2"'* Reference to winning+
Non-regular	Very few recorded	Questions relating to confusion and non-understanding – 'What's going on here?'* Statements related to confusion and non-understanding – 'I don't understand this'* Miscellaneous – 'I think I'll get a bag of chips after playing this'*

Table 5.4 Summary of the verbalisations of the players (All quotations of utterances are taken from Griffiths, 1994, pages 358–9.) Note that only those marked * are significantly different. Utterances marked + are interesting differences but not statistically significant.

performance was mostly due to chance, but the regular gamblers said it was equal chance and skill. In response to questions about their own level of skill in comparison to the average person, regular gamblers perceived themselves to be average or above, whereas non-regular gamblers thought they were average or below.

The participants were asked to identify certain 'skills' used when playing fruit machines. The responses of regular and non-regular gamblers were compared and a number were found to be significantly different. The skills related to knowledge were regarded as more important for regular gamblers; these included knowledge of the gamble button, 'feature skills' and when the machine will pay out. Regular gamblers also regarded not playing when the machine has just paid out as an important skill.

Finally, of the 60 participants, 21 managed to break even and stay on for 60 gambles. The successful 21 participants included 14 regular gamblers and 7 non-regular gamblers. What was particularly significant was that 10 regular gamblers carried on until they had lost everything and only 2 non-regular gamblers continued.

Regular gamblers are clearly more skills orientated than non-regular gamblers and therefore these findings support the hypothesis that regular gamblers would report themselves as being more skills focused. The skills they reported are related to knowledge about the features of a fruit machine, which may be used to turn small wins into bigger wins by using 'nudges' and 'holds'. This enables them to spend longer on a machine by re-investing their winnings as they play. In reality, there is little scope for skill, as the machines are designed to work purely by chance. The perception that skills are important could be due to an 'illusory correlation' heuristic. This is where variables (nudges etc.) seem to have an impact on other variables such as winning or losing, though in reality they do not.

What did Griffiths conclude?

The difference between regular and non-regular gamblers is related to how they deal cognitively with the idea of skill in relation to fruit-machine gambling. Regular gamblers think there is more skill involved than there actually is, as the skills identified seem to have a minor influence on the outcome of fruit-machine gambling. Griffiths considers that the regular gamblers' 'irrational gambling bias' can be modified and indicates some level of success by allowing them to listen to recordings of their verbalisations. Participants were surprised to hear what they said and how they were thinking. Once they are made aware of their irrational thoughts it becomes easier to change them.

Summary of the main points

1   Regular and non-regular fruit-machine gamblers think differently about the role of skill and its effect on gambling success.

2   There may be some skills related to the knowledge of fruit machines that can be used to boost small wins into larger gains.

3   Thinking aloud has the potential to be an effective therapeutic treatment for gamblers who may be addicted to playing fruit machines.

Evaluating the study by Griffiths

What are the strengths of the method used in this study?

The ecological validity of this study is very high. The experiment was conducted in a local amusement arcade on a typical fruit machine that required decisions to be made on how to use various gaming features to win money or extend playing time.

The risk and excitement of playing were maintained by providing participants with enough money for 30 gambles and after this the challenge was to reach 60 gambles.

A variety of techniques were used to attempt to understand the cognitive processes used by gamblers. These included observation of behaviours, recording of verbalisations and semi-structured interviews. This enabled the data-gathering to be enriched and also allowed for triangulation.

Key term

triangulation the use of a variety of methods to study one issue in an attempt to avoid bias and reduce the limitations of using one technique

What are the weaknesses of the method used in this study?

The validity of the 'thinking aloud' technique can be questioned. On a simple level it is a very hard thing to do. Griffiths himself notes that most of the verbalisations are descriptive and this does not explain or give a rationale for gambling behaviour. It is the cause of these descriptions that is of real interest and this requires more research.

The inter-rater reliability was low, which suggests that the descriptions of categories offered by Griffiths are fully understood only by him. Ironically, this can also be viewed as a strength,

Figure 5.12 Amusement arcade

as the context (observing a participant playing a fruit machine) is only understandable within each separate playing session.

The understanding required about how to play fruit machines and the language used by the gamblers is not well known. Griffiths has spent many years studying this behaviour and is respected as an expert in this area, and it could well be that he is one of the few people who would be able to define the categories of the verbalisations made by fruit-machine gamblers. The ethics can also be questioned as Griffiths was standing close to the fruit-machine player, which may have encouraged longer periods of gambling.

How representative was the sample of participants?

As with many studies the participants were recruited after responding to posters placed in a local university and college. It is therefore possible that the group selected did not represent a full section of society.

The regular gambling group suffered from a considerable gender imbalance, consisting of 29 males and 1 female. Although this is not ideal, it does represent the nature of problem fruit-machine gambling, which is that it is dominated by young males.

It would appear that males and females have different roles within amusement arcades, where the males play on machines and females offer social support. Griffiths considers the females to be fulfilling the role of cheerleaders.

What type of data was collected in this study?

This is a data-rich study that has been enhanced by the variety of techniques used. The behavioural data are quantitative and allow comparisons and statistical analysis to be made.

The analysis of the verbalisations is initially qualitative due to the intuitive way in which Griffiths selected the various utterance categories. These categories are then turned into quantitative data by identifying the frequency

of use and ranking these to provide statistical comparisons.

The transcripts are used to provide detailed qualitative data of the 'thinking aloud' process. Finally, the semi-structured interviews provide a detailed qualitative and quantitative insight into the possible heuristics used by the gamblers.

How useful was this research?

An important feature of this research is that it raises the profile of a 'forgotten addiction' among adolescents and one that could lead to further gambling problems in adulthood. This research also suggests that problem fruit-machine gamblers could be treated by allowing them to listen to 'thinking aloud' recordings. It is suggested that the insight gamblers gain into their thoughts could be used as part of a cognitive behaviour-modification programme.

> ### Check your understanding
>
> Why is fruit-machine gambling thought to be a 'hidden' addiction?
>
> Briefly explain the 'thinking aloud' method.
>
> The verbalisation categories had a very low inter-rater reliability. Discuss why this may be a strength.
>
> How might the findings from this study be used to help those with addictive behaviours?

Exam Café

How useful was the 'thinking aloud' method?

Answers to this question need to consider two main areas.

1   Is this actually an easy thing to do? (Have you tried it?)

2   What level of insight do we get into cognitive processes? Are the participants simply describing what they are doing and not actually offering any explanation?

Be prepared to offer your own ideas as to how to carry out an investigation to discover the thought processes of individuals.

Exam Café
Relax, refresh, result!

Relax and prepare

What I wish I'd known at the start of the year...

Mike

Design a poster for each study to show new AS Psychology students why that study is important. The poster doesn't need to concentrate on the methodology but should highlight what it tells us about human behaviour. It's really useful to concentrate on how the study has helped us understand human behaviour – this is what makes Psychology so interesting.

Daphne

Try to draw a 'timeline' for the events during the study. This should show the order in which things happened during the study and help to untangle some of the more difficult experimental designs. My timeline for going to school is:

----↓------------↓------------↓------------↓---------↓

| Stroke the cat | Meet Tracey | Buy crisps | Wait in the bus stop | Skip into class |

Refresh your memory

A simple revision aid is to make a checklist to help you evaluate the methods used in a study. Try copying and completing the example below.

Study	Alternative sample	Different method	Different ways of measuring	More ethical	Improvements
Thigpen and Cleckley	Gathered data from other cases		Observations from other therapists		
Rosenhan		Used questionnaires		Did not deceive the medical professional	
Griffiths					Discussed 'utterances' with other fruit-machine players

Exam-style question

We are going to look at a student response written under exam conditions to the following question:

Outline an alternative method that could have been used to investigate your chosen study. Discuss any methodological implications this may have. (8 marks)

Student answer

Griffiths carried out an investigation into whether the thought processes of regular fruit-machine gamblers were the same as those of non-regular gamblers. He used a technique known as 'thinking aloud' to enable him to hear what the gamblers were thinking during gambling.

Thinking aloud is difficult, as you have to be able to say what is in your mind while you are playing. Another problem was that very few people could interpret the phrases the gamblers used and it seemed that only Griffiths knew exactly what they meant.

An alternative method would be to use a self-report questionnaire to ask the participants about how they were thinking while playing the game.

This would mean that the participants could play the game normally and not be disturbed by thinking aloud.

It would also allow them to explain their thoughts in phrases that non-regular gamblers understood. The questionnaires could also be shown to other people to discuss their meaning. This would increase the inter-rater reliability.

Examiner says:

This is a good start as it lets the examiner know that you understand the investigation.

Examiner says:

This is a reasonable suggestion, I wonder if you could add examples of the sorts of questions you think would be helpful.

Examiner says:

This is helpful as it reminds the reader of one of the fundamental problems with this study.

Examiner says:

It is helpful to identify areas you think could be improved before you suggest changes.

Examiner says:

It would be useful to indicate how thinking aloud had an effect. For example time taken to gamble.

How can this question be related to the other two studies?

You need to be prepared to be able to answer the question about alternative methods for each of the three studies, so it is useful for you to consider what the alternatives may be. For example:

Rosenhan

Carry out a case study on a medical professional to obtain rich data on the experience and process of carrying out diagnostic procedures. This would not involve deception and would remove the possible influence of the participant observers.

Thigpen and Cleckley

This is a case study on one individual. An alternative method could be to allow observers other than the two therapists to see Eve's behaviour. This would allow for greater objectivity in describing Eve's behaviour as Thigpen and Cleckley could be influenced by their belief that Eve had MPD.

Psychological investigations

Hypotheses

The word 'hypothesis' is seldom used in everyday conversation; it is mainly found in scientific texts. Despite this we are all involved in making up hypotheses most of the time, and therefore hypotheses are far more common feature of our lives than you might expect. A hypothesis is simply a statement that can be tested to see if it is true. In other words it is a prediction.

Every day is full of little hypotheses. When the alarm goes off in the morning you may lie in bed and consider whether getting up first or waiting for the morning rush to be over is more likely to give you maximum time in the shower. The only way to find out is to make the decision to either lie there or get up straight away. Psychologists endeavour to understand how and why humans behave as they do, and to do this they devise and test hypotheses. When a hypothesis is developed psychologists need to find a way to test it and see whether it should be accepted or rejected from the evidence obtained from their research. This is not easy and it is important to write hypotheses carefully and clearly, to make sure everyone understands what you are trying to find out. Therefore there are three types of hypothesis:

The *research hypothesis* is rather like the beginning of a debate, as it is a general prediction. An example may be 'Eating oily fish will make children do well at school.' This does not give enough information on which to base an investigation, therefore another type of hypothesis is needed.

The *alternative* (or *experimental*) *hypothesis* is similar to the part of the debate when more information is needed to see if the research hypothesis can be accepted or rejected. How can we find out if eating oily fish makes children do better at school? The alternative hypothesis states how the research hypothesis can be

operationalised, or carried out. For this to happen it must identify what variables are to be measured. For our example this could be '5-year-olds who eat 10 grams of oily fish each day will do better in spelling tests than 5-year-olds who do not eat any oily fish.' This statement is now more precise and indicates what will happen in the investigation. Once the results have been obtained, a statistical test must be carried out to find out if the results are due to chance or if there really is an effect between the variables. (See page 162 for more information on analysing data.)

Statistical analysis will be used to test if the result happened by chance and therefore there needs to be another hypothesis. The *null hypothesis* is a statement of no difference (or correlation) between the variables being measured. So in our example this would be 'There will be no difference in the spelling test scores of 5-year-olds who eat 10 grams of oily fish each day and those who do not eat any oily fish.'

The direction of the hypothesis

The final point to highlight regarding hypotheses is whether they are *directional* or *non-directional*. It is important to know this, as it will have an effect on the statistical analysis.

A directional hypothesis is also known as a *one-tailed hypothesis*. In this case the hypothesis will be predicting the direction the result will go in, such as 'The more time A-level students spend revising the more A grades they will get.' Psychologists tend to choose hypotheses like this if there is already a lot of research that suggests the prediction is going to be correct. If an increase in the independent variable brings about an increase in the dependent variable, this is said to have a positive direction.

It is more common for psychologists to choose a non-directional or *two-tailed hypothesis*, as this suggests that the direction of the results is uncertain, which for most complex human behaviours tends to be the case. This type of hypothesis does not predict any direction in either the difference or correlation between the variables. In our example this would be 'The amount of time A Level students spend revising will have an effect on the number of A grades they get.'

If you look back through the core studies, you will notice that that several studies relate to memory and learning. Think about the following studies for a few minutes and identify the aspect of memory being investigated in each of them:

◆ Loftus and Palmer (pages 12–19)

◆ Freud (pages 56–62)

◆ Dement and Kleitman (pages 76–83)

◆ Maguire et al. (pages 68–75)

◆ Thigpen and Cleckley (pages 132–139)

Can you find links to memory in any of the other core studies?

If you think about the studies listed above it should also be clear that they used a variety of methods to investigate aspects of memory. These include laboratory experiments and self-reports.

In this unit we are going to look at four main research methods used by psychologists. You should be familiar with these methods already, as they were all used in the core studies. As memory is such an important topic in psychology, we are going to look at how each of these methods could be used to investigate an aspect of memory.

Try this ...

Are these hypotheses experimental or null?

◆ Sunlight improves mood.

◆ Eating breakfast will affect scores on a test.

◆ Eating breakfast will have no effect on scores on a test.

◆ There will be no difference between test scores of males and females.

Try this ...

Are these hypotheses one-tailed or two-tailed?

◆ Sunlight improves mood.

◆ Sunlight affects mood.

◆ Room temperature will affect test scores.

◆ People will perform a task faster in a warm room than a cold room.

Psychological investigations

Experiments

Experimental methods involve the manipulation and measurement of variables. In a standard laboratory experiment the researcher manipulates one variable (the independent variable) and measures the effect that this has on another variable (the dependent variable). A good example of a laboratory experiment is the core study by Loftus and Palmer (pages 12–19), where the researchers manipulated the way that a question was asked and measured its effect on the response that the participants gave.

The strengths of laboratory experiments are that cause-and-effect relationships can be established. Laboratory experiments also allow the researchers to control other variables that may have an effect on the results. By bringing participants into controlled environments it is easier to study the effects of single variables. However, laboratory experiments also have their weaknesses. The controlled environments are often unlike real life (referred to as low ecological validity) and it can be difficult to know if this is how people would behave in real-life situations. Participants also know that they are being studied, and this may affect the way they behave.

Sometimes experiments can be conducted in real-life situations. These are referred to as field experiments. An independent variable is still manipulated and a dependent variable is still measured, but not in a controlled laboratory environment. The core study by Piliavin et al. (pages 112–119) is a good example of a field experiment. Field experiments have higher ecological validity and it is generally easier to assume that this is how people would behave in a real situation. This would be particularly true if they were unaware that they were taking part in an experiment, which is the case in Piliavin, Rodin and Piliavin's study. However, such research might raise ethical issues.

Other experiments are conducted with naturally occurring independent variables such as age or sex, which cannot be manipulated experimentally. These are referred to as natural experiments or quasi-experiments. The core study by Baron-Cohen et al. (pages 20–27) uses the naturally occurring variables of autism, Asperger's Syndrome and Tourette's Syndrome. The core study by Samuel and Bryant (pages 40–47) uses the naturally occurring variable of age and the core study by Maguire et al. (pages 68–75) uses the variable of whether or not people are licensed London cab drivers and how long they have been licensed.

This allows researchers to manipulate variables that would otherwise be unavailable to them, but there is less control over other variables and it sometimes harder to draw cause-and-effect conclusions.

To conduct a laboratory experiment into memory, you need to choose a variable to manipulate and you need to decide how you are going to measure memory.

Remember the ethical guidelines – you cannot manipulate variables that might mean that you are causing people distress.

Some examples of research questions might be:

- Does background noise affect our ability to remember?
- Does eating breakfast affect our ability to remember?
- Does chewing gum affect our ability to remember?
- Do we remember better at different times of day?
- Does diet affect our ability to remember?

As these are stated here they are simply research questions. Before we can begin, we need to state them as hypotheses and then operationalise the variables.

1 Manipulating the independent variable

Start with the research question: 'Does eating breakfast affect our ability to remember?'

The independent variable in this question is whether or not the participants have eaten breakfast. We could manipulate this directly by asking participants to arrive at the lab without eating anything and then give breakfast to one group of participants and not to the other group. Does this raise any ethical issues?

Alternatively we could conduct a more natural experiment where we select participants who have or have not eaten breakfast and test them. This might have the advantage that you are not artificially interfering in their normal everyday lives, but conversely you have less control – perhaps people with better memories are more likely to eat breakfast?

Both of the above ideas are using an independent measures design. This means using different participants in each condition of the experiment. It would be possible to conduct a repeated measures design here, using the same people in both conditions. This would involve asking them to eat breakfast on the first morning and testing them, and then not allowing them to eat breakfast on the second morning and testing them again.

What strengths and weaknesses do you think that a repeated measures design would have for this experiment? (You can find suggested answers to this question on page 175.)

Which design do you think would be best to use? There is no right or wrong answer here. Both designs have their strengths and weaknesses.

2 Measuring the dependent variable

We still need to decide how to operationalise 'ability to remember'. There are probably thousands of ways that this variable could be operationalised. Some are listed below:

◆ Give participants a list of words to learn and then recall.

◆ Give participants one minute to look at a tray of objects and then one minute to recall.

◆ Give participants a short passage to read and then question them on it.

◆ Show participants a short film clip and then ask them questions.

If we chose the first example above then our operationalised hypothesis might read as follows:

Participants who have eaten breakfast will remember more words from a list of 20 words than participants who have not eaten breakfast.

Null: There will be no difference between the number of words recalled from a list of 20 words by participants who have eaten breakfast and participants who have not eaten breakfast.

or

Eating breakfast will have no effect on the number of words that can be recalled from a 20-word list.

You should be able to see that we have become much more specific in what we are looking for. You could argue that this is reductionist – we have reduced memory to 'the number of words someone can remember', which is clearly a simplistic view of a complex topic. If you refer to the discussion on reductionism on page 186, you will remember that we have said that the advantage of reductionism is that it allows us to conduct controlled studies and when a large number of studies have been conducted they fit together like the pieces of a jigsaw puzzle.

Now we are ready to start. Let's assume that you are using an independent measures design and your participants are all students.

Write a brief procedure for this study, including any instructions (time limits, etc.) that you would give to the participants.

Once you have conducted your research, you will need to evaluate what you have done. What improvements would you make if you conducted this experiment again?

Observations

Sometimes psychologists simply observe behaviour in real-life situations or in the laboratory without manipulating an independent variable. This can be extremely useful when it is not possible to manipulate variables or simply as a starting point for research. Observations usually involve the categorisation or rating of behaviour in precise ways.

Some studies are entirely observational, but more frequently, researchers use observational techniques as a way of recording behaviour as part of an experiment. The core study by Bandura, Ross and Ross (page 48–55) is an example of this kind of research. The researchers conducted a laboratory experiment but used observational techniques to code the children's behaviour.

The core study by Rosenhan (page 124–131) is another example of observation. In this study Rosenhan conducts a participant observation. This means that he (and some other researchers) went 'undercover', posing as psychiatric patients in order to observe the interactions between hospital staff and patients. Research like this has very high ecological validity as it is conducted in real-life environments and the participants were unaware that they were being observed. However there is a lack of control in such research and serious ethical issues are often encountered.

Observational research is also difficult to replicate. You will never be able to observe the exact same environment in the real world, as you have little control over confounding variables. This is very different from experimental research, where it is possible to reconstruct the exact same environment within a laboratory. It is not always possible to be sure that you are drawing the right conclusions from your observation. Perhaps asking people why they behaved in particular ways would generate different kinds of information.

Observations can also suffer from observer bias. Perhaps the observer is more likely to record things that fit in with the aim of the research, or simply has a bias towards certain kinds of behaviour. Another observer may see very different things. This is why it is important in many observations to develop a coding scheme to record the behaviour. The clearer the coding scheme, the easier it becomes for different observers to use this scheme and be sure that they are using it in the same way.

If you have high levels of agreement between observers this is called inter-rater reliability.

To conduct an observation it is necessary to decide how the data will be recorded. Some observations can be conducted with the researcher simply writing down everything that he or she observes and analysing it later by looking for patterns in the information that has been recorded. This is very useful if you are studying a behaviour for the first time. This type of observation might lead you to generate hypotheses that could be investigated experimentally or suggest more structured observations that could be conducted.

However, as we stated above it is usually easier to construct a coding scheme. For example if you were going to conduct an observation looking at whether girls or boys choose healthier meal options at lunchtime, you would need to decide on your definition of healthy and unhealthy and construct a coding scheme like the one below.

Participant no.	Male / Female	Healthy choice	Unhealthy choice
1			
2			
3			
4			

This is a very simplistic coding scheme. What problems can you imagine encountering if you tried to use it? How might you overcome these problems?

If you were observing the amount of aggression displayed by children in a playground, you might not want to simply record each child once. You might use an event-sampling technique. In this kind of observation you list all the behaviours you might see and tick every time you see them. In this scheme you simply tick every time you see a behaviour on the list, as in the example on the next page. What strengths and weaknesses do you think this type of observation might have?

Behaviour	
Hitting	✓✓✓✓
Kicking	✓✓
Pulling hair	✓✓✓
Aggressive role-play	✓✓✓✓✓✓
Other behaviours	✓✓✓✓✓

Using observation to investigate memory

Initially this appears more difficult. However, it is possible to observe the behaviours that people show when they are trying to remember something. If someone asks you for directions, what do you do? Do you stand absolutely still and explain, or do you use your arms to direct them?

Try this ...

Choose a well-known place relatively close to where you are going to conduct your observation. This could be a particular office in your school or college or a well-known building in your town. Work in pairs and construct a checklist like the one below.

Participant number	Eye movements	Head movements	Hand gestures	Orients whole body	Facial touching	Lip biting	Other
1							
2							
3							
4							
5							
6							
7							

1   Now go and ask people to direct you to your chosen place. One person should ask for directions and the other person should observe them and tick the appropriate box if a person shows that behaviour.

2   Which movements are the most common?

3   What other movements could you have added to your list?

4   How easy was it to do this – did the person observing manage to code all the behaviour or was this too difficult? How could you improve this?

5   Do you think that this study was ethical?

Self-reports

Psychologists carry out research to find out how and why humans behave as they do. Human beings are complex and often irrational, and finding out exactly what their thoughts and feelings are can be difficult. If psychologists design experiments or carry out observations, this usually involves interpreting the behaviour of the participants. And it is this interpretation that may cause the findings to lack validity.

To emphasise this point, consider how you may feel when adults make assumptions about how you feel and what you want to do. For example: it is Sunday afternoon. You have spent the morning doing homework and then had a monster lunch. You settle down to catch up on the week's soaps and start to drift off to sleep, only to be disturbed by an adult who claims 'What you want is a good dose of fresh air and a long walk'. But what you actually want is a quiet afternoon, a bit of a nap and the chance to catch up on the latest soap gossip.

The psychologist carrying out experiments or making observations and the unhelpful adult are both making assumptions or judgements on how other people feel. This judgement is from their perspective and not that of the participant (or the soap viewer!). The irony is that psychologists are trying to find out about the behaviour of individuals, but they do not always ask them. Investigative techniques that focus on the participants' perspective are known as self-report methods and can be regarded as more likely to produce findings that reflect the participants' point of view. The two main types of self-report are questionnaires and surveys and interviews.

Questionnaires and surveys

Questionnaires contain a number of questions that are intended to find out how people think and feel. The questions could be closed and only allow certain responses, or open to allow more detailed replies (see the examples on page 158). A survey usually consists of highly structured questions and has a clear focus.

Interviews

Interviews are really spoken questionnaires, but they also allow the researcher to observe body language and to ask further questions if this is thought to be useful. If the researcher uses a very rigid set of questions the interview is said to be structured. However, interviews that use more open questions and are prepared to respond to participants' replies are said to be semi-structured.

Strengths and weaknesses

Self-report type	Strength	Weakness
Questionnaires and surveys	Record the participant's experiences. Response rate can be high. Can sample a very large target population. Can contain questions on issues that are difficult to talk about.	Often influenced by bias. Difficult to design well. Response rate can be low. The data gathered can be complex and difficult to interpret. Participants may not answer truthfully.
Interviews	Provide large amounts of qualitative data. Enable the researcher to respond to the participant's experiences. More likely to gain insight into the participants world. Can use body language to confirm verbal responses.	Difficult to carry out. May be influenced by experimenter bias. Can be difficult to analyse. Take a long time to carry out. Participants may not answer truthfully.

Using self-report to study memory

In this section we are going to look at the use of different kinds of self-report to investigate memory. Rather than manipulating the factors that might affect memory, we are going to ask people how good their memory is.

Closed questions

These can be analysed quantitatively, for example:

Do you regard yourself as having a good memory? Yes/No

Try this ...

Write some more closed questions asking more specific questions.

Hint: you could ask people about different aspects of memory such as memory for faces, revision, etc.

Likert scale questions

How good a memory do you think you have?

Very poor 1 2 3 4 5 6 7 8 9 10 Excellent

Open questions

These do not give people fixed-choice answers. Respondents can write whatever they want and the researcher will analyse their responses, for example:

Describe how good your memory is.

Try this ...

Write some more open questions. They could ask about the same aspects of memory as the closed questions you wrote for the last task.

Try this ...

1   Put together a short questionnaire on memory. This should include at least one closed question with fixed-choice answers, one with a rating scale and one open question. Ask 10 people to complete your questionnaire.

2   Did any of your questions seem to confuse people? How could you improve them?

3   Do you think that people told the truth? If not, why not?

4   Do you think that this kind of method is the most appropriate for studying memory? If so, why? If not, why not?

Correlation

Strictly speaking, correlation is a technique for data analysis rather than a research method. It is used to establish whether there is a relationship between variables. Correlation involves the measurement of two variables and does not involve any manipulation. It is a useful technique when variables cannot be manipulated for either practical or ethical reasons. Maguire et al. used it to investigate the relationship between the volume of grey matter in the hippocampal region of the brain and the length of time participants had spent as licensed London cab drivers. Although no variables were manipulated in this study, the researchers showed that a clear relationship existed between these two variables.

Correlation only demonstrates the strength of a relationship. It does not allow us to conclude that changes to one variable cause change in another variable. However, correlational relationships may be positive or negative. A positive correlation is a relationship between variables where as one increases so does the other. A negative relationship is where one increases as the other decreases.

Correlational research can be a useful technique in psychological research as there are so many variables that cannot be manipulated. It can also act as a starting point for research. Once relationships have been established, more research can be conducted to investigate them further.

Using correlation to investigate memory

Remember that correlation simply shows you a relationship between two variables. In this example we are going to use the rating scale scores from your self-report activity and correlate them with another measure of memory.

Correlational hypotheses

Correlational hypotheses predict relationships between variables. They are usually worded as follows:

There will be a significant relationship between a person's self-rating of memory ability and their memory score.

You should never write a hypothesis for a correlation that includes the words 'difference' or 'effect'. We are not investigating how these variables affect each other; we are simply investigating the relationship between them.

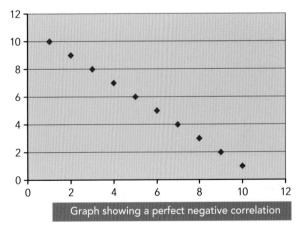

Graph showing a perfect negative correlation

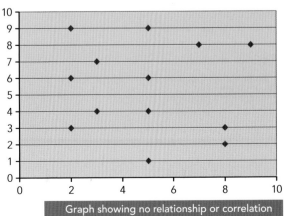

Graph showing no relationship or correlation

Graph showing a perfect positive correlation

Think about the example above. If we find a positive correlation between a person's self-rating of memory ability and their score on a memory test, we do not conclude that the rating caused the score. We are simply concluding that there is or isn't a relationship between them.

For example, you might have asked your participants to answer the question:

How good an eyewitness do you think you are?

Very poor 1 2 3 4 5 6 7 8 9 10 Very good

This is your first variable.

Your second variable needs to be another measure of eyewitness ability. For example you could show people a short film clip and then ask them some questions. The number of questions they get right will be the score on the second variable.

Try this ...

1 Conduct this correlational activity – it needn't be as complex as using a film clip – ask people to rate their memory ability and then give them a simple word-list task, such as the one you might have used for your experiment.

2 When you have collected your data, plot them on a scattergraph (see page 164 for more details on this). What conclusion can you draw from this scattergraph?

3 Were the measures that you used appropriate?

4 Would you change them or improve them if you conducted this investigation again?

5 What other improvements could you suggest?

Sampling

The first step in carrying out a psychological investigation is to develop a suitable hypothesis. The next step is to consider what group of people to test this hypothesis on. If the research hypothesis has been clearly operationalised into an experimental hypothesis, this group may be quite clear. For example, the hypothesis that 'Sleep has an effect on children's ability to memorise numbers' can be operationalised as 'Children aged 5 and 6 will memorise more numbers if they have had 8 hours or more sleep each night'. The group the psychologist needs to find in order to carry out this investigation are children aged 5 and 6.

This group of children is referred to as the target population. A target population includes all the members of the group who are included in the study. In this case the target population would be all children aged 5 and 6. Obviously it is impossible to carry out this investigation on all children of this age and therefore a smaller group or sample of this population is needed. What the researcher will attempt to do is to select a sample that represents the target population. What the researcher must take care not to do is to select a sample that is biased and does not fully represent the original group. The importance of this can be illustrated by the example of a local council that decided to find out what changes people wanted in the local park. The target population included everyone who lived in the town, but the council only sampled the people who were in the park during the day, on weekdays. Thus the sample was biased towards pensioners and mothers with young children. As a result the park has lots of seats and a fenced-off set of swings, but no space for ball games or skateboards. Remember: choosing a representative sample is very important.

How to select a sample

Random sampling

Random sampling should produce an unbiased sample. This would involve including everyone in the target population and then selecting a number of these to make up the final sample. A common way to do this would be to give each person a number and to select a sample by using a random number generator or even pulling them from a hat.

Opportunity sampling

This method is probably the most widely used as it is convenient. An opportunity sample will include individuals from the group the research is focused on, but those selected are the ones the researcher is most likely to come into contact with. They may be friends, work colleagues or people who live nearby.

Self-selected sampling

This type of sample is often called a volunteer sample. They are usually chosen by responding to adverts or simply being in the right place at the right time.

Strengths and weaknesses

Sample type	Strength	Weakness
Random	The group will be unbiased	Often difficult to carry out and not all people selected are willing to take part
Opportunity	Provides easy access to participants	Sample can be biased due to social and cultural groups. May only contain individuals from your friendship group
Self-selected	Fairly easy to administer	May be biased towards the sort of people who reply to adverts and therefore keen to impress the researcher. The researcher has to rely on who ever happens to be around

Psychological investigations

Analysing your data

Descriptive statistics

Measurement of central tendency

At AS level you are not expected to conduct complex statistical analysis on your data, but you are expected to be able to interpret and describe your findings. One of the simplest places to start is to learn to calculate measures of central tendency.

1 The mean

The mean is the mathematical average. To calculate the mean from a list of scores, simply add them up and divide by the number of scores.

What is the mean of these scores?

- 9, 9, 11, 12, 14, 14, 15, 17, 18, 19
- 2, 2, 3, 5, 5, 6, 6, 7, 7, 20

These numbers are scores out of 100 on a memory task:

- 43, 45, 46, 49, 52, 52, 54, 57, 57, 58
- 11, 14, 16, 21, 28, 68, 71, 73, 74, 79

Calculate the means for the two sets of scores above. What do you think the strengths and weaknesses of the mean are?

2 The median

The median is the middle number when you have placed all the numbers in ascending order.

What is the median of these scores?

- 9, 9, 11, 12, 14, 14, 15, 17, 18, 19
- 2, 2, 3, 5, 5, 6, 6, 7, 7, 20

What do you think the strengths and weaknesses of the median are?

3 The mode

The mode is the most common number in a set of scores.

Calculate the mode in the following sets of scores:

- 9, 9, 11, 11, 11, 12, 14, 17, 18, 19
- 2, 2, 2, 2, 5, 7, 9, 9, 10, 10

How useful do you think the mode is?

Try this …

Work out the mean, median and mode for the following sets of data:

- 45, 34, 23, 56, 34, 41, 51, 36, 42, 39
- 12, 14, 15, 11, 12, 56, 57, 49, 47, 51
- 5, 5, 5, 5, 5, 11, 45, 67, 68, 71

Complete the table below.

	Description of measure	Major strengths	Major weaknesses
Mean			
Median			
Mode	The most common number		

Visual representations of data

It is often useful to find a way to display your results in a simple visual form. This could be in the form of a table or graph. The best type of tables and graphs are simple ones, which have been clearly labelled. Imagine you turned over a page in a book and came face to face with a huge table containing hundreds of numbers. Most people would either shut the book or keep turning the pages until they found a short summary of what the table showed or a much simpler table. Keep that in mind as you read these pages – you are trying to convey information in the simplest possible format.

Examiner's tip

Students often think that the most complicated tables and graphs are the best ones. This is not true. In the Psychological Investigations exam you will be awarded marks for clarity and simplicity. Summarise the data by calculating measures of central tendency and ensure that you label everything clearly.

Tables

One of the simplest ways to display your data is to construct a simple table. In most research reports you will not find tables of raw data but tables of measures of central tendency or other summaries of the data such as percentages.

The most important thing to remember when you are constructing a table is to label it correctly. Remember that the person who is reading your report is not as familiar with the data as you are.

What conclusions can you draw from the following table?

	Condition A	Condition B
Mean	16.5	12.5

The answer is 'not a lot'. The best we could do here is to say that the mean in condition A is higher than the mean in condition B, but since we do not know what the conditions are or what the numbers represent we cannot draw any other conclusions.

Look at the table below, which has appropriate titles and labels. Now what conclusions can you draw?

	Noisy conditions	Quiet conditions
Mean time taken (seconds)	16.5	12.5

Mean time taken to solve an anagram in noisy and quiet conditions

From this table we can conclude that participants completed the anagram faster when they were in quiet conditions than when they were in noisy conditions.

Examiner's tip

If you are asked to draw a table in the exam, make sure that it contains a summary of the data rather than all the raw data. You should also make sure you have included all the correct labels. A title helps too!

Bar charts and histograms

A bar chart shows the data in a more visual form. A bar chart showing the same data as the table above would look like this:

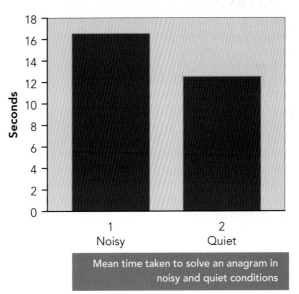

Mean time taken to solve an anagram in noisy and quiet conditions

Pie charts

A pie chart shows the proportions of different scores. This might be suitable for the sort of data that you collected for your observation. The example below shows the sort of results

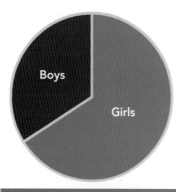

Pie chart to show percentages of boys and girls making healthy food choices

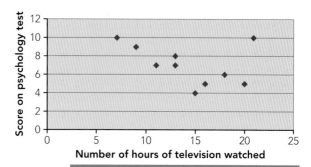

The relationship between number of hours of television watched in a week and the score achieved on a psychology test

you might have got if you had conducted the observation into healthy eating on page 155.

You can easily see that girls made more healthy food choices than boys.

Try this ...

Would a pie chart be suitable for displaying data from any of your four investigations into memory? If so, sketch one and label it appropriately.

Scattergraphs

A scattergraph is only used for displaying relationships between two variables. This means that we can use a scattergraph to display the data that we have collected in our correlational investigation. Note that here we are using the raw scores; we have not worked out means or other measures of central tendency as we are looking for relationships between the scores.

We have already looked at scattergraphs on page 159, where you will find an example of scattergraphs showing:

◆ a positive correlation

◆ a negative correlation

◆ no correlation.

The example below shows the relationship between the number of hours television that students watched between a particular Monday and Thursday and the score that they achieved in a psychology test on the Friday morning.

You can see from this scattergraph that there does appear to be a relationship between the two sets of scores. Generally speaking, the more television the students watched over the four days, the worse they did in the psychology test, making this a negative correlation (as the score

on one variable increases, the score on the other variable decreases). However, we have not shown that watching television means that you will do badly as correlational research cannot show cause and effect. All we have shown is that there is a relationship. Although in this example the relationship is perhaps likely to be a causal one, we would need to conduct an experiment to demonstrate this.

There are other interesting aspects to this scattergraph. The person who did best on the test watched the least television, which fits with our prediction; but the person who watched the most television came second in the test scores. This data point sits outside the general pattern of the results and is called an 'outlier' in statistical terms.

Try this ...

Plot the results from your correlational activity. Can you see a pattern? Does it suggest a positive or a negative correlation? Write a conclusion that can be drawn from this scattergraph – remember to use the words 'relationship' or 'correlation' and not 'difference' or 'effect'.

Taking it further

You have seen how to calculate measures of central tendency and how to construct simple visual representations of your data. Although these are very useful, you will have realised from reading the core studies that most researchers use statistical analysis to test their hypotheses. Statistics tell you how likely it is that your results are due to chance and allow you to formally reject either the alternate or the null hypothesis. You will learn how to conduct simple statistical tests if you continue your studies at A2 level.

Evaluating your research

For this exam, the evaluation issues you should concentrate on are the primarily methodological ones. This might include the following:

1   What are the strengths and weaknesses of the method used?

You should be aware of the strengths and weaknesses of each method in general (see pages 153–164), but you should also be able to apply those strengths and weaknesses to the specific topic being investigated. A better question to ask yourself might be 'is the research method the best one that could be used to investigate this topic?'.

For example, if you were given details of a self-report study into helping behaviour you could state that people's responses to self-reports are not always truthful. You would then have to take this a little bit further and relate it to helping behaviour, perhaps by saying that people might want to appear more helpful than they really are. Perhaps you could argue that people are giving the answer that reflects how they would like to think they would behave in a real-life situation, but if they have never been in this situation they may not know how they might behave. In this situation you could argue that you might get more valid results from a field experiment but that this might raise ethical issues.

2   What are the strengths and weaknesses of the experimental design used? If the researcher has used an independent measures design, what are its strengths and weaknesses? Could they have used a repeated measures design instead?

For example, a study into whether people complete a jigsaw puzzle faster with music playing or in silence could use either design. An independent measures design would mean that people only had to take part in one condition and so would only have to do the puzzle once. However the people in the silence condition might be better at jigsaws anyway than the people in the music condition, and you wouldn't know this. If you used a repeated measures condition you wouldn't have this problem, as the same people would take part in each condition, but if you used the same jigsaw they might be faster at doing it the second time because they have done it before. If you used a different jigsaw, one might be easier than the other, even though they had the same number of pieces.

One solution to this might be the use of matched pairs design. This is time consuming, as you would have to measure the participants' jigsaw ability to begin with and then pair the participants. This means that the two best scorers would be put into different groups and so on, down to the two worst scorers. You then have two groups of different people who have similar abilities. Another solution might be the use of the repeated measures design with counterbalancing. This means that the participants take part in both conditions, but some do the music condition first and some do the silence condition first. This means that you have 'evened out' any possible effects of everyone doing one condition first and the other second.

3   How did they select the sample? What are the strengths and weaknesses of this sampling method? What are the strengths and weaknesses of this sample for this particular study?

For example, could a study on memory using A-level students be generalised beyond A-level students? You could argue that A-level students are more used to learning and remembering things than the wider population. They have regular tests, so testing is not a new and stressful experience for them. This means that results obtained from just A-level students may not be generalised beyond A-level students. A more representative sample of participants from different occupations and of different ages should give results that could be generalised more widely. You could also consider the sampling method. If samples are obtained by opportunity then maybe the people who were around are all similar in some way. If people volunteer to take part, are they representative? Might the sort of people who volunteer to take part in research be somehow different from those who don't volunteer? Maybe this doesn't really matter, but if you were studying conformity or obedience or helpfulness it might matter a great deal.

4   Were there any problems with the way the research was conducted? Could people have discussed their answers to questionnaires? How do you know they are telling the truth? What might make them lie to you?

For example, conducting a self-report in a busy student common room could mean that people discuss their answers. It could also mean that people are not taking the study seriously or do not want to give honest answers in case someone sees what they are writing or hears what they are saying.

5   Are there any ethical issues? How could these be overcome?

This is very important. Review the ethical guidelines on page 9. For example even a simple study on stress might be asking people for sensitive information that they do not wish to share. Not only does this have implications for your research, it also potentially leaves your participants in a distressed state. Sometimes it is not possible to conduct the research that you would like to conduct, and at other times you have to consider alternatives. For example, asking people if they ever get stressed might be acceptable, but asking them for details of stressful events is not.

Try this ...

Evaluate each of the activities you have conducted, using the following headings:

- Strengths of the method (and design if applicable)
- Weaknesses of the method (and design if applicable)
- Strengths of sample and sampling method
- Weaknesses of sample and sampling method
- Other strengths of the way the research was conducted
- Other weaknesses of the way the research was conducted
- How could these weaknesses be overcome?
- Ethical issues.

ExamCafé

Relax, refresh, result!

Refresh your memory

The exam is 1 hour long and there are 60 marks. This means you are working to a 'mark-a-minute' rule. Try not to spend more than four minutes on a 4-mark question. If a question is worth 10 marks you probably need to spend 10 minutes answering it, but some of that is thinking time.

This exam is all about methods. This means that you will need to review the whole Psychological Investigations section, but don't forget that a lot of your knowledge about research methods has come from the core studies. Copy and try to complete the table below without looking back through the book.

Method	Strengths	Weaknesses
Experiments		
Observations		
Self-reports		
Correlation		

Get the result!

Exam-style question

Section A

A researcher conducted an experiment to see if people can solve anagrams faster in a quiet room or a noisy room. They conducted this study using an independent measures design.

The results were as follows:

Condition 1: Noisy room	Condition 2: Quiet room
53 sec	48 sec
47 sec	51 sec
62 sec	44 sec
58 sec	46 sec
49 sec	50 sec
55 sec	48 sec

Time taken in seconds to solve 10 simple anagrams

1 a) Suggest an appropriate null hypothesis for this experiment. (4 marks)

b) Identify the independent and dependent variable in this experiment. (2 marks)

c) Outline one other way in which the dependent variable could have been measured. (2 marks)

2 a) What is meant by an 'independent measures design'? (2 marks)

b) Outline one strength and one weakness of using an independent measures design for this experiment. (6 marks)

3 Outline two conclusions that could be drawn from this data. (4 marks)

Student answer

1 a) A suitable null hypothesis would be as follows: there will be no difference in the time taken to solve ten simple anagrams between participants working in a quiet room and participants working in a noisy room. Any difference is due to chance.

1 b) The independent variable is whether the participants complete the task in a noisy room or a quiet room. The dependent variable is the time taken in seconds to solve ten simple anagrams.

c) The dependent variable could have been measured by giving people a time limit of 2 minutes and counting how many anagrams they could solve in this time.

2 a) An independent measures design is when different participants are used in each condition of the experiment.

b) A strength of using an independent measures design for this experiment is that participants only have to do the anagram-solving task once. This means that they do not get bored or tired or manage to work out the aims of the study. The weakness is that different people may be better or worse at solving anagrams anyway, so it may be difficult to conclude that it was the noise level in the room that affected their score.

3 People took longer on average to solve ten simple anagrams in a noisy room than a quiet room. The range of scores is much smaller in the quiet room.

Examiner says:

This is a clearly written null hypothesis. The 'any difference is due to chance' is not strictly necessary but shows that the student is aware that this is what the null hypothesis predicts.

Examiner says:

Absolutely right!

Examiner says:

A good suggestion, still measuring the same variable but in a different way.

Examiner says:

Again a correct answer.

Common mistakes

Students sometimes think of the null hypothesis as being the opposite of the alternate hypothesis. If the alternate hypothesis says 'People will do better in a quiet room compared to a noisy room' then they think that the null hypothesis is 'People will do worse in a quiet room.' This is wrong – the null hypothesis states that the independent variable will have no effect on the dependent variable.

Section B

A researcher wishes to conduct an observation of students' use of the computer rooms in the sixth-form centre.

4   Describe and evaluate a suitable procedure for this observation. (10 marks)

5   Describe one methodological problem that the researcher might come across when conducting this observation and suggest how this issue might be dealt with. (6 marks)

6   Outline one strength and one weakness of using observational methods in psychological research. (4 marks)

Examiner's tip

You have about 10 minutes for the 10-mark question. You need to spend a couple of minutes planning your answer. Don't forget that there are two parts to this question. First you need to describe the procedure that you would follow – this should include the categories of behaviour that you are looking for and the way that you will code them. You also need to evaluate this – describe the strengths and weaknesses of this procedure – not of observations in general terms – but of the procedure that you have proposed. You could think about practical problems, ethical issues or general design issues.

Look at question 6 carefully – this time you are not being asked about the activity described in the exam paper, but about the strengths and weaknesses of observational methods in general.

Student answer

4 To conduct this observation I would need to construct an observation schedule. I would go to the computer room and observe every person in the room. I would record what they were doing as follows:

Participant number	Male or female	Working on computer (not internet)	Working – not on computer	Playing games on computer	Surfing the net – working	Surfing the net – not working
1						
2						
3						
4						

This would allow me to see what people were doing at the time that I observed.

The strengths of this would be that it would be simple to conduct and I would not be invading people's privacy, so it would be quite ethical. The categories are fairly straight-forward so several observers could be used to cover the whole day or even a whole week. The weakness is that I am only observing a person for a minute or two and they may be working all day and just playing for a few minutes while I was observing. It might have been better to observe people using a time-sampling frame to observe a smaller number of people for the whole time they were in the computer room, noting down what they do every minute or every five minutes. Also, although the categories are fairly simple it might be difficult to decide whether people online are looking for work stuff, especially if they were computer studies or media studies students.

5   One methodological problem that the researcher may encounter is that of demand characteristics. If the people in the computer room know that they are being observed they will probably all start working. This means that the behaviour I observe is probably not what they would have been doing if I hadn't been there. To overcome this I would have to sit at a computer in the corner and pretend to be working – I could even have my coding scheme on the computer so that it was possible to check boxes without people being aware that they were being observed.

6   One advantage of observational methods in psychology is that they can have very high ecological validity. If people are observed in their natural environment and without knowing that they are being observed, their behaviour is likely to be entirely natural. One disadvantage is that researchers generally have much less control in observational research compared to experimental research. This means that it is difficult to draw conclusions from observational research.

Examiner says:

A good answer, showing awareness that all observational research is not the same – the candidate has said that observations can have high ecological validity and that usually they have less control – this shows clearly that the candidate is aware that observations can be conducted in a variety of ways.

Section C

A researcher has conducted a correlational study to investigate the relationship between how good people think their problem-solving skills are and how well they do on problem-solving tasks. The first variable was 'self-rating of problem-solving skills' and this was measured by asking people to rate their own problem-solving skills on a 10-point scale where 1 = very poor and 10 = excellent. The second variable was 'problem-solving ability' and this was measured by giving people two pictures with 20 very minor differences between them and measuring how many differences they could find in 90 seconds. Results were as follows:

Participant no.	Self-rating of problem-solving ability (1= low 10=high)	No. of differences found in pictures within 90 seconds (max 20)
1	3	5
2	3	7
3	5	10
4	6	9
5	6	11
6	7	12
7	8	9
8	9	14
9	9	8
10	10	16

7 a) Sketch an appropriately labelled scattergraph displaying the results. (4 marks)

   b) Outline one conclusion that can be drawn from this scattergraph. (2 marks)

8   Suggest two problems with the way 'self-rating of problem-solving ability' has been measured in this investigation. (4 marks)

9   Describe and evaluate two other ways in which actual problem-solving ability might be measured. (10 marks)

Student answer

7 a)

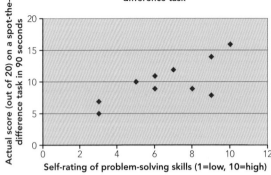

A graph to show the relationship between self-rating of problem-solving skills and actual score on a spot-the-difference task

b) One conclusion that can be drawn from this scattergraph is that there is a positive correlation between a person's self-rating of problem-solving ability and their ability to find differences in a spot the difference task.

8   One problem is that people may be subject to social desirability bias. They may want to present themselves in the best possible light and so they may rate their problem-solving ability as high so as not to appear stupid. Conversely they may rate it as low in order not to seem arrogant or big-headed. A second problem is that likert scales like the 1–10 scale used in this self-report are subject to different interpretations by different participants. For example one person may think that they have good problem-solving skills and give themselves an 8 and another person may think that they have brilliant problem-solving skills and also give themselves an 8. This means that it is difficult to interpret the results of these self-reports.

Examiner says:

A good answer again. The candidate has suggested two alternatives and given both strengths and weaknesses of each.

9   Problem-solving ability could be measured by the length of time it takes someone to complete a jigsaw puzzle. This would be good as everyone could be given the same jigsaw puzzle with the same number of pieces and simply timed. However some people may enjoy doing jigsaw puzzles and do them frequently, whereas other people may not have done a jigsaw for years. This might mean that they didn't complete the puzzle as quickly even though their problem-solving skills are just as good. Another way that problem-solving could be measured would be to use maths problems. The person could be given five minutes to answer as many questions as they can. This would be easy to measure as the more they got right the better their problem-solving ability would be, but some people might be good at other sorts of problem-solving and not at maths problems, or the other way round so I don't think this is the most valid way to do this.

Suggested answers to the research question on page 154

Strengths might be that you are using the same people in both conditions of the experiment. This means that you are removing the likelihood that individual differences are responsible for any differences in results. You also need fewer people in total to take part in your study. The weaknesses are that you would need two different memory tests (one for each day), and if these were not equivalent in difficulty then any differences in the results might be due to the test rather than the breakfast. You could also argue that there are ethical issues surrounding allowing or not allowing people to eat breakfast, and an experimenter should be aware of possible harmful effects caused by denying food to participants who usually eat breakfast.

Synoptic issues

Issue 1: Ecological validity

Ecological validity refers to the extent to which findings from a study can be related to behaviour in everyday life. After all, the purpose of psychological research is to understand the way people behave and function in their everyday lives, the things we read about in the papers and the behaviour of people we meet every day.

Much research is conducted inside a laboratory environment, where the situation is controlled and manipulated in the way the researcher determines. In everyday life, situations are not so easy to control or manipulate and there are many factors or variables that influence the way a person behaves or reacts.

A difficult task for any researcher is to decide how behaviour can be studied in a realistic way, in which the behaviour of the people being studied is natural and unaffected by the research process. In laboratory experiments, participants know that they are being studied and are often inquisitive about the nature of the research, they may look for clues about how to behave, wanting to please the experimenter, or more negatively do the opposite of what is expected ('the screw you effect'!). It is human nature to want to be seen to behave in a way that is more socially acceptable (the 'social desirability effect').

Aspects of the experiment that lead participants to behave in an unnatural way are called demand characteristics; these cause behaviour to be less like natural reactions found in everyday life.

Loftus and Palmer's study on eyewitness testimony could be considered to be low in ecological validity. The study was carried out in a laboratory and participants had volunteered to take part; they therefore knew they were being studied and when asked questions about film clips of car crashes were more likely to give an answer that they felt was expected by the experimenter: 'the experimenter said the cars smashed into each other; therefore they must

want me to estimate that the cars were travelling at a high speed'. This effect may not be present when eyewitnesses are questioned by the police, as being in an experiment is not like any other situation since there is pressure to meet the demands of the experimental situation.

Another way in which this study was low in ecological validity is the use of film clips rather than real car crashes. There are differences between witnessing a real crash and watching a film of a crash; emotions would be more intense with involvement in a real crash and this might affect one's ability to recall information.

Researchers can achieve much greater ecological validity when field experiments are used. For example, the study by Piliavin, Rodin and Piliavin was conducted on a real train. The participants were not aware that they were in a study and so their behaviour was unaffected by factors such as demand characteristics, wanting to please the experimenter or the social desirability effect. As a result the findings can be generalised to everyday behaviour much more confidently than those from a laboratory experiment.

Try this ...

Choose five core studies that you feel were low in ecological validity, and for each one:

◆ suggest two ways in which the ecological validity could be improved.

◆ discuss the implications of each improvement.

Take it further

Why don't psychologists conduct all their studies in everyday life settings if they are more ecologically valid?

How can demand characteristics be reduced in laboratory experiments?

Issue 2: Application to everyday life

One of the things teachers learn when teaching psychology is that many students find the subject interesting. This may sound strange, but it highlights one of the fundamental issues that psychologists have to deal with: whether their research is of any use to individuals. The ultimate goal of psychology is to understand people better and to use this knowledge to help us live fulfilled lives. Many students will therefore find psychology interesting because they can apply what they learn to themselves and others. This means that the research psychologists carry out needs to be useful. There needs to be a word of caution as psychologists can often be accused of telling us things we already know. This can be a good thing, as we may experience things in life but not really know why. For example how we learn is still a big debate that has not been resolved. Also, we should not dismiss research that seems to have no immediate use, as it may be part of a big jigsaw still being assembled.

Griffiths' study on regular fruit machine gamblers is an example of a piece of research that provides psychological insight into the thought processes of people with addictive behaviours. He does not just describe and explain how these individuals think, but goes further and suggests how this information could be used to provide support to help people reduce their addiction to gambling. In this study Griffiths has used the 'thinking aloud' technique as both a research process and an effective tool to be used in therapy to deal with gambling addictions.

Rosenhan's research 'On being sane in insane places' has had a significant impact on the mental health profession as it deals with the problems of accurate diagnosis. When this research was published the impact was similar to the young boy pointing out that the emperor was not wearing fine clothes but was unfortunately naked. His findings opened up the debate about the reliability of diagnosing mental illness, despite the fact that many people already felt uncomfortable with this process. Rosenhan provides no solution to the problem and just highlights where the inaccuracies may be coming from. Even though this study was written in 1973 the debate still rages, with many psychologists still unsure about the reliability of diagnostic procedures.

Try this …

It is hoped that ultimately all studies can be applicable and useful to everyday life. Re-read the studies listed below and consider whether they really are useful, or indeed if they have uses that their authors have not mentioned.

◆ Samuel and Bryant (pages 40–47). How can these findings help educational professionals improve the learning experience?

◆ Maguire et al. (pages 68–75). If the size of the hippocampus can change, what are the implications of this?

◆ Reicher and Haslam (pages 104–111). How might this information be used by the prison service or the army, and should psychologists be involved with these services?

Take it further

Which of the core studies do you think are the most useful? Why?

A winning line on a fruit machine

U2

Synoptic issues

Issue 3: Representativeness of sample / generalisability

One issue you could consider when evaluating research is whether the researcher has chosen an appropriate sample for his or her research. Is it possible to generalise the results from this piece of research to a larger population? You need to be sensible when considering this issue – it is not appropriate to criticise a researcher because their research does not reflect the whole world, but it might be appropriate to criticise a researcher who over-generalises the findings from their research, for example claiming that their research applies to children generally when the sample were all from one very small area.

Think about Sperry's research. Sperry had a sample of 11 people who had undergone surgery to sever their corpus callosum. Eleven people is quite a small sample for this kind of research, but this sample did reflect virtually all the patients who had undergone this operation. This means that we can be fairly sure that the results apply to those people who have that operation. However, it is slightly harder to determine whether Sperry's results tell us anything about the way 'normal' brains function. It is possible that these 11 people had atypical brain functioning (perhaps due to their epilepsy) before their operation and if this were the case then it is more difficult to apply these findings to the functioning of normal brains.

Another way of looking at the representativeness of samples is illustrated in Savage-Rumbaugh et al.'s study. This study used two pygmy chimpanzees, one male and one female, with comparisons made to two other chimpanzees whose learning is reported in more detail in other studies. Clearly, two is a very small sample, although an appropriate one for such an in-depth study of language development. However it would be unwise to generalise the findings gleaned from two pygmy chimpanzees to pygmy chimpanzees in general. The chimpanzees used in this study may have been significantly more or less able than other pygmy chimpanzees, and to draw generalised conclusions about the abilities of pygmy chimpanzees could be potentially inaccurate and misleading.

There are many other issues that you could consider when thinking about the representativeness of the samples used in the core studies. You could consider whether the sample was all from one culture. This is not a problem in itself, but would be considered a problem if the researchers attempted to apply their findings beyond that culture. The same issue might apply when looking at the age or sex of a sample. You might also consider whether a piece of research conducted 30 or 40 years ago can still be used to explain people's behaviour today.

Try this ...

Make a list of all the core studies. Identify the sample for each one and briefly comment on the sample. The list has been started for you.

Study	Sample	Comments
Loftus and Palmer	American college students	May not represent Americans generally; sample likely to have limited driving experience, used to learning / testing situations, may be prone to demand characteristics if they are students of the researcher
Baron-Cohen et al.		

Take it further

1   What are the problems in attempting to achieve a representative sample?

2   Does psychological research really reflect the whole human race or is it simply the psychology of white American college students?

Issue 4: Ethics

The ethical guidelines are in place to protect participants in psychological research.

They cover all aspects of the research, from gaining consent before a study to debriefing participants at the end. As a general rule, participants should be the same at the end of a study as they were at the start, that is, they should not have been *harmed* in any way.

Certain groups are more vulnerable to harm than others, for example children and animals are not able to withdraw from studies or give consent, and for this reason it is especially difficult for psychologists to work with them in an ethical way. However, some psychologists view studies on children as central to developmental psychology and to helping us to understand how adult behaviour is shaped.

The ethical guidelines present a great dilemma for psychologists because adhering to them strictly can render research useless. Take for example the guideline to avoid deception: by informing participants of the aim of a study their behaviour can change. Imagine if Milgram had told his participants the true aim of his study, that they were being observed to see whether they would obey to the point where they thought they had killed someone, they would have behaved very differently, not least because they did not want to look like bad people (the social desirability effect).

In fact, in a survey Milgram carried out before the study, he asked members of the public how likely they thought it was that they would shock a person in response to a request from an authority figure: only 3% predicted that they would.

Another ethical guideline that presents a dilemma for psychologists is protection from harm: studies often induce stress or anxiety in participants that may last longer than the duration of the study. The participants in the Milgram study, for example, showed signs of extreme stress including digging their fingernails into their flesh, biting their lips and in one case having a seizure. Milgram did attempt to assess whether this stress was long-lasting by interviewing the participants some time after the study, and claimed that the participants were not harmed in the long term. It has also been asserted that the knowledge gained from the study was worth the temporary stress experienced by the participants.

In Reicher and Haslam's prison study a great deal of frustration and stress was experienced by both prisoners and guards as a result of the experimental situation and although this is an important area of research, we have to ask ourselves whether this was ethical. A further consideration is whether it is the procedure in this study that caused the stress or the ways the participants chose to behave. The researchers could argue that the participants were free to behave in either a positive or negative way and that the stress was of their own making. The same could also be said for the participants in the Milgram study, after all they could have chosen not to obey the experimenter at all and thus avoided the stress they experienced. When looked at this way, perhaps the studies were not unethical.

The other ethical guidelines include the requirement to maintain confidentiality, and to carry out observations only with permission or in public places.

Try this ...

For each of the studies listed below, suggest the implications of making them ethical.

◆ Bandura, Ross and Ross (pages 48–55)

◆ Rosenhan (pages 124–131)

◆ Savage-Rumbaugh et al. (pages 28–35).

Take it further

Do you think there is ever a justification for breaking ethical guidelines?

Signs of tension were seen in the participants

U2

Synoptic issues

Issue 5: Nature and nurture

This debate is a very important one in psychology and concerns the relative influences of inheritance and experience. Nature refers to the inherited or genetic make-up of a person and nurture refers to all other influences from the moment of conception. Some of the core studies suggest the influence of inheritance and others suggest the influence of experience. As with many of these debates, some research suggests an interaction between the two.

For consideration:

◆ Which of the core studies offer a 'nature' explanation of the behaviour they are investigating?

◆ Which of the core studies offer a 'nurture' explanation of the behaviour they are studying?

◆ Are some 'a bit of both'?

Drawing definite conclusions about the relative contributions of nature and nurture is difficult because the type of research that might need to be conducted is often impossible for ethical or practical reasons. It is impossible to isolate a human being from all 'nurture' influences and so controlled experiments are difficult to conduct. Even if you demonstrate a relationship between for example, the IQ scores of parents and their children, it is difficult to interpret this relationship. If the children have been brought up by their biological parents it is difficult to know if the relationship is due to the influence of nature or the influence of nurture. Researchers should also consider the ethical implications of their research before publication. For example, what do you think would be the effect of publishing research that claimed that one sex was naturally more intelligent than the other, or that one race was naturally more intelligent than another?

If we consider the core study by Maguire, it is clear that there is another issue to consider. Environment and experience can affect biology and this can complicate the picture. Maguire claimed that the experiences of

spatial navigation that the cab drivers had was actually represented by an increased hippocampal volume. Whilst it is still possible to debate the possibility that people with either an increased hippocampal volume or the potential for an increased hippocampal volume are more attracted to work that requires good spatial navigation skills, this study clearly demonstrates the complexity of working in this area.

The core study by Samuel and Bryant suggests that both nature and nurture contribute to the development of cognitive skills. Samuel and Bryant confirmed Piaget's findings that cognitive ability increased with age, although they did suggest that the children they studied were able to conserve at an earlier age than Piaget's subjects. The study also suggests that the experiences children have also determine the levels of cognitive ability that they are able to demonstrate. In the study the specific focus was on the way the children were questioned, but it is also probable that the educational experiences the children had would also have played a part.

Try this ...

Design a study to test whether aggression is innate or learnt.

What ethical issues would you face in conducting your research?

What problems might you experience in interpreting the results of your research?

Do you think that your research would be useful?

Children are capable of a greater understanding than Piaget thought

Issue 6: Individual and situational explanations

This refers to the explanations of behaviour offered by the studies. An individual explanation would be about the person (they fell over because they are clumsy) and a situational explanation would be about the situation (they fell over because the floor was slippery). Some research suggests individual explanations of behaviour and some suggests situational explanations.

Consider the research by Milgram. Milgram found that the majority of participants in his research obeyed the experimenter. In other words Milgram concluded that the reason why people gave severe electric shocks to other people was not because they were sadistic (this would be an individual explanation) but because there were powerful social forces operating on them that they found difficult or impossible to resist. In other words, they behaved in this way because of the situation they were in and not because of the type of people that they were.

Now think about the research by Rosenhan. Rosenhan found that once patients were labeled as mentally ill, that label stuck to them. Everything they said or did was interpreted as typical of a schizophrenic (or manic depressive) patient. This means that the situation that the pseudopatients were in had a powerful impact on the way they were judged. The hospital staff were not able to perceive the pseudopatients in isolation from their labels and the fact that they were already in a psychiatric hospital. This raises serious doubts about the validity and reliability of psychiatric diagnosis and also shows how powerful situational effects are. The doctors and nurses no doubt believed that they were judging the individual ('he is behaving this way because he is schizophrenic'), but Rosenhan's research showed that in fact they were strongly affected by the situation that the person was judged in.

Social psychology tends to focus on the situational determinants of people's behaviour whereas individual differences perhaps focuses more on individual explanations for behaviour. However, you should realise that both types of explanations are suggesting causes for behaviour, and this debate overlaps with the free-will determinism debate discussed on page 187.

Try this ...

How easy is it to investigate whether behaviour is situational or individual?

First, it is possible that behaviour is determined by a complex interaction of both situational and individual factors. It is difficult to isolate just one variable to study. Even in highly controlled experimental research there are numerous individual factors that cannot be controlled for.

1   With reference to the study by Milgram and the study by Reicher and Haslam, make a list of all the individual factors that may have contributed to the behaviours shown.

Even if you could think of individual variables that might have a role in the behaviour, they may not be variables that can be manipulated. This might be for practical or ethical reasons.

2   Make a list of individual factors that can't be experimentally manipulated for either practical or ethical reasons, e.g. age, sex, intelligence.

Finally, people are not always aware of the factors that determine their own behaviour and so even self-report research may not give you clear answers.

Take it further

1   How useful do you think self-reports would have been after the studies by Milgram and Piliavin, Rodin and Piliavin?

2   What sort of questions could you have asked people? Do you think the participants in this study would identify the same reasons for their behaviour as the researchers did?

Issue 7: Reliability

The psychological definition of reliability is not very different to how we use it in our everyday lives. For psychologists, reliability refers to how well a way of measuring something gives a consistent result. The most reliable ways of measuring will give the same result each time. If a questionnaire is being used to describe personality, then a reliable questionnaire will always describe you in the same way. This is just like our everyday lives, where a reliable friend never lets you down. When psychologists measure human behaviour they always try to use a method or device that can provide an accurate result whenever it is used, and one of the features of good research is that the findings are seen to be reliable. If a piece of research is replicated by someone else using the same procedure, the same findings should be obtained. If this does not happen then the original research is questioned.

The issue of reliability can be discussed in all the studies, but this section will focus on two: Thigpen and Cleckley's case study of Eve White, and Bandura, Ross and Ross's experiment on the transmission of aggression.

Thigpen and Cleckley obtained their data about the various personalities that inhabited Eve White's body by using descriptions from their own therapeutic sessions and also from a number of psychological tests. It is difficult to test the reliability of the observations made by Thigpen and Cleckley on Eve White or the other personalities, as they were the only people present. We have no assurance that someone else may have described Eve differently. Psychometric tests on IQ and memory can be regarded as being reliable, as the tests used were well established. The projective tests to identify the dominant personality characteristic may have their reliability questioned as they are based on an individual's subjective interpretation.

In the study on the transmission of aggression, children were observed playing in certain experimental conditions with a selection of toys provided by the researchers. The children were not observed in normal everyday activities but within an experimentally controlled 'play' environment. This unnatural environment may lead us to question whether the behaviours observed can reliably be regarded as aggressive acts, or simply just how children responded to the demand characteristic of the environment. So it could be that the behaviours being measured were not in fact the aggressive behaviours that occurred in everyday life. Despite this it is fair to conclude that what was measured was recorded reliably as the inter-rater reliability of the observers was very high and this meant that they had a very close agreement between them when they described the behaviours.

Try this ...

Consider the issues of reliability in a number of other studies. For example, how reliable are:

- the measurement of speed in Loftus and Palmer's study (pages 12–19)
- the description of Little Hans's behaviour (pages 56–62)
- the ability to carry out conservation tasks in Samuel and Bryant's study (pages 40–47)
- the measurement of brain activity during dream states in Dement and Kleitman's study (pages 76–83)?

Would this behaviour occur in everyday life?

Issue 8: Validity

Validity refers to whether a measure really measures what is intended. We have seen that if a study is low in ecological validity it is not really measuring how people behave in everyday life. It is often difficult to devise a way of measuring or studying behaviour, especially because the method itself can change the way people behave due to their awareness of being studied. Think about having your blood pressure taken: the procedure itself could make you feel stressed or nervous, which could alter your blood pressure.

Cognitive processes are also difficult to measure, mainly since they can't be seen and measuring how someone thinks or processes information is a difficult task. Imagine a questionnaire on racist attitudes: would people be keen to expose themselves as racists? Since it is not socially desirable to be racist, people may alter their responses accordingly.

So the whole business of measurement is difficult in psychology. It is much easier to measure physical features about a person, such as their height or their weight, because there is an objective measuring system that can be used, e.g. kilos and centimetres, but measuring psychological and behaviour features is much harder. The natural sciences do not have this problem to the same extent, since the material they are dealing with such as atoms, chemicals and cells do not think like humans do, in fact the main problem for psychologists is how to study or measure characteristics of people who are aware of what you are doing.

Psychologists therefore spend a lot of time devising tests, tasks and situations that can be used to study and measure behaviour and cognitive processes.

For example, in the study by Baron-Cohen et al., a series of tasks were used to measure whether adults with autism or Asperger's Syndrome had a theory of mind. A theory of mind is a cognitive skill which 'normal' adults use subconsciously to predict the behaviour of others. To find a task that would test just this skill was difficult to achieve, but here the researchers feel that the Eyes Task did indeed measure theory of mind.

They checked the validity of the Eyes Task by comparing the participants' performance with their performance on another test of theory of mind; Happé's (1994) 'strange stories'. The thinking behind this was that if the Eyes Task was indeed tapping theory of mind, then performance on the Eyes Task should correlate with performance on Happé's 'strange stories'. A series of other tasks were also done to check the validity of the Eyes Task; the gender recognition task and the basic emotion recognition task. Where one measure is correlated with another measure of the same thing, this is known as concurrent validity.

Another study that demonstrates the issue of validity is Reicher and Haslam's prison study. Here the researchers measured the reactions of the prisoners and guards in the mock prison by using a variety of measures including video- and audio-recordings, daily psychometric testing, a battery of scales, and daily swabs of saliva. When a variety of measures are taken this can improve the validity of the study as the variety of measures used allows the weaknesses of some measures to be overcome by the strengths of others. A more comprehensive picture of events can be developed where more than one measure is used. We must remember however, that the validity of a measurement depends heavily on the overall ecological validity of the study.

Try this …

For each core study, think about what behaviour or process was being measured and identify factors that may have affected the validity of the measurements taken. These factors might include quantitative or qualitative data, social desirability effect, demand characteristics, artificiality, uncontrolled variables.

You may like to do this in a table like the one below.

Core study	Variable being measured/studied	Factors affecting validity
Loftus and Palmer		
Baron-Cohen et al.		

Issue 9: Qualitative and quantitative data

Psychologists collect two main types of data: qualitative and quantitative. They each provide different kinds of information. Let's say you were discussing who are the greatest rock beat combo of the modern era. Two arguments could be put forward:

1   The Beatles are the greatest because I love the songs and they can make me feel happy and sad.

2   The Beatles are the greatest because they have sold millions of records.

The first point is a qualitative measurement as it relies on description and interpretation by an individual. Many people will not agree with the first point, but it is the experience of the person who said it.

The second point is a quantitative measurement because it is based on numeric measurement. You may not like the Beatles, but the numbers clearly suggest that many people do. These data are reliable as they cannot be denied!

The problem psychologists have is how to investigate and report the human experience. If they use only qualitative data they can be accused of dealing only with the subjective experience of those involved and their findings are not reliable and cannot therefore be generalised. If they use only quantitative data this may be more reliable and easily applied to other people, but it may not give us a description of the experience being investigated. No one way is correct, as both can be used to inform the research process.

In their study on MPD, Thigpen and Cleckley were attempting to provide evidence that the condition actually existed. They did this by using qualitative and quantitative data. The qualitative data were the detailed descriptions of the behaviour of Eve White and her other personalities. They even recorded their own feelings, which is an important feature of the therapeutic process, to add additional evidence. It was noted that they felt attracted to Eve Black. To back up these descriptions of their experience they asked another psychologist to carry out a series of psychometric tests on IQ and memory. The intention of this was to provide harder, more reliable data to back up their subjective descriptions.

In Freud's case study on Little Hans and the development of his phobia of going outside and fear of horses, no quantitative data were recorded. Freud also made few observations himself, as the task of recording Hans's behaviour was left to his father. Freud justified this by

Why was Hans afraid of horses?

suggesting that the sort of information he wanted could only be obtained by someone who knew Hans well and was trusted by him. Freud later used these reports to interpret why Hans developed phobic behaviours. Although the data only describe the experience of one boy, Freud used this to explain wider human behaviours.

Try this …

Identify what sort of data have been collected in the studies listed below, then consider how they have been used to inform our understanding of human behaviour. If the data have been quantitative, do you think any other information would be useful to provide insight into the situation? If qualitative data are used, is this sufficiently reliable to be applied to other peoples' experiences?

◆   Rosenhan (pages 124–131). Think about the experience of the pseudo-patients.

◆   Samuel and Bryant (pages 40–47). Does this experiment really provide information on how children think?

◆   Maguire et al. (pages 68–75). Does measuring a brain region really help us to understand memory systems?

Issue 10: Control

To see the effect of one variable on another variable, laboratory experiments are often used, due to the amount of control the researcher has over the situation. Laboratory experiments are also popular in scientific fields of research for the same reason; take for example a scientist who wants to find out the effect of using fertiliser on the growth of roses. It would make sense to compare the growth of roses grown with the fertiliser and roses grown without it, but it would also be important to control any other variables that may affect the roses' growth, including the amount of water and sunlight, the quality of the soil, etc. These variables are called extraneous variables. In this example the use of fertiliser is the independent variable and the growth rate is the dependent variable.

The laboratory provides the perfect environment for psychologists to control such extraneous variables, whereas in everyday situations it is much harder to have control. It is only by controlling extraneous variables that a 'cause-and-effect' conclusion can be drawn and the psychologist can be confident that it is the independent variable that is causing the effect in the dependent variable.

The study by Loftus and Palmer was conducted in a laboratory setting, which allowed the researchers to control various aspects of the situation. One important aspect of control is that every trial of the experiment could be standardised and kept exactly the same for each participant, for example the conditions in which the film clips were viewed, such as background noise. This is important as any variation in the procedure could have affected the participants' estimates of speed. A further example of control in this study was the ability for the researchers to select who took part in the study – had the study been conducted in everyday life it would have been difficult to select specific people to view a car crash!

The study by Piliavin, Rodin and Piliavin on the other hand was a field experiment where it was difficult to control extraneous variables. The subway trains were carrying passengers going about their business and so there was no control over who took part in the study. In fact one difficulty for the researcher was to avoid the same passengers seeing the victim collapse more than once, as this would have aroused suspicion. Further variables which could not be controlled included: possible intervention from emergency services, difficulty in debriefing passengers, and inability to control the number of passengers on the train or their view of the victim's collapse.

So it can be seen that laboratory experiments provide the most control for researchers to establish causal relationships, much as scientists studying atoms, chemicals or cells.

Try this ...

For each of the core studies that are laboratory experiments, identify which variables were controlled. For those studies that used other research methods, for example case studies, suggest one variable that should have been controlled.

Take it further

What are the disadvantages of high levels of control?

How might using high levels of control be considered reductionist?

Passengers read their morning newspapers en route to work, New York 1963

Issue 11: Reductionism

This is the way in which psychologists often explain complex psychological phenomena by reducing them to a much simpler level, often focusing on a single factor. Most research is reductionist to an extent, as most experimental studies choose to examine the influence of single factors on complex behaviours. This can be a problem sometimes, as the explanations for complex behaviours may appear over simplistic because other contributing factors have not been investigated. However, reducing concepts to simplistic levels makes them easier to test and often means that researchers can use controlled laboratory experiments that are easy to replicate. Remember also that each study you look at is just part of a whole body of research which taken as a whole shows a much less reductionist viewpoint as many factors and different levels of explanations are incorporated. The type of explanation that is offered for a behaviour is also relevant here. Physiological explanations are seen as more reductionist than social explanations.

Dement and Kleitman investigated dreaming. They did this through a physiological approach using electroencephalography to measure the changes in brain activity while a person was asleep. In a sense they have reduced dreaming to a simple physiological measure; it could be argued that this oversimplifies a very complex phenomenon. However it allowed them to establish a link between rapid eye movement and dreaming that had not been established previously and since their research was conducted, many other studies have investigated other aspects of dreaming.

Baron-Cohen et al. studied the theory of mind ability of autistic adults. In this study they could be seen to have reduced theory of mind to a simple task of inferring a person's mental state of just from the information in photographs of their eyes. Clearly this study represents just one aspect of autism that has been extensively researched recently. You could regard this study as one piece of a complicated jigsaw: each piece isolates one factor to study, but the more pieces that are completed, the clearer the whole picture becomes. This is a good example of the advantages of isolating single variables to make them easier to study.

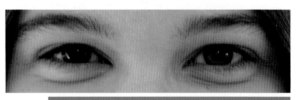

Can you judge how these people are feeling?

Try this ...

Choose one of the following studies:

- Bandura, Ross and Ross (pages 48–55).
- Samuel and Bryant (pages 40–47).

Suggest how the behaviour being investigated in this study might be reduced to a simpler level of explanation.

How could this be tested?

What problems might there be in testing this explanation and/or in interpreting the results of this investigation?

Take it further

Make a list of the advantages and limitations of a reductionist approach in psychology.

Issue 12: Determinism

The issue of determinism refers to the idea that our behaviour is controlled by external factors over which we have little or no control. The opposite view is that we have free will, which means that we are free to make our own decisions. This debate is not as straightforward as it may sound, as most psychological research is trying to find out what factors cause us to do what we do and can therefore be regarded as deterministic. Imagine going for a big night out in town with your friends. What makes you do this? Is it a decision based on your own free will, or are other factors involved? Maybe you go out because of social pressures and you want to be part of that group. Or it could be that your hormones are encouraging you to meet people of the opposite gender. Or you could just be one of those 'party people' who are always up for a good time!

Samuel and Bryant investigated the way children think, and were testing previous theories that children's thinking was qualitatively different from that of adults. The previous theory by Piaget suggested that children develop through a series of age-dependent stages and within each of these stages their thinking was very different. Samuel and Bryant 'fine tuned' this original research and provided some evidence that these stages were not as fixed as Piaget had first theorised. Their findings did not refute the existence of stages, and they would suggest that the way children think is therefore dependent on their age. This is a deterministic point of view as it indicates that our thought processes are not decided by us but are determined by whatever age we happen to be. Consequently our thoughts are controlled by the external factor of our age-related brain development, not what we 'want' to think.

The case study of Little Hans and his phobias carried out by Freud sought to identify what unconscious processes were responsible for his seemingly irrational behaviour. This study focused on one child's early experiences and used these to develop a theory of human behaviour and how an individual's personality may develop. Freud argued that we do not always make rational conscious decisions, but that the root cause for behaviour is the result of resolving the unconscious tensions between sexual and aggressive urges. His views are similar to Piaget's in that he considered that individuals go through developmental stages and that the experiences during these periods can determine later personality. It would appear from this that as individuals are not consciously aware of what causes their behaviour, free will can play little part. What Freud does argue, however, is that by using psychoanalytical techniques people can become more aware of the unconscious causes of their behaviour and therefore learn to make more conscious and ultimately fulfilling decisions. It is possible to view this process as, at least, approaching free will.

Try this …

Review the core studies and try to identify the issues related to determinism in all of them. For each one, try to identify what the researcher has hypothesised to be the cause of the behaviour being investigated.

Take it further

These questions may be difficult, but discuss them and do not be afraid to grapple with some really difficult ideas.

If people have free will, what is the point of psychology?

If our behaviour is determined by external factors, can we ever be held accountable for our actions? Think about getting good exam grades; telling lies; falling in love or even committing murder.

Synoptic issues

ExamCafé
Relax, refresh, result!

Core study summaries

To help you to understand and remember the core studies it is useful to make a summary of each one. Below is a summary sheet filled in for the Loftus and Palmer study. You can use this as a template for the other study summaries.

This will help you prepare information for the **Section A** and **Section B** exam questions, which require knowledge of details from the studies.

Study: Loftus and Palmer

Aim of study: (*hypotheses, variables*)

To investigate the effect leading questions on eyewitness testimony

Experiment 1: the verb used in the question will have an effect on the speed estimate given

Experiment 2: the verb used in the question will affect whether the participant recalls seeing broken glass one week later

Independent variable: verb used in leading question (e.g. 'smashed')

Dependent variable: Experiment 1: estimated speed; Experiment 2: broken glass recalled

Method: laboratory experiment

Participants: (*sampling technique, numbers, ages...*)

Experiment 1: 45 students, *Experiment 2*: 150 students

Procedure: (*how the study was conducted, controls used...*)

Experiment 1:

▷ Students shown 7 film clips of traffic accidents

▷ Then given questionnaire to i) give account of accident just seen ii) answer specific questions

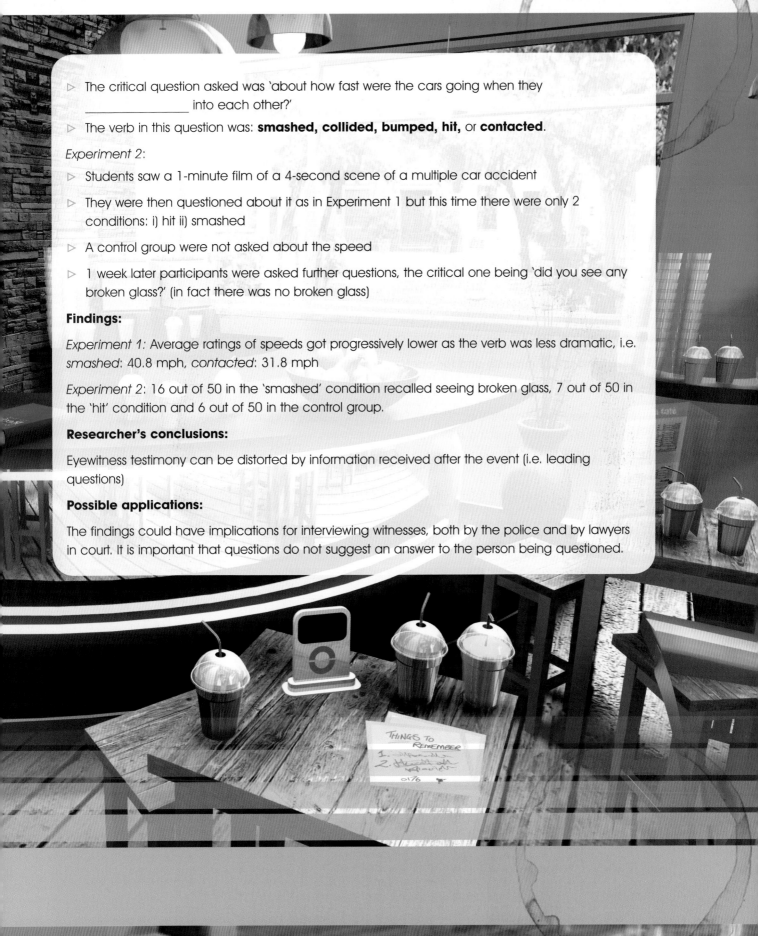

▷ The critical question asked was 'about how fast were the cars going when they _____ into each other?'

▷ The verb in this question was: **smashed, collided, bumped, hit,** or **contacted**.

Experiment 2:

▷ Students saw a 1-minute film of a 4-second scene of a multiple car accident

▷ They were then questioned about it as in Experiment 1 but this time there were only 2 conditions: i) hit ii) smashed

▷ A control group were not asked about the speed

▷ 1 week later participants were asked further questions, the critical one being 'did you see any broken glass?' (in fact there was no broken glass)

Findings:

Experiment 1: Average ratings of speeds got progressively lower as the verb was less dramatic, i.e. *smashed*: 40.8 mph, *contacted*: 31.8 mph

Experiment 2: 16 out of 50 in the 'smashed' condition recalled seeing broken glass, 7 out of 50 in the 'hit' condition and 6 out of 50 in the control group.

Researcher's conclusions:

Eyewitness testimony can be distorted by information received after the event (i.e. leading questions)

Possible applications:

The findings could have implications for interviewing witnesses, both by the police and by lawyers in court. It is important that questions do not suggest an answer to the person being questioned.

Evaluation

Choose four evaluations issues and briefly discuss each one:

Ecological validity: the study used film clips rather than a real-life car crash, these are two very different experiences and factors such as emotional response and attention would be very different. So the study is low in ecological validity.

Sample: Students were used in both of the experiments. Students are not representative of the general population in terms of age, driving experience or attention span; these factors make this sample difficult to generalise from.

Demand characteristics: the participants knew they were taking part in an experiment that would affect their behaviour in a number of ways. They would be looking for clues as to how to behave and may have given speed estimates they felt were expected.

Quantitative data: the speed estimates and answers 'yes' or 'no' to seeing broken glass provide quantitative data. This is useful for making comparisons but also reductionist in that they do not tell us why participants gave the answers they did.

Suggest two improvements and for each one outline the effect it would have on the study:

Improvement 1: could use a more realistic actual event rather than a film clip

Effect: this would increase the ecological validity of the study and may decrease the amount that people are affected by leading questions

Improvement 2: could use a wider range of participants, e.g. age, occupation, driving experience

Effect: this would make the sample more representative and increase the generalisability of the findings, the results may be very different from those found by Loftus and Palmer, who used only students.

Evaluating across the studies

Many of the evaluation issues relate to several studies and it is useful to plot the connection between the studies on each issue. On the next page is an example of how you could see the connection between the studies in terms of some ethical implications.

You could use this as a template to plot connections in other issues, including:

- application to everyday life
- determinism and free will
- ecological validity
- generalisability of sample
- individual and situational explanations

- nature/nurture
- quantitative and qualitative measures
- reductionism
- reliability
- validity and control.

Not all of the issues relate to each study, but you can fill in the boxes for the studies for which you feel the issue is relevant.

This will help you prepare information for the **Section B** and **Section C** exam questions, which require evaluation of the core studies.

The ethical aspects of the core studies

Sperry
- Fully informed consent
- Possible stress caused by inability to do task

Loftus and Palmer
- Possible distress from watching car accidents
- General consent was given

Milgram
- Deception about nature of task
- Severe stress caused by task, possible long-term effects
- Withdrawal issues due to payment and prompts

Baron-Cohen et al.
- Possible distress from inability to do task and strange situation

Savage-Rumbaugh et al.
- Interference with natural behaviour and development of species

Reicher and Haslam
- Participants had the right to withdraw
- Stress and anxiety caused by situation

Samuel and Bryant
- Problems with consent when working with children
- Withdrawal issues when working with children
- Possible stress from strange situation

Ethics: Which ethical issues are raised or broken in relation to the following guidelines?
- Deception
- Debriefing
- Observation
- Consent
- Withdrawal
- Protection
- Confidentiality

Piliavin, Rodin and Piliavin
- No consent given by participants
- No right to withdraw
- Possible distress caused by victim's collapse/failure to help

Bandura, Ross and Ross
- Problems with consent when working with children
- Withdrawal issues when working with children
- Distress from exposure to aggressive model and strange situation

Rosenhan
- No consent given by doctors or patients
- Damage to reputation of doctors/hospitals

Freud
- Confidentiality issues
- Intrusive questioning may cause harm/long-term effects

Thigpen and Cleckley
- Confidentiality issues
- Possible deterioration in patient's condition due to study

Maguire et al.
- Fully informed consent given by cab drivers
- Possible stress from process of MRI scan

Griffiths
- Fully informed consent given
- Participants were given money to gamble
- Not all participants were given therapy

Dement and Kleitman
- Fully informed consent given
- Possible effects from interference with sleep patterns

Relax and prepare

Hot tips

What I wish I'd known at the start of the year...

Ivan

It's really useful to consider the strengths and weaknesses of each set of studies. Often the same issues or strengths and weaknesses are appropriate for several studies within one approach. I revised the cognitive studies together, then the developmental studies and so on. I felt that I had a much better grasp of the approaches doing it this way.

Rashid

I find evaluation really difficult. One thing that really helped me was to try to tell someone in very simple terms what the study was all about and how it had been conducted. Then I tried to tell them what was good about it and what was bad about it. It was even better when the person I was telling wasn't a psychology student, because I had to explain things to them.

Refresh your memory

The student answers on the next few pages are all focused on the strengths and limitations of the five approaches that you have studied. Before you read the model answers, you might find it useful to complete a table like the one below.

Approach	Major strengths of approach – try to give an example of a study that illustrates the strength	Major weaknesses of approach – try to give an example of a study that illustrates the weakness
Cognitive (Loftus and Palmer, Baron-Cohen et al., Savage-Rumbaugh et al.)	Use of controlled lab experiments, e.g. Loftus and Palmer	
Developmental (Bandura, Ross and Ross, Freud, Samuel and Bryant)		Difficult to isolate single variables that are responsible for development, e.g. Samuel and Bryant
Physiological (Dement and Kleitman, Sperry, Maguire et al.)	Use of scientific apparatus, e.g. MRI scan (Maguire et al.)	
Social (Milgram, Reicher and Haslam, Piliavin, Rodin and Piliavin)	High ecological validity, e.g. Piliavin, Rodin and Piliavin	Ethical issues, e.g. Milgram
Individual differences (Rosenhan, Thigpen and Cleckley, Griffiths)		Can be subjective and subject to researcher bias, e.g. Thigpen and Cleckley

Sample answers

Cognitive approach exam-style question

We are going to look at a student response written under exam conditions to the following question:

Discuss the strengths and weaknesses of the cognitive approach, using examples from any of the cognitive approach studies. (12 marks)

Student answer

One strength of the cognitive approach is that many cognitive studies are experiments carried out in laboratories. This is probably due to the desire to control variables. This was the case in the study by Baron-Cohen and his colleagues, where they were able to select participants with the desired characteristics and to maintain a standard procedure for all participants during the various tasks involving looking at eyes and faces. By controlling variables, cause and effect can be established, in this case the effect that autism and Asperger's Syndrome have on theory of mind skills.

However, laboratory experiments are not without their weaknesses and by studying cognitive processes in a laboratory, ecological validity is often compromised and people are more aware of being studied which may change the way they think and react. For example in the study by Loftus and Palmer films of car crashes were used as it would have been difficult to stage realistic crashes in a laboratory setting. As a result the ecological validity was low, making it very difficult to generalise to eyewitness testimony in everyday life.

Examiner says:

A good choice for the first strength and a clearly explained example.

Examiner says:

Good to explain that lab studies have both strengths and weaknesses.

Examiner says:

Another good strength with a clear example.

A further strength of the cognitive approach is the practical applications that can arise from studying the way people process information. Practical applications provide ways of helping people or improving performance in some way. For example the study by Loftus and Palmer offers us an insight into the factors that can affect the reliability of eyewitness testimony, in particular the use of leading questions in interviews which can distort a witness's memory of an event. This could prove vital for police questioning techniques.

A final weakness of the cognitive approach relates to finding valid measures of cognitive processes. It is difficult to measure how cognitive processes work because they are 'mental' processes and cannot be seen. For example in the study by Savage-Rumbaugh and her colleagues they attempted to measure Kanzi the pygmy chimpanzee's use of language. There is no doubt that the chimpanzee could recognise and use words but it is still difficult to tell whether this is the same as language use in humans, who use language in very complex ways.

Examiner says:

Overall a good answer which demonstrates how all of the issues can be applied across an approach as well as to a single study.

Developmental approach exam-style question

We are going to look at a student response written under exam conditions to the following question:

Discuss the strengths and limitations of the developmental approach, using examples from any study. (12 marks)

Student answer

One of the strengths of developmental psychology approach is in the rich data that can be obtained. Rich data provides a lot of material for psychologists to discuss and interpret and can provide lots of evidence that is useful to understand people. The study by Freud on Little Hans was a case study that was carried out over a 2-year period and involved his father recording behaviour and conversations. This allowed Freud to get lots of information on Hans that would not have been possible if more children had been involved. Samuel and Bryant were able to get lots of information on how children think by selecting a sample to study that had an age span from 5 to 8 years. By investigating this age range they were able to obtain evidence on how children's thinking changed.

Another strength of the developmental approach is that it provides useful information that can be applied to everyday life. Bandura, Ross and Ross's study on how children may learn aggressive behaviour can be used to inform decisions on what children can watch on television. The findings from Samuel and Bryant indicate how children think and this can be used to help teachers understand learning.

A limitation of this approach is due to how difficult it is to have participants that are representative samples of the population and without this it is difficult to generalise the findings to more people than those in the studies. The children in Bandura's study were all from a particular nursery and did not represent other social and cultural

Examiner says:

A good start, getting lots of data is important.

Examiner says:

Helpful, but the bit on Samuel and Bryant could have an example.

Examiner says:

You could also have used Freud, he only had one young boy.

groups. This was also a problem for Samuel and Bryant, as although they selected children from many schools they were all from the same area. It is difficult to suggest that all children all over the world will respond in the same way.

Another limitation is due to development being a very complex process and it is difficult to isolate any one cause for behaviour. The children in Bandura's study could have shown aggressive behaviour because that is what Bobo dolls were for. Freud's case study on Little Hans suggests that his phobia is due to unconscious anxiety related to the Oedipus complex. Other people think that Hans could have learned to be afraid of horses or that his behaviour was due to attachment problems. It is very complicated and hard to find any one reason why children do what they do.

Examiner says:

Making this point again successfully brings this question to an end.

Physiological approach exam-style question

We are going to look at a student response written under exam conditions to the following question:

Discuss the strengths and weaknesses of the physiological approach, using examples from any of the physiological approach studies. (12 marks)

Student answer

One strength of the physiological approach is the high levels of control that are gained when researchers are able to use scientific and technical equipment to measure variables. This gives objective, reliable data. For example in the study by Maguire et al., the measure of hippocampal volume was taken through scientific analysis of MRI scans.

Another strength of the physiological approach is that it demonstrates clear links between biology and behaviour and these links can often lead to practical applications. For example, the Maguire study demonstrates that the brain has plasticity and changes in response to the demands placed upon it. This may have positive implications for the rehabilitation of those who have suffered brain damage through injury and disease.

Examiner says:

This is a good first point. It has been clearly made and the example is an appropriate choice. The writer could also have used the study by Dement and Kleitman as one that uses technical measuring equipment.

Examiner says:

Another well made point. The Maguire example has been used well. There are obviously other examples that you could have used instead, but you only need one example for each strength/weakness.

One weakness of the physiological approach is that where
researchers use highly controlled lab experiments the
research may lack validity. For example, studying sleep
and dreaming in a laboratory environment as Dement and
Kleitman did may lack ecological validity as we do not know
if the data collected would be the same if the research had
been conducted in the participants' own homes.

Another weakness of the physiological approach is that
studies sometimes use very small or very specific samples of
people who have had suffered a similar type of brain damage
and it may not be possible to generalise these results to the
wider population. For example the participants in Sperry's
study had all undergone an operation to control severe
epilepsy and it may be that their brains had been damaged in
some way by the epilepsy. This means that the study of these
participants may not tell us anything about the working of a
normal brain.

Social approach exam-style question

We are going to look at a student response written under exam conditions to the following question:

Discuss the strengths and weaknesses of the social approach, using examples from any of the social approach studies. (12 marks)

Student answer

One strength of the social approach is the use of field experiments, which allow for much more ecologically valid evidence to be collected. For example the experiment by Piliavin took place on a subway train with real passengers who were going about their daily lives. By witnessing the victim's collapse in a normal environment the participants were more likely to react in a natural way rather than acting in a socially desirable way as a result of being in a laboratory situation. This ultimately helps researchers to avoid demand characteristics and to collect more valid data.

A weakness of the social approach relates to the frequent use of laboratory experiments to study social processes. For example the study by Milgram was the opposite to Piliavin's, it was conducted in a laboratory setting, strange to the participants and in addition involving an unusual task (shocking another person!). Such artificial surroundings and tasks tend to produce demand characteristics where the participant does not behave in a natural way but responds to the unusual situation in a way they feel is expected of them. This can affect the validity of the data gathered.

Examiner says:

A good first point focusing on methods, with a clearly explained example.

Examiner says:

A good comparison has been drawn here. The strength in the first paragraph is also to do with methods.

Examiner says:

This is an important strength. It is always important to consider the extent to which the findings of a study can be applied in the real world. The writer could have used any of the social approach studies as examples here.

Another strength of the of the social approach is the wide variety of applications that come from investigating important social issues, for example the effects of group membership and social roles in the study by Reicher and Haslam. From this study it can be seen that failure of a group to establish control, as in the case of the guards, can lead to very negative consequences including tyranny and abuse of power. Findings such as this can be used to inform the running of our prison system.

A final weakness of the social approach relates to the ethics of subjecting people to stressful situations or procedures in an attempt to understand social processes. For example, in the obedience study by Milgram the participants suffered from extreme stress as a result of the conflict they experienced in wanting to obey the experimenter and wanting to help the victim they thought they were shocking. Although the results from this study provide us with useful insights into how far people will go in the name of obedience, we have to question the ethics of social studies that harm participants in the process.

Examiner says:

Again, another important point linking to the previous one. Although it is a clearly a strength to have research with clear applications to the real world, there is also a limitation to consider if such research puts people into unacceptable situations.

Individual differences approach exam-style question

We are going to look at a student response written under exam conditions to the following question:

Discuss the strengths and limitations of the individual differences approach using examples from any study. (12 marks)

Student answer

When studying individual differences it is useful to use qualitative and quantitative data. This is a strength because it allows the researcher to be able to use quantitative data for accurate objective information and also use qualitative data to provide more descriptive information. Thigpen and Cleckley tried to distinguish between Eve White and Eve Black by using their own qualitative observations within the therapy sessions and also used psychological data such as IQ scores. The study on fruit-machine gamblers by Griffiths was similar as he used quantitative data about how long the gambling lasted along with the utterances from 'thinking aloud'.

Another strength of studying individual differences is that it helps us to understand human behaviour and help those who have problems. Griffiths was able to suggest that addictive gamblers may have different ways of thinking about gambling compared to others. He was also able to suggest ways to help people addicted to gambling by letting gamblers hear their own thoughts from thinking-aloud tapes. When they did this they were more likely to gamble less. Rosenhan's study raised lots of questions about how good medical professionals are at diagnosis and this could be used to help them understand their mistakes.

Examiner says:

A good mix of qualitative and quantitative data. You could also have mentioned Rosenhan because he used numbers and description.

Examiner says:

Useful applications are important. Thigpen and Cleckley provided information to help in the diagnosis of MPD.

A limitation of the individual approach is that it often relies on the subjective opinion of one person about somebody else's behaviour. This means that they will often interpret what they see in a way that may only make sense to them. Most of Thigpen and Cleckley's data came from their observations of the two Eves and they may have 'wanted' to discover someone with MPD. In the study of fruit-machine gamblers Griffiths was one of the few people who understood what the gamblers' utterances meant. This could mean that he gave them a meaning that matched his own views as the study does say the inter-rater reliability is very low.

Another limitation that is linked to the problems of using people's subjective opinion is related to demand characteristics and how this can have an effect on the validity of the findings. In Rosenhan's investigation the pseudopatients may have behaved in a certain way due to the fact that they were participant observers and this may mean that their findings are not what really happens. This means they are not valid. In Thigpen and Cleckley's study of Eve it is possible that the two therapists led themselves and other psychologists into thinking that the behaviour they witnessed was due to MPD rather than another mental illness.

Glossary

agentic state when individuals relinquish their personal views and act as an agent of someone else's will

anecdotal evidence evidence gathered without a systematic approach – often just researchers' accounts of what they have observed – and therefore open to bias

Asperger's Syndrome a mild version of autism

assent a child's agreement to participate in an activity, having had it made it clear to them that they can start and stop the activity whenever they wish. It is worth noting that an adult's consent for a child to take part in an activity may not reflect the child's wishes

attitude scale a way of measuring a person's attitude towards something; it provides a quantitative measure

blind test the use of an experimenter who does not know the details of a study and so cannot influence the outcome

bystander behaviour the reactions of those who witness an emergency

cause and effect refers to the ability to establish that one variable is having an effect on another. By controlling all variables other than the independent variable, you can be sure it has caused any effect found. In Baron-Cohen et al.'s study it was clear that the characteristics of autism caused poorer performance on the Eyes Task, as all other variables were controlled

commune a democratically-run society whose members all have a say in its organisation

confederates actors who take part in experiments

confounding variable a feature that is not controlled for but could affect the outcome

controlled observation observations of the reactions of participants in a specific situation. It differs from natural observation, where people are in their usual environments and nothing is set up by the researcher

corpus callosum the bundle of nerve fibres that connects the two hemispheres of the brain

cover story a false explanation of the aim of a study, told to participants in order to change their behaviour

culture learning the role of culture and socialisation in learning language

demand characteristic a feature of a procedure (other than the independent variable) that influences a participant to try to guess what a study is about and look for clues as to how to behave

dependent variable in an experiment, the variable that is affected by the researchers' manipulation of the independent variable

determinism the idea that our behaviour is determined by factors beyond our control, e.g. the situation, the environment, and our biology

dispositional hypothesis the idea that a person's characteristics determine their behaviour, e.g. personality traits

EEG see electroencephalography

electroencephalography a non-invasive method for measuring the electrical activity of the brain by recording from electrodes placed on the scalp. The resulting traces (printed out by the machine) are known as an electroencephalograph (EEG). They represent the activity of a large number of neurons and are sometimes called 'brainwaves' due to the wave-like patterns seen on the traces

ethnocentric favouring one group of people

experimental realism the extent to which the participants perceive an experimental situation to be real

free association is a psychoanalytical technique that encourages the speaking out of whatever thoughts a person has, whether they make sense or not. This is meant to provide an insight into unconscious thoughts

fugue a state of mind in which an individual forgets who they are, characterised by loss of their memory and personality

genocide deliberate and systematic destruction of a racial, political, or cultural group

Happe's 'strange stories' a test of advanced theory of mind skills that involves answering questions on a selection of stories and the characters in them

heuristic device a framework that can be used to predict behaviour

heuristics common-sense sets of rules that are used to solve problems

hippocampus the part of the brain that is concerned with memory and spatial navigation

hysteria the display of physical symptoms like paralysis with no obvious cause

independent variable the variable that researchers manipulate in an experiment

independent measures design a method that involves comparing the results from separate groups or populations

inter-rater reliability describes how well independent observers score events: 1 is an exact match

IQ intelligence quotient, a numerical representation of intelligence. IQ is derived from dividing mental age (result from an intelligence test) by the chronological age

lexigram a visual symbol system, a board covered with geometric symbols that brighten when touched

limbic system a set of brain structures including the hippocampus and the amygdala that support a variety of functions including emotion and long-term memory

model in Social Learning Theory, a person whose behaviour is imitated

modelling the way behaviours can be changed by observational learning, when participants in a study base their behaviour on the behaviour of a model

MRI (magnetic resonance imaging) scan method that uses radio waves to obtain 3D images of brain and body tissue

mundane realism the extent to which a procedure or task relates to everyday life

neurosis a mental illness in which the individual remains in touch with reality but suffers psychological problems related to anxiety

neurospecificity the way in which neurons are hard-wired to attach to one another in certain predetermined ways during the development of the brain

observational learning is when we acquire new behaviours by observing the actions of others and selecting those that are perceived to receive social rewards, such as affirmation

Oedipus complex the conflict between a boy's desire towards his mother and the associated fear that his father will punish this desire by castrating him

order effects effects such as improvement in performance, boredom or tiredness, that occur as a result of the order in which conditions or tasks are experienced

pathological a behaviour that is unusual and interferes with everyday life

phobia a fear that is out of proportion to reality

psychoanalysis a form of therapy based on psychoanalytical theory, which regards unconscious thoughts and feelings as the cause of human behaviour

psychometric testing tests that attempt to measure psychological characteristics such as mood and self-esteem. These normally produce a quantitative score

psychosis a mental illness in which the individual has difficulty relating to reality, and their intellect and emotions are often divorced

quasi-experiment an experiment where the independent variable varies naturally without the need for manipulation by the experimenter

random number tables computer-generated lists of random numbers

reductionist any explanation or method that simplifies behaviour and experience in such a way that the complexity of the human condition may be lost or underestimated. When referring to quantitative data this means that the data do not allow for more detailed evidence to be recorded and may display an overly simplistic picture of events

repeated-measures design where the same participants experience each condition of the independent variable

Sally-Anne test a simple test involving two dolls. One doll leaves the room, the other moves an object, the first doll returns and the child is asked where that doll will look for the object. It is assumed that basic theory of mind skills are required in order to pass this test

schema a framework of knowledge about some aspect of the world

self-efficacy belief in one's ability to bring about change

significant difference there is a significant difference between results if the probability of a chance result is less than 1 in 20 ($p<0.05$)

situational hypothesis the idea that conditions in a situation determine behaviour, e.g. orders from an authority figure

Social Identity Theory a theory that proposes that group membership affects our identity, self-esteem and behaviour

Social Learning Theory tries to understand social behaviour by focusing on how individuals imitate the actions of others to model their own behaviour

standardised this refers to any aspect of the procedure that is kept exactly the same for each participant. This is to control for variations in the procedure that could affect the outcome statistical tests tests that let you know how likely your results are to be due to chance. The lower the probability of a chance result, the more likely your results are to be due to the manipulation

of the independent variable. If the probability of a chance result is less that 1 in 20 (written as $p<0.05$), we can say that there is a statistically significant difference between the conditions and accept our hypothesis

subjectivity bias created by a person's own interpretation or point of view

stages of development in the oral stage children derive pleasure from their bodies by sucking; in the anal stage children experience control of their bodies by retaining or expelling faeces; in the phallic stage children become aware of their genitals and sexual differences

theory of mind an individual's theory about how minds in general work, including their own and other people's

time-series approach a study that introduces changes to the independent variable over time

Tourette's Syndrome a neurological disorder characterised by recurring movements and sounds (called tics)

trial each time an experiment is carried out

triangulation the use of a variety of methods to study one issue in an attempt to avoid bias and reduce the limitations of using one technique

unsolicited participants people who are not aware that they are taking part in a study

References

Aserinsky, E. and Kleitman, N. (1955) 'Two types of ocular motility occurring in sleep', *Journal of Applied Physiology*, 8, 1–10.

Banyard, P. and Grayson, A. (1996) *Introducing Psychological Research: Sixty Studies that Shape Psychology*, Basingstoke: Macmillan.

Bettelheim, B. (1967) *The Empty Fortress: Infantile Autism and the Birth of the Self*, New York: The Free Press.

Bryan, J. H. and Test, M .A. (1967) 'Models and helping: naturalistic studies in aiding behaviour', *Journal or Personality and Social Psychology*, 1967, 6, 400–7.

Carter (2000) *Mapping the Mind*, London: Phoenix.

Crick, F. and Mitchinson, G. (1983) 'The function of dream sleep', *Nature*, 304, 111–14.

Darley, J. and Latane, B. (1968) 'Bystander intervention in emergencies: diffusion of responsibility', *Journal of Personality and Social Psychology*, 1968, 8, 377–83.

Devlin Committee Report (1973) Report of the Committee on Evidence of Identification in Criminal Cases, Scottish Law Commission.

Donaldson, M. (1978) *Children's Minds*, London: Fontana.

Ekman, P, (1992) 'An argument for basic emotions', *Cognition and Emotion*, 6, 169–200.

Freud, S. (1900) *The Interpretation of Dreams*, originally published 1899, published by Penguin, 1991.

Green, S. (1994) *Principles of Biopsychology*, Hove: Lawrence Erlbaum Associates Ltd.

Griffiths, M. D. (2002) *Gambling and Gaming Addiction in Adolescence*, Oxford: BPS Blackwell.

Haney, C., Banks, W. C. and Zimbardo, P. G. (1973) 'Study of prisoners and guards in a simulated prison', *Naval Research Reviews*, 9, 1–17.

Kirk, S. A. and Kutchins, H. (1992) *The Selling of DSM: The Rhetoric of Science in Psychiatry*, New York: A. de Gruyter.

Loftus, E. F. and Zanni, G. (1975) 'Eyewitness testimony: the influence of the wording of a question', *Bulletin of the Psychonomic Society*, 5, 1, 86–8.

Porpodas, C. D. (1987) 'The one question conversation experiment reconsidered', *Journal of Child Psychology and Psychiatry*, 28, 2, 343–9.

Haslam, S. D. and Reicher, S. A. (2005) 'The Psychology of Tyranny', *Scientific American*.

Rose, S. A. and Blank, M. (1974) 'The potency of context in children's cognition: an illustration through conservation', *Child Development*, 45, 499–502.

Spritzer, R. L. (1976) 'More on pseudoscience in science and the case for psychiatric diagnosis', *Archives of General Psychiatry*, 35, 773–82.

The Times, 19 January 1970, 'The Subway Samaritan'.

Tinbergen, N. and Tinbergen, E. (1983) *'Autistic' Children: New Hope for a Cure*, London: George Allen & Unwin.

Wagenaar, W. (1988) *Paradoxes of Gambling Behaviour*, London: Erlbaum.

Index

Index

Your Exam Café CD-ROM

In the back of this book you will find an Exam Café CD-ROM. This CD contains advice on study skills, interactive questions to test your knowledge and many more useful features. Load it onto your computer to take a closer look.

Among the files on the CD are editable Microsoft Word documents for you to alter and print off if you wish.

Minimum system requirements:
- Windows 2000, XP Pro or Vista
- Internet Explorer 6 or Firefox 2.0
- Flash Player 8 or higher plug-in
- Pentium III 900 MHZ with 256 Mb RAM

To run your Exam Café CD, insert it into the CD drive of your computer. It should start automatically; if not, please go to My Computer (Computer on Vista), click on the CD drive and double-click on 'start.html'.

If you have difficulties running the CD, or if your copy is not there, please contact the helpdesk number given below.

Software support
For further software support between the hours of 8.30am and 5.00pm (Mon–Fri), please contact:
Tel: 01865 888108
Fax: 01865 314091
Email: software.enquiries@pearson.com